Quaker
Carpetbagger

ALSO BY MAX LONGLEY

*For the Union and the Catholic Church:
Four Converts in the Civil War*
(McFarland, 2015)

Quaker Carpetbagger

*J. Williams Thorne,
Underground Railroad Host
Turned North Carolina Politician*

Max Longley

McFarland & Company, Inc., Publishers
Jefferson, North Carolina

LIBRARY OF CONGRESS CATALOGUING-IN-PUBLICATION DATA

Names: Longley, Maximilian, 1971– author.
Title: Quaker carpetbagger : J. Williams Thorne, Underground Railroad host turned North Carolina politician / Max Longley.
Description: Jefferson, North Carolina : McFarland & Company, Inc., Publishers, 2020 | Includes bibliographical references and index.
Identifiers: LCCN 2019055235| ISBN 9781476669854 (paperback : acid free paper) ∞
ISBN 9781476637747 (ebook)
Subjects: LCSH: Thorne, J. Williams (Joseph Williams), 1816–1897 | Quakers—Pennsylvania—Chester County—Biography. | Quakers—North Carolina—Biography. | Legislators—North Carolina—Biography. | North Carolina—Politics and government—1865–1950.
Classification: LCC BX7795.T5834 L66 2020 | DDC 289.6092 [B] —dc23
LC record available at https://lccn.loc.gov/2019055235

BRITISH LIBRARY CATALOGUING DATA ARE AVAILABLE

ISBN (print) 978-1-4766-6985-4
ISBN (ebook) 978-1-4766-3774-7

© 2020 Max Longley. All rights reserved

No part of this book may be reproduced or transmitted in any form or by any means, electronic or mechanical, including photocopying or recording, or by any information storage and retrieval system, without permission in writing from the publisher.

On the cover: photograph of J. Williams Thorne, ca. 1870
(courtesy Nancy Plumley)

Printed in the United States of America

*McFarland & Company, Inc., Publishers
Box 611, Jefferson, North Carolina 28640
www.mcfarlandpub.com*

Acknowledgments

First and foremost, I would like to acknowledge Nancy Plumley, a descendant of J. Williams Thorne, who not only gave me copies of the Thorne family papers, but shared the notes, annotations, and transcriptions she made on much of this voluminous material. She also looked at drafts of the chapters in my manuscripts and gave me comments and encouragement. Any errors that remain in this book are mine alone.

My bibliography lists several archives whose more-than-helpful staff were happy to meet my research requests. The Chester County Archives and Lancaster County Archives in Pennsylvania provided highly relevant court and government documents. The Chester County Historical Society has correspondence by J. Williams with many figures in and outside of the county. The Friends Historical Collection at Swarthmore College, Pennsylvania, had valuable documents. The Warren County Memorial Library in North Carolina has a very informative letter about J. Williams.

Dr. Kevin Luskus, MD, gave me some information about 19th-century medicine and how some of it holds up (or doesn't hold up) today.

I received a grant from the National Coalition of Independent Scholars which helped during the early stages of my research—thank you!

My thanks to my mother, for minimizing errors in the book. Remaining errors are my own.

Table of Contents

Acknowledgments   v

Preface   1

1. The Ecclesiastical Trial   3
2. Born into a Cold World   5
3. Let Truth and Error Grapple   20
4. The Federal Invasion and the Progressive Friends   35
5. Reform, Slave Raid, War   49
6. Keystone Stater and Tar Heel   65
7. Cast Out   87
8. The Carpetbagger and the Carpet Will   106
9. Returning Home   126
10. Speaking His Mind   142

Epilogue   156

Appendix I. Memorial Resolution on J. Williams Thorne Adopted by the Progressive Friends Meeting, Longwood, 1897   163

Appendix II. J. Williams Resorts to Satire to Defend What He Considers the Principles of a True Republic, 1877   165

Chapter Notes   171

Bibliography   193

Index   203

Preface

If anyone embodied Thomas Jefferson's ideal of the virtuous patriotic yeoman farmer better than Jefferson himself, it was Joseph Williams Thorne. A Pennsylvania family farmer who late in life moved to North Carolina as a so-called "carpetbagger" (a Northerner who went South after the Civil War), J. Williams associated himself with many of the reform causes of the day. He debated his ideas with all comers—in person if possible, through the medium of print if a suitable oral debate couldn't be arranged.

This was Jefferson's ideal—sturdy sons of toil managing their own farms as well as assisting in the affairs of the Republic. J. Williams was more Jeffersonian than Jefferson in that he shared Jefferson's opposition to slavery without adopting any compromises with the system. Jefferson pursued his fugitive slaves, while J. Williams ran a station on the Underground Railroad, helping fugitive slaves to freedom. This was more in accordance with the Jeffersonian ideal than Jefferson's actual practice.

Like Jefferson, J. Williams was hostile to evangelical Christianity, denying many parts of the Bible and opposing the efforts of Christians in politics. J. Williams was far more open and public than Jefferson when insisting on these views.

Again like Jefferson, J. Williams had great confidence in his ideas in the face of messy reality, giving an impractical cast to some (though not all) of his ideas.

In a deviation from Jefferson, J. Williams took his faith in the common people into outright populism—distrusting the wealthy and educated and suspecting their designs against the poor.

1

The Ecclesiastical Trial

Raleigh, North Carolina: February 1875

Raging waters and furious winds battered North Carolina. The Yadkin, Roanoke and Tar rivers rose to high levels, doing "damage ... to mills, dams and bridges." On February 20, a hurricane hit the central part of the state, wreaking destruction. Wake County, site of Raleigh, the state capital, saw many trees toppled by the force of the blast.[1]

In storm-tossed Raleigh, the state House of Representatives was conducting a stormy hearing. A member of the House, Joseph Williams Thorne (who generally went by "J. Williams"), was accused of atheism, which would disqualify him from office under the Reconstruction-era constitution of the state. By this constitution, to "deny the being of Almighty God" barred a person from officeholding. The Clerk of the House read out loud a pamphlet which Thorne had published a couple of years previously, vehemently denouncing Christianity, Christian morals, and Christian leaders.[2]

Raleigh was small, with 4,000 white and 4,000 black inhabitants, wrote a *Scribner's* correspondent, Edward King. King had spent 1873 and early 1874 exploring the South for the benefit of *Scribner's* readers, and in 1875 he published his collected sketches in a book grandiloquently titled *The Great South: A Record of Journeys in Louisiana, Texas, the Indian Territory, Missouri, Arkansas, Mississippi, Alabama, Georgia, Florida, South Carolina, North Carolina, Kentucky, Tennessee, Virginia, West Virginia, and Maryland*.[3] The author's tour included the eleven states of the now-defeated Confederacy—states, including North Carolina, which had been readmitted to the Union on condition of respecting the rights of the freed slaves and rejecting their rebel past.

King was one of several Northern (often Republican) authors at this juncture who were denouncing Reconstruction as a failure. King gave his opinion that "the white population" of North Carolina had suffered "villainy

Quaker Carpetbagger

and robbery ... at the hands of the [Republican] plunderers maintained in power by the negro." The Conservatives (Democrats) had taken the legislature away from the Republicans four years previously, though a Republican (Curtis Brogden) remained in the governor's mansion. An earlier Republican governor, William Woods Holden, whom King blamed for the prior abuses, had been a North Carolina native, not a "carpetbagger" who had migrated from the North. Thus, King assured his readers, North Carolina whites did not blame the North for imposing carpetbag rule. Indeed: "The North Carolinians are accustomed now-a-days to wonder why immigrants do not rush into their state, and settle upon the lands which can be had so cheaply."[4]

King added, "[F]inding that but few [immigrants] come, and that the State is in a general condition of discouragement and decay, financially," the whites "have relapsed into an indolent attitude, and let progress drift by them. In some of the small towns I found the people more inclined to bitterness and less reconciled to the results of the war than anywhere else in the South."[5]

To hear King tell it, J. Williams Thorne would face no special prejudice because of his status as a carpetbagger. This was one of many areas in which King could be seen as unduly optimistic about conditions in the Tar Heel State.

If Raleigh was fairly small, the capitol building had high aspirations. "The State-House at Raleigh," wrote King, "is delightfully situated in the midst of lovely foliage, and its massive granite columns and superb dome, modeled after the Parthenon, are very imposing."[6]

On the 23rd, as the House met again to consider Thorne's case, the galleries filled up with a highly interested audience, curious to learn about the alleged atheist and find out his fate. By noon, when the proceedings began, both the legislative galleries and the lobbies were full of people.[7]

J. Williams Thorne faced a highly unsympathetic audience in a majority–Democratic House that had had enough of "radicalism," and J. Williams made no secret that he had what others would consider radical ideas. A Republican and racial egalitarian, Thorne had been elected to the House from black-majority Warren County. He had come to North Carolina over five years previously, from his home in Chester County, Pennsylvania. He had hoped to be able to uplift the people of his new home. They did not all want to be uplifted.

2

Born into a Cold World

When Joseph Williams Thorne was born of Quaker parents on Christmas 1816, much of the world had gone through several months of freezing weather. It had snowed in the United States that summer, and while the snow had not reached Chester County in the southeast corner of Pennsylvania, it had hit the northern part of the state. This, and renewed cold weather in September, greatly damaged crops. Many New Englanders, driven to emigration by the summer snow and ice, sought new homes in the West, traveling through Easton, Pennsylvania, under a hundred miles north of East Fallowfield. "One family of eight," write William and Nicholas Klingaman, "bound for Indiana arrived in Easton in late December after walking all the way from their farm in Maine, pulling a cart loaded with their youngest children and a few possessions." In nearby Philadelphia, a boatload of Irish immigrants, fleeing the cold in their own country, were landed in the city and, according to a newspaper, "were actually dying in the streets."[1]

Scientists now trace the cause of 1816's freezing weather to the 1815 eruption of Mount Tambora in what is now Indonesia.[2] Metaphorically speaking, the newborn Joseph Williams Thorne would go through a lifetime of storms, eruptions and chilly climates. Much of this was through his own choice in battling for unpopular causes. Some of these causes were dubious, and others were matters of basic human rights and dignity. It was the just causes that tended to get him into the most trouble. And for the first half-century of his life, he didn't have to go far from home to find occasions of conflict. When fifty years of strife was not enough, he left home to find some more.

In 1810, "Mary Thorn," perhaps the same person as Joseph Williams's grandmother Mary, was on a committee to help establish a separate Fallowfield Monthly Meeting in East Fallowfield, Chester County. A Monthly Meeting, comparable to a congregation of a local church in another denomination, was the local body in which Quakers (Friends) met to worship and (once a month) to conduct business. In 1814, the Fallowfield Monthly Meeting approved the marriage of Joseph Jonathan Thorne (probably the son of the Mary Thorn who helped established the meeting) to Margaretta (or Margaret) Williams of Sadsbury Monthly Meeting in adjacent Lancaster County. (There is also a Sadsbury in Chester County, as we shall see, and there was an East Sadsbury Quaker Meeting). After learning of the Fallowfield Meeting's action, the Sadsbury Meeting agreed to the marriage as well. These approvals were necessary for any Quaker who wanted to remain a Quaker; those who got married without the approval of their meetings would have to repent or be "disowned," deprived of membership in the Quaker body. Approvals were not granted for marriages to non–Quakers, though this may not automatically have been a hardship given the large number of Quakers in Chester County.[3]

Joseph and Margaret had their first child, Mary Dubree Thorne, in 1815. Joseph Williams, their first son, followed in 1816. James was born in 1818, Lydia Ann in 1821, Ann Eliza in 1825, and twins Caroline and Lucretia—Lucretia died after two weeks—in 1831.[4]

Joseph's parents lived in West Fallowfield, just under ten miles away from their place of Quaker worship, the Fallowfield Monthly Meeting in the hamlet of Ercildoun in East Fallowfield. The 1830 census shows that Joseph the elder had two white males aged between 10 and 15 in his household, presumably his sons Joseph and James. (The census of 1830 records a man between 30 and 40 living in Joseph Thorne's household, and the census of 1840 records a man between 40 and 50. These men—or perhaps the same man—could have been relatives or workers living with the family. The 1840 census records a male household member between 15 and 20, likewise perhaps a relative or worker.[5])

George Johnston, the editor of *The Poets and Poetry of Chester County, Pennsylvania*, informed his readers in 1890, "Mr. Thorne from his earliest youth was charmed with poetry, and memorized much of it without effort."[6]

Not that J. Williams was a reclusive child who stayed indoors. That wouldn't have been much of an option growing up in a farm household, and Joseph, judging from a reminiscence he wrote many years later for a children's magazine, *The Children's Friend*, sometimes enjoyed farm work, or liked to grow nostalgic over it.

> There is scarcely anything now as it was forty years ago. A great change has come over nearly every rural scene. The growing and preparing of flax has passed away. The sickle has long ago yielded to the swift horse-powered reaper. The merry ring

2. Born into a Cold World

of mowers whetting their scythes in the neighborhood field of cloves [clover?] on a bright June morning, will soon be but a pleasant memory of the past. Forty years ago the hand rake for the gathering of hay gave place to the revolving horse-rake. Now the revolving horse-rake is among the things which have passed away.... Most of our threshing is now done in summer or autumn. Formerly it was reserved for the leisure of winter and while deep snows were spread over the earth preventing out-door work the regular alternate frail-beast would be heard in every barn for miles around.[7]

The elder Joseph Thorne took many of his agricultural goods to market in Philadelphia, often accompanied by his daughter Lydia.[8] We don't know if he made a family trip in 1824 to see the Marquis de Lafayette in his last American tour, but Lafayette did visit Philadelphia that year and would have been quite an attraction for any local farmers who could spare the time. On July 26 the following year, Lafayette came by again, this time to West Chester, the county seat. As one local recalled later: "Although it was the midst of harvest, farmers and men left their grain fields standing that they might see and honor" Lafayette. About ten thousand people from Chester and neighboring counties came to get a look at the hero. Whether Joseph's Quaker family was in the audience, to celebrate a military man however distinguished, is again not clear.[9]

In another article, J. Williams fondly recalled helping wash sheep before their shearing. The children helped herd the sheep into a special enclosure in a local lake, where a "washer" squeezed the water out of the wool and put it in a clean condition. "Although 'sheep washing day' was a fine holiday for the boys, it was otherwise for the sheep who ... made the hills resound with their plaintive bleatings."

One incident Thorne recalled shows his childhood sensitiveness and reflects his vegetarianism as an adult. During one sheep washing, a snake was "sunning himself on the warm bank of the stream. He was severely and perhaps mortally wounded by a person who attempted to kill him. In a short time after another snake appeared and in the gentlest manner coiled himself around the wounded serpent, and began to carry him towards the water. It pains me to think that in the performance of this kind offer he was killed by the same person who had so rudely and ruthlessly wounded the first, not that he was really a hard-hearted man, but he was strongly prejudiced against 'snakes.'" From this, Joseph drew this conclusion: "Even among the lowest and most despised animals, there are lessons of kindness and sympathy we would do well to heed."[10]

Human cruelty in Chester County was not limited to animals.

"It's life for life!" proclaimed John Read.

Quaker Carpetbagger

It was midnight on December 14, 1820. Two white men, Samuel Griffith and Peter Shipley, had invaded Read's home in Kennett Township in the southern part of Chester County. Griffith was a slave-owner from Baltimore and Shipley was an overseer. The pair (accompanied by two other ruffians) claimed that Read, a black man, was Griffith's runaway slave from Maryland. Read disputed that claim in an unmistakable way—by shooting Griffith and attacking Shipley with a club. The slaveholder and his assistant both died. Read was tried for murder in both killings.

The prosecution proved that Read was the son of a slave—his mother was a queen who had been "legally" kidnapped from Africa—but Read's lawyers claimed that even if the deceased had legitimate ownership claims on Read, they had gone about asserting their claim in the wrong way. The deceased, argued the defense lawyers, had not intended to bring Read before a judge in Pennsylvania to determine his slave status—and a recent Pennsylvania statute said that anyone who tried to seize or entice a black person to enslave him outside the state was a kidnapper. Griffith and Shipley had allegedly meant to drag Read, without trial, into Maryland to be held as a slave. By ignoring due process of law, Read's defense went, the attackers were legally kidnappers and had been killed in lawful self-defense. The court in Griffith's case agreed that if Griffith had meant to drag Read into slavery without a trial, Griffith was a kidnapper and could be shot. The jury acquitted.

Then Read was tried for Shipley's death and attempted the same defense. This time the presiding judge, Isaac Darlington, had been the prosecutor in the previous case. Judge Darlington said that, contrary to the first court, slave-owners could take their runaway slaves out of Pennsylvania without a trial. Thus it was a crime for slaves to resist their masters' efforts to seize them without due process. Read got a manslaughter conviction and a nine-year sentence.[11]

Read's case illustrated Chester County's vulnerability to slave raids, as well as the conflation of legitimate arrests of fugitive slaves and outright kidnapping of black people, slave or free. Pennsylvania in general, and Chester County in particular, were on the front lines of this conflict: Pennsylvania and Chester County both had the Mason-Dixon Line as a southern boundary. This famous boundary line had been drawn by its namesake surveyors to resolve a longstanding boundary dispute between Pennsylvania and Maryland. While this line solved one dispute, it did not solve others, specifically the crossing of the boundary by Marylanders—and often people from other slave states. Fugitive slaves in search of

2. Born into a Cold World

freedom, and white kidnappers in search of fugitive slaves and free blacks to send south into bondage, made Chester County, like many Northern counties throughout the North-South border, into an arena of conflict.

Until the 1820s, a particularly bold gang of kidnappers operating in Philadelphia seized free black children in the city in order to take them into slavery. A ship belonging to the kidnap gang often docked at the Arch Street wharf—the same street that contained a famous Quaker meetinghouse. A Mississippi plantation owner helped alert Philadelphia authorities when the kidnappers tried to sell some of the children to him. The dispersal of this gang, of course, did not stop the operation of other kidnap gangs throughout the state, targeting children and adults in the free black community. As historian Julie Winch put it: "The 'underground railroad clearly operated in two directions.'"[12]

The threat slave-hunters posed to free blacks in Pennsylvania was a key impetus behind the formation in Pennsylvania of the country's earliest antislavery groups in 1775. The Society for the Relief of Free Negroes Unlawfully Held in Bondage was a largely Quaker group, later known as the Pennsylvania Abolition Society (PAS). The PAS monitored and sought to stop the various attempts by kidnappers to bring free blacks into servitude, or to evade Pennsylvania's pioneering emancipation law by taking slaves outside of the state so their children would not be freed by state law. With its watchful members and high-powered lawyers, the organization sought to prevent kidnapping, liberate the victims, and prosecute the kidnappers, as well as strengthening the antislavery and antikidnapping laws and uplifting the free blacks.[13]

A dispute between Pennsylvania and Virginia in the Republic's early years sparked federal action. Kidnappers took a freed slave into Virginia, and Pennsylvania unsuccessfully tried to have Virginia return the kidnappers to Pennsylvania for trial. In response to the dispute, Congress then passed a law in 1793 to implement key provisions in the federal Constitution concerning interstate fugitives from justice (alleged criminals) and fugitives from "service or labor" (runaway slaves). Under the new statute, both groups—criminal suspects and runaway slaves—had to be sent back to the states from which they had fled, to face either a trial (in the case of accused criminals) or renewed slavery (in the case of runaway slaves). The Constitution was not specific as to how the relevant constitutional provision was to be enforced, so Congress was trying to fill in the gaps with this new statute. Under the statute's provisions, someone claiming a black person as a fugitive slave from another state could seize that person and

Quaker Carpetbagger

bring him before a nearby state or federal court in the state of capture, for an adjudication of his or her status. If the court certified the person as a fugitive, the claimant could take the person back to his or her alleged master in another state. In the case of an accused criminal, proof of guilt was not required, but the governor of the state that charged the fugitive must send the paperwork to the state that sheltered him, after which the governor of the latter state was responsible for sending the suspect for trial in the state where he had been charged.[14]

Kidnappers continued to ignore the distinction between fugitive slaves and free blacks. If they could seize black people, why go to the expense and delay of getting a court to certify the person as a fugitive slave? Southern kidnappers kept coming to Pennsylvania to drag black people down South. Pennsylvania passed a law in 1820—the law that featured in Read's case—providing strict penalties for anyone who took a black person out of the state in order to enslave him or her. Maryland's legislators and officials complained about Pennsylvania's alleged sheltering of fugitive slaves, and in 1826 the Pennsylvania legislature passed a law specifically dealing with fugitives. Pennsylvania's courts could issue warrants for the arrest of an alleged fugitive, and the person would then have a trial in one of the higher trial courts (but not in a lower trial court). If the court found that the person was a fugitive, (s)he would be sent South; otherwise, (s)he would be released. This law was meant to encourage kidnappers to follow judicial processes in seizing black people. Legislators warned that taking blacks out of the state without following proper judicial proceedings was kidnapping, but the slave raids continued, with both free blacks and fugitive slaves getting caught in the net.[15]

While J. Williams was growing up, he probably didn't have any contact with a prominent religious radical who shared Joseph's later suspicion of Christianity but not Thorne's later political views, calling into question (if Thorne had kept up with the matter) whether freedom from Christian doctrine necessarily led to reformist, radical views. A Pennsylvania scientist named Thomas Cooper taught chemistry in Pennsylvania's Carlisle College (later Dickinson College). Cooper was a religious radical originally from England and a friend of fellow radical scientist J.B. Priestley, with whom he emigrated to Pennsylvania. As well as being a scientist, Cooper was a lawyer, a Jeffersonian, a victim of the Federalist Sedition Act, and a Pennsylvania judge until the state legislature removed him (one charge against the non–Quaker Cooper was that he punished a Quaker for not removing his hat in court). In religion, Cooper scandalized more orthodox

2. Born into a Cold World

believers by his denial of the soul (while affirming the Resurrection). After leaving Pennsylvania, Cooper became president of South Carolina College in Columbia. Because of his religious views, the South Carolina legislature debated Cooper's fitness to hold such a position at a state college. The trustees sustained him and he was allowed to retire honorably. By this time, the 1830s, Cooper had considerable backing from the dominant pro-slavery, nullificationist party in South Carolina, because Cooper had been a pioneer in arguing the rightfulness of slavery (revising earlier views) and in defending nullification and secession.[16] If Cooper's notorious career led J. Williams to question his facile equation of orthodox Christianity with slavery, and freethinking with reform and abolitionism, then J. Williams left no indication of this.

When J. Williams was ten, his Quaker world was shaken by a serious division. Starting in 1827, American Quakers broke into two branches, the "Orthodox" and the "Hicksites." Briefly, the Orthodox were sympathetic to evangelical Protestantism, then undergoing a revival in America's Second Great Awakening. The Orthodox believed that Quakers needed to revere the Bible in the evangelical Protestant manner, relying on its authority against an alleged tendency of Unitarian and deist ideas being spread throughout American Quakerdom. The main culprit, in the eyes of the Orthodox, was an elderly Long Island farmer and itinerant Quaker minister named Elias Hicks. Hicks and similarly-minded Quakers were not necessarily deists or Unitarians (though, as it turned out, some were), but they believed that the Orthodox were using the Bible as a club to repress the "Inner Light" traditionally valued by Quakers. To make things worse, the Orthodox leaders tended to be rich Philadelphia merchants, while Hicks's sympathizers tended to be farmers and artisans, adding another source of irritation to the conflict. To the Hicksites, the arrogant Orthodox activists were suppressing humble Hicksites and their leadings of the spirit, even while the Orthodox diluted Quaker purity by joining with evangelical Protestants in charitable and religious groups.

After 1827, the Orthodox/Hicksite split led to separate organizations. There were two Philadelphia Yearly Meetings, Orthodox and Hicksite (each Yearly Meeting supervised, at least nominally, the affiliated Quaker Monthly Meetings in Pennsylvania). The Fallowfield Monthly Meeting split along Hicksite/Orthodox lines, with the majority of the members, including Joseph's parents, joining the Hicksites and keeping the old meetinghouse. (The Orthodox tried for a few years to maintain their own

Quaker Carpetbagger

Monthly Meeting and cemetery, but soon merged with a nearby Orthodox Monthly Meeting).[17]

In October 1833, J. Williams enrolled at the Westtown Friends Boarding School, to the southeast of West Chester, the county seat. The Quakers had founded this institution for Quaker boys and girls in 1799. After the schism, Westtown remained under Orthodox control, though a large number of Hicksite families, such as the Thornes, continued to send children there. The trustees thought that education of young Quakers had grown more important than ever after the schism, so to make the institution within parents' means, they had lowered the fees to sixty dollars per year for tuition, room and board. Correctly guessing that these fees would not be sufficient to support the school—even with a farm attached to the property—the trustees relied on subsidies from the Orthodox Yearly Meeting to make up the difference. The lower tuition and fees—which the school committee claimed were only half that of a typical boarding school—led to increased enrollment.[18]

A few years before young J. Williams's arrival, at the time of the schism of 1827, there had been problems with certain students who were apparently stirred up by a talk Elias Hicks gave in the area. Rejecting the Bible-centered approach of the Orthodox faction, Hicks had said that the Popes had had the Bible for centuries. Perhaps his point was that during this period the Scriptures' supposed reformatory tendencies were not apparent, a dig at the evangelical Protestantism of the Orthodox. Perhaps taking an overzealous approach to Hicks's words, some male students, denouncing Bibles as papal, set fire to as many Bibles as they could get their hands on—and given the mandatory Bible-readings in the school, there were Bibles available for burning purposes. The school expelled several students and labored with others to get them to repent of their behavior.[19]

The Bible-burning incident behind it, the school sought to instruct the pupils, ranging in age from nine to eighteen, in science, religion, classic literature, and mathematics. The school had a special fondness for math instruction, supposedly spurred on by student demand, and prided itself in its focus on this practical subject. The students' behavior, at least on the boys' side of the institution, was monitored by an employee, Daniel Reece, appointed for that purpose. While reserving corporal punishment for egregious behavior, the school rarely used this disciplinary option, in contrast to the early years when floggings were as routine as at other schools of the era.[20]

In a memoir of his school experiences, written many years later for

2. Born into a Cold World

a local newspaper, Joseph called to mind affectionate memories. These memories included the instructors, the outings allowed on the school grounds, and the occasional opportunities of the older boys to bypass faculty surveillance and slip love notes to students from the girls' side of the school. There was a contrast between the official rules of the school and the "common law of the boy-democracy" by which the schoolboys governed their actions when they could get away with it. One of the offenses forbidden by the schoolboy common law was snitching on other students: "Tale-bearing was the 'sin against the holy ghost' that could not be forgiven." One persistent snitch was "swung in a sheet from an upper chamber window."[21]

Another provision of the schoolboy common law was that it was OK to get "pies and cheese from the table or the pantry." This may explain part of a letter which young J. Williams wrote to his mother in 1834. The lonely schoolboy, while wishing for more family visits, asked his family not to bring him food. The early part of the letter shows that Joseph had begun honing the rhetorical skills he would show throughout his life. His mother had reproached him for not writing more, and Thorne protested that his previous letters, while not addressed to his mother, had been meant for the whole family. To prove this, Thorne said that he had used the plural form of address in his previous letters, indicating that he was writing to his whole family.[22]

In the same year as Joseph wrote his letter, his younger brother James died, leaving Joseph as his parents' only son, an increase of responsibility which could certainly have made an impression on the youth.[23]

Another event at the school gave J. Williams a chance to use his skills at argument. The boys liked to read books regarded by the school as improper, including romances. At one point, a teacher caught Joseph and some friends reading a biography of Lord Byron. In light of the scandalous incidents in Byron's life, the teacher questioned whether this book was appropriate reading material. Joseph replied that many of the books the pupils read with the school's approval included lives of rulers and generals like Napoleon—war leaders whose bloody battles, Joseph indicated, were just as unedifying as Byron's romantic misadventures.[24]

From J. Williams's perspective many years later, only about a fifth of the 129 boys with whom he attended Westtown benefited from the course of instruction. Most of the students needed more practical skills than the curriculum focused on, in J. Williams's estimation. J. Williams was also critical of the religious instruction, consisting of regular Bible readings

Quaker Carpetbagger

and readings from 17th-century Scottish Quaker Robert Barclay's catechism. In giving their periodic Bible readings, Joseph remembered, the teachers skipped over parts of the Old Testament, which reminded the older Joseph of Martin Luther's attempt to exclude certain books from the Bible.[25]

It would be tempting to speculate that, as part of his school curriculum or outside reading, J. Williams may have read about a controversy relevant to his later career. This controversy arose in 1809 and involved Jacob Henry, a slave-owning Federalist from coastal Carteret County and a member of the North Carolina House of Commons (later the House of Representatives). Henry's fitness for his position had been called into question. Henry was Jewish, and the state constitution provided: "That no person, who shall deny the being of God or the truth of the Protestant religion, or the divine authority either of the Old or New Testaments, or who shall hold religious principles incompatible with the freedom and safety of the State, shall be capable of holding any office or place of trust or profit in the civil department within this State." Henry gave an eloquent speech in defense of his right, as a Jewish citizen, to hold public office. Contrasting the exclusionary provisions of the state Constitution with the state Declaration of Rights, he said that the Declaration, which affirmed everyone's right to worship God in his own manner, took precedence over any religiously discriminatory law. Religion "is surely a question between man and his Maker," said Henry. Judaism "inculcates every duty which man owes to his fellow men," and Henry did not seek either to proselytize, or to refuse friendship to, his Christian brethren. There was no cause to deny him his rights. The House decided that Henry could keep his seat on a technicality (the legislators did not consider themselves part of "the civil government").

Henry's triumph was publicized throughout the country as a broader victory for freedom than it actually was. The *American Orator,* a popular collection of speeches to be studied and recited by schoolchildren, included Henry's speech. During a lengthy, and ultimately successful, campaign in Maryland to allow Jews to hold office, H.M. Brackenridge, a supporter of Jewish rights, read parts of Henry's speech out of a copy of the *American Orator* and added: "Mr. Henry prevailed, and it is a part of our education, as Americans, to love and cherish the sentiments uttered by him on that occasion." Mr. Brackenridge's own speech was published in a pamphlet printed in Philadelphia.[26]

Many Chester County Quakers, including young J. Williams, gave

2. Born into a Cold World

a renewed focus on the evils of slavery in the 1830s. The American Antislavery Society (AASS), a national organization espousing the principles of immediate abolition, held its founding convention in Philadelphia in December 1833. Many Pennsylvanians were present, including some members of Pennsylvania's older antislavery group, the Pennsylvania Abolition Society. These people attended in their personal capacities, since the Pennsylvania Abolition Society had not endorsed the new national movement.

The East Fallowfield Antislavery Society was founded in 1835 and had regular meetings in the Fallowfield Friends meetinghouse. There seems to have been considerable, but not complete, overlap between the local Quakers and the membership of the East Fallowfield Antislavery Society. For a time, J. Williams Thorne was clerk of the Fallowfield Meeting, which would have made it easier to have antislavery meetings in the building, since J. Williams had developed strong abolitionist views. J. Williams was one of the many Pennsylvania abolitionists who wanted to establish a state affiliate of the American Antislavery Society, which would be more militant than the older and more cautious Pennsylvania Abolition Society. Calls for a state convention were published in the *National Enquirer and Constitutional Advocate of Universal Liberty*, a Philadelphia abolitionist newspaper edited by Benjamin Lundy. The name of "Joseph Thorne" was included in a December 1836 list of those supporting the convention call. Another convention call printed in January 1837 included "Joseph Williams Thorne" as a signatory from Chester

The Jewish citizen Jacob Henry, whose Carteret County, NC, house is commemorated by this plaque, eloquently defended his right to sit in the lower house of the North Carolina legislature despite his minority religious views. J. Williams Thorne would find himself beleaguered on account of his own religious views when he tried to serve in the same body (Wikimedia Commons).

County—indicating that young Joseph was active among East Fallowfield's abolitionists.²⁷

Early 1837 was a busy time for the East Fallowfield Antislavery Society. Connecticut abolitionist C.C. Burleigh reported how he had addressed two crowded meetings of the society on January 9. Some unspecified individuals tried to make trouble outside the meetinghouse, but they did not succeed, and either had to depart or sit and listen. While Burleigh's well-attended meetings were presumably held to rouse up support for the state antislavery convention at the end of the month, the *National Enquirer*'s account does not indicate that the East Fallowfield society, as a body, was represented when the new Pennsylvania Antislavery Society was formed. On March 12, the East Fallowfield society debated four antislavery resolutions, the first three introduced by the ladies of the meeting. Resolutions 1, 2, and 4 were adopted, urging citizens to speak and work for the end of the sin of slavery, and "to cultivate the moral condition of *our own* vicinity." The third resolution, declaring that religious ministers "*do not declare the whole counsel of God*" unless they denounced slavery, was deferred for the next meeting.²⁸

On March 16, the Board of Managers (male and female) of the East Fallowfield Antislavery Society joined with the Clarkson Antislavery Society to call for a Chester County Antislavery Society. J. Williams was not on the Board of Managers.²⁹

By 1838, the East Fallowfield society was listed as part of the Pennsylvania Antislavery Society's Eastern District. The *National Enquirer* had a new editor, an up-and-coming poet from Massachusetts named John Greenleaf Whittier, and a new name: the *Pennsylvania Freeman*. Abolitionists and reformers commissioned work on a new building in Philadelphia, to be called Pennsylvania Hall, a gathering place for reform activities, the renamed newspaper, and free debate.³⁰

Apparently, the East Fallowfield Antislavery Society resolved their disagreement about how to deal with non-abolitionist clergy. In a meeting of March 3, 1838, the society debated, and unanimously adopted, a resolution announcing that antislavery principles applied to everyone, especially Christians, and that the society "view with feelings of deep regret and astonishment" the lack of support for the abolitionist cause from "many whom we have been taught to look up to as lights in the world, and promoters of every good work."³¹

By the end of 1838, the hopeful prospects, as they may have appeared from East Fallowfield, were met with setbacks, showing the difficulties the

2. Born into a Cold World

Gutted remains of Pennsylvania Hall, burned by an anti-abolitionist mob in Philadelphia (*History of Pennsylvania Hall, Which Was Destroyed by a Mob, On the 17th of May, 1838* [Philadelphia: Printed by Merrihew and Gunn, 1838], opposite p. 140).

abolition movement would have to overcome even in the Quaker state. First an anti-abolitionist mob burned Pennsylvania Hall to the ground. Then antislavery Governor Joseph Ritner went down to defeat. And the voters endorsed a new state Constitution that limited the vote to whites only—which, together with a state high court decision the previous year, concluded a decades-long ambiguity over whether blacks could be voters. The ballot box would be closed to Pennsylvania blacks for the next three decades.[32]

A Quaker minister named Jesse Kersey visited the area around this time, and provided J. Williams with some spiritual inspiration. Kersey, a Pennsylvanian, was an old man who had led a Job-like life. Constantly plagued by poverty and illness, Kersey outlived his wife and ten of his eleven children. For a time, rather than seek comfort with his friends like Job did, Kersey sought to console himself with the bottle. This led to his being removed from the position of elder, until he broke with his drinking habit and was reinstated. Visiting different Quaker meetings as a traveling minister, the reformed and spiritually reinvigorated Kersey brought a message of spiritual peace. He spoke of the need to "strip" Christianity "of all the dead formalities that have been unwisely heaped upon it." J. Williams was quite inspired by one of Kersey's messages during Quaker worship, and wrote a poem paraphrasing the message. Joseph's poem would play an important role in a crisis in Thorne's life later on. J. Williams may also have imbibed (so to speak) a lesson on the dangers of alcohol, and he may have noted that Kersey's drinking habit began when his physician prescribed brandy and laudanum for his illness.[33]

Some parts of Kersey's message would have been less welcome to J. Williams. One of Kersey's key teachings was to warn fellow Hicksites against the sort of thing J. Williams was doing—cooperating with non–Quaker abolitionists. To Kersey, the Hicksites should have learned from their encounter with the Orthodox that Quakers should not compromise their special position as a people apart. For years, Quakers had been deliberately insular, keeping the non–Quaker world at arm's length to avoid spiritual contamination. Those outside the Quaker fold did not hold to the doctrine of the Inner Light, and might lead Quakers away from God with purely private notions, even in the context of working for a good cause like abolition. To Kersey, the "darkness" into which the church had fallen in the past had come from abandoning the "Light of Christ." "Therefore," as Kersey later wrote in his memoirs,

> I have felt concerned to warn the society of Friends against entering upon this descending ground, and downward course ... many of our parents are apparently joining with those who are acting their part in what are called works of reform, under the guidance of the natural understanding; for, among the people at large the necessity for any higher principle to govern or influence, than the natural faculties of man,—is not admitted. Therefore when Friends join with them and attend their meetings, they cease to maintain a state of humble dependence upon the gospel power, and expect to be sufficiently wise of themselves.[34]

Kersey's concerns were not unique among Hicksite Quakers. In 1830, soon after establishing an independent existence, the Philadelphia Yearly Meeting of the Hicksites (with authority over Chester County) warned the faithful not "to mingle with other professors [a Quaker term for outsiders who professed to be Christians] in what is called religious concerns, though professedly to promote the cause of Christ...."[35]

Echoing these concerns with great fervor was an itinerant Hicksite minister named George Fox White. To White, Hicksites who consorted with non–Quaker abolitionists were engaging in the same errors as the Orthodox from whom the Hicksites had just split. As with all Quakers of the time, White believed slavery was wrong—among all branches of Quakerism, owning or trading in slaves was a disownable offense. White

2. Born into a Cold World

(like Hicks himself) refused to purchase the products of slave labor. But Quaker collaboration with the abolitionist movement, from White's point of view, was not only diluting Quakers' witness as a distinct people, but was endangering the American Union and doing more harm than help to the slave.

White's views were popular among many Hicksites, though those who were dedicated to the abolitionist cause saw White as a source of moral corruption, teaching indifference to the slave's plight. For the abolitionist Hicksites, White compounded his evildoing by preaching against the participation of reform-minded Quaker women in abolitionist and other reform causes. In a visit to Chester County in 1839, White said women should attend to their domestic duties, not "roam over the country from Dan to Beersheba spurning the protection of man." White's influence may have been helped by a personable one-on-one attitude, contrasting with his harsh public words: a Chester County Quaker, Benjamin Swayne, called White "agreeable and cheerful."[36]

The 1840 census listed a young man between 20 and 30 years old living in the elder Thorne's household. This could have been J. Williams, who in his mid–20s would have been about the right age.[37]

The strife between freedom and slavery continued to bring itself to Chester County's doorstep. In mid–1841, a purported slave owner and two policemen from neighboring Lancaster County seized a black woman in Chester County whom they said was a fugitive slave. As the cops were taking the woman away in a carriage, some black men, about five or six in number, beat the carriage-horses with clubs to get the carriage to stop. Though the cops didn't have jurisdiction in Chester County, they fired at the rescuers, wounding one, until the black men beat the cops and forced them to give up their victim.[38]

3

Let Truth and Error Grapple

In January 1842, a convention of slave-owners met in Annapolis, the capital of Maryland, to consider the crisis of absconding slaves. What to do about the large number of Maryland slaves who crossed into Pennsylvania and, often with the help of sympathetic blacks and whites, eluded pursuers?[1]

The United States Supreme Court came to the aid of slave-owners in a decision in March. Several kidnappers from Maryland had been charged under Pennsylvania's Personal Liberty Law of 1826 for seizing a black woman and her children and bringing them into slavery, without first obtaining a judicial ruling that the family were in fact fugitive slaves. In order to induce the kidnappers to surrender, Pennsylvania negotiated a deal with Maryland to make the kidnappers' prosecution into a test case for the U.S. Supreme Court. As part of the deal, Pennsylvania stipulated that the woman was a fugitive slave, while Maryland stipulated that one of her children had been born in Pennsylvania.[2]

In its decision in *Prigg v. Pennsylvania*, the Supreme Court held that a master from a slave state, or his agent, could enter a free state and seize a fugitive slave without trial and bring him or her back into slavery. All he had to do was avoid a breach of the peace. The states had no role to play in enforcing the Constitution's fugitive slave clause, or making sure it was fairly enforced—that was solely a federal responsibility. The only role for the states to play was to stay out of the way while masters, with or without federal assistance, seized their slaves and brought them back to bondage.[3]

In the 1840s, black migration continued into Chester County and the neighboring border county of Lancaster. Some of them had been emancipated by owners across the border, and others were fleeing from slavery. The poor black population as a proportion of the total increased until they made up about a quarter of blacks. This process continued as white

3. Let Truth and Error Grapple

migrants also inundated the area. As traditional crafts were replaced by small industry, the competition among members of the different races increased considerably, and the growing power of Jacksonian Democrats allowed a climate in which the whites openly sought to seize the jobs that were on offer.[4]

At the top of the black community were some well-off entrepreneurs, like Abraham Shadd. Below them were a beleaguered middle class and working class, and finally were the great proportion of paupers who sought to eke out a living by seasonal labor, while often reporting to the almshouse in the off season.

The working-class and pauper-class blacks also came to the attention of whites when they showed up in court, charged with brawling or theft, or with petty pilfering on the part of those who were hungry and desperate. Blacks were obliged to fight on many fronts on behalf of their community: fighting slave raiders from across the border and their white local accomplices, newly emboldened by the Supreme Court; seeking the elusive goal of equal opportunity in a community which, overall, practiced racial oppression against the disenfranchised blacks, while also seeking the economic uplift of their less-well-off compatriots. The African Methodist Episcopal Church provided a spiritual home for the middle class; the entrepreneur class supported that church while often co-worshipping with sympathetic whites.

Sympathetic whites still existed, though they faced hostility from other whites as well as divisions among themselves. The large Hicksite Quaker population of Lancaster and Chester Counties provided the main support of a group of antislavery whites who worked against the institution of slavery, often facing obstruction from their coreligionists.

The East Fallowfield Antislavery Society continued to meet at the Fallowfield Monthly Meeting house, and Joseph Williams Thorne was one of many who had overlapping memberships in both the society and the meeting. Meanwhile, the antislavery movement throughout the country was afflicted with bitter divisions. If he had had such a frame of reference, J. Williams would have been reminded of the rival anti–Roman opposition groups in *Monty Python's Life of Brian*. Some review of the confusing factionalism of the abolitionist movement is necessary to understand local developments in Chester County and East Fallowfield.

Before 1833, the Pennsylvania Abolition Society had been established for several decades. In the country as a whole, many opponents of slavery supported sending freed slaves to an American-sponsored colony in west

Quaker Carpetbagger

Africa, known as Liberia. The Liberian project was promoted, out of a variety of motives, by the American Colonization Society (ACS). Colonization was unpopular among most free blacks, who did not wish to be deported from their native country. Many white abolitionists likewise rejected the "negrophobia" reflected in proposals to separate the black and white populations. One of the planks of the American Antislavery Society (AASS) platform, upon the founding of the organization in 1833, was rejection of colonization in favor of elevating blacks, as rapidly as possible, from their status as slaves or as free members of a degraded class, into the status of full citizens.[5]

This agenda was considered sufficiently "radical" in itself to provoke often violent white opposition, in the North as well as the South. A central figure in the AASS, William Lloyd Garrison, added some extra elements of radicalism to his personal philosophy, positions which he often seemed to combine with the AASS agenda in his newspaper, the *Liberator*. In addition to scathing denunciations of the clergy for their softness on slavery, Garrison by the 1840s had developed into a militant pacifist. He also was evolving into a secessionist, preaching that the North should withdraw from the American Union in order to separate itself from the South and the allegedly proslavery Constitution. As the years progressed, Garrison and his followers also rejected voting—they believed true abolitionists should not taint themselves with association with the political system, relying instead on "moral suasion" Finally, Garrison accepted, at least in theory, an equal role for women in abolitionist activism and endorsed the newborn feminist movement. Garrison's controversial views, and his vehement quarrels with abolitionists of other perspectives, led to a schism in the antislavery movement in 1840, as a dissident group broke away from the American Antislavery Society to form the American and Foreign Antislavery Society. The latter group, referred to as the "New Organization" as opposed to Garrison's "Old Organization," did not categorically reject voting, it was more sympathetic to mainstream Protestantism (many leaders were ministers and former ministers), it was not absolutist on pacifism, and it only accepted women in auxiliaries, not in the main organization.[6]

By the mid-1840s, the squabbling New and Old Organizations were overshadowed by a new antislavery political party, the Liberty Party. Many abolitionists put their energies into this new third party, prompting the founding of several party newspapers and the nomination of a repentant ex-slaveholder, James G. Birney, for president. The party platform in 1844 declared that the federal government must divorce itself from slavery—

3. Let Truth and Error Grapple

which meant no slavery in Washington, D.C., the federal territories, or federal buildings, etc., and no new slave states. The Fugitive Slave Act of 1793 was pronounced unconstitutional, and the Fugitive Slave Clause of the Constitution was pronounced contrary to the divine law. The election of 1844 divided Americans over the question of whether to annex the slaveholding Republic of Texas, something abolitionists opposed because Texas had slavery. Birney got enough votes to deny the election to the waffling Whig Henry Clay and elect the annexationist Democrat James K. Polk.[7]

In Eastern Pennsylvania, the abolitionists, who were mostly Hicksite Quakers, had stuck with the Old Organization, and had not formed a strong Liberty Party organization. But beneath the surface, Chester County's abolitionists were divided over the same issues that sparked disagreement among abolitionists throughout the North. After the 1844 election, the Chester County Antislavery Society, affiliated with the national group, announced a forthcoming meeting on November 29 in the Fallowfield meeting house. Explaining the purpose of the meeting in the Old Organization newspaper, the *National Antislavery Standard*, the leaders of the county society complained that "instead of presenting one unbroken front to the enemy, we have pressed onward, attacking on every side ... each one doing what his judgment dictated." The announcement called for a discussion "in that spirit of forbearance that made us one in the beginning, ready to assert or yield" their various opinions "as truth may convict us of their rightfulness or error." The issue of whether to stay in the Union with the slaveholding states was a matter "of great interest" on which members would attempt "reasoning together." "Other matters of interest, it is expected, will come before the meeting," apparently including the legitimacy of taking part in elections.[8]

The Fallowfield conclave was probably inconclusive. On the national level the Garrisonian Old Organization wanted to rally its membership in Eastern Pennsylvania in support of proper Garrisonian principles. Though the mainly-Quaker abolitionists of eastern Pennsylvania had remained faithful to the Old Organization, they still had to be sold on the new, uncompromising Garrisonian program. A lecture tour of eastern Pennsylvania was planned, and the main attraction would be the fervent Garrisonian Abby Kelley. Her nomination for the AASS leadership had been the final straw that prompted the schism of the New Organization, but the presence of a female lecturer would presumably be less offensive to Quaker audiences, accustomed as Quakers were to traveling female

Quaker Carpetbagger

ministers. Kelley would help the cantankerous Quakers see the proslavery nature of the U.S. Constitution, the need for disunion, and the need to separate from non-abolitionist churches. Assisting Kelley would be two male lecturers, Erasmus Hudson and Benjamin Jones. Armed with the recently published notes of James Madison on the Constitutional Convention debates in 1787, Kelley prepared her case against the Constitution. She often met with rowdy heckling and threats, though these tended to come from non–Quakers.[9] Mob disruption from Quakers themselves may not have been something she anticipated.

The appearance of Kelley and the other lecturers had originally been scheduled for December 19, 1844, but for whatever reason was rescheduled for January 17 and 18 in the Fallowfield Meetinghouse. In addition to the hostility of the white population in general, she faced unrest among the Quakers themselves. Fallowfield Meeting, like other Hicksite Meetings in Chester County, was part of the Hicksite Pennsylvania Yearly Meeting and its regional subdivision, the Western Quarterly Meeting. At the April 1844 Western Quarterly Meeting in London Grove, one disgruntled Quaker reformer claimed that the leadership slighted the abolition and temperance crusades in favor of enforcing Quaker peculiarities like plain dress and naming months by numbers (April was "fourth month"). Quaker Ministers like Jesse Kersey and George Fox White had helped turn many Hicksites away from political activism, and toward suspicion of the politically active members of their own denomination, whose cooperation with professional non–Quaker reformers was compared to the Orthodox Quaker friendliness with non–Quaker "hireling ministers."[10]

On January 17, 1845, the first day of the speeches at the Fallowfield Meetinghouse, the lectures dealt with disunion and voting, and proceeded without interruption. On the 18th, the topic under discussion was the need to separate from churches which were proslavery or lukewarm. Dr. Edwin Fussell, a Chester County physician (who with his uncle Bartholomew would promote the establishment of a woman's medical college in Philadelphia), was warming up the audience with his discourse on slavery while the main attraction, Abby Kelley, waited her turn. What happened next was described by Philadelphia's Joseph Liddon Pennock, who covered the meeting for the *National Antislavery Standard*. The audience during the evening's talk was made up of about three hundred women and men, and a few "mobocrats" and troublemakers. One man yelled during Fussell's speech that Fussell had talked long enough, and other disruptive individuals made noises to drown the speaker out. Some people knocked

3. Let Truth and Error Grapple

out the windows, and someone threw brimstone (sulfur) on the stove that warmed the building. The infernal stench, and the turbulence, led some to flee the building, at times by jumping out the windows. Some "brave men" (the sarcastic term was Pennock's) moved from the men's side of the room to the women's side (Quaker meetings at the time were divided into rooms for the men's and women's meetings).[11]

Charles Lukens, a Hicksite Quaker and apparently a member of the Fallowfield Meeting, tried unsuccessfully to drag Fussell out of the building. Kelley urged respect for free expression and offered to answer anyone with specific arguments against her position. Charles Lukens's father William replied to Kelley that she had been "cursing the Bible," and called on Fussell to leave, saying Fussell was desecrating the building where William's late mother, a Quaker minister, used to speak. Others in the audience insisted on hearing the speakers, and finally the tumult subsided and Fussell and Kelley were able to give their talks. Fussell spoke of the importance of free expression and Kelley spoke of the need to "come out" from the churches and from "the American compact" (in Pennock's paraphrase, presumably describing the federal Constitution).[12]

William Lukens and seven others were charged with rioting. Only Lukens could be found, and he faced a trial of several days in West Chester during February. Lukens denounced the speakers as treasonous, and said that it was not the proper business of the Fallowfield Meeting to invite them. The judge found this explanation legally irrelevant to the issue of guilt, though the jury acquitted Lukens. The local Democratic newspaper in West Chester, the *Jeffersonian*, praised the jury for acquitting Lukens and denounced the speakers he had interrupted.[13]

Cleared by a jury, William Lukens still had to face his own meeting. The sparse records of the Fallowfield Meeting suggest that Lukens made some kind of apology for his behavior and was allowed to retain his membership.[14]

In April, at the call of the Fallowfield Preparative Meeting, Fallowfield's Quakers debated for around seven hours about the use of the hall by abolitionists and for other outside purposes. The majority group in the meeting approved of the way the meeting hall had previously been opened to reform and radical speakers. A determined minority, probably including some of the disruptors from January, expressed their dissatisfaction with outsiders using the meetinghouse premises. This could have ended in a schism, but the majority group adhered to customary Quaker practice, which emphasizes obtaining a sense of the whole meeting, not

Quaker Carpetbagger

simply having a majority impose on the minority. The majority faction in the meeting agreed with the minority not to use the meetinghouse for outside non–Quaker purposes any longer.[15]

In lieu of having speakers at the meetinghouse, the majority group constructed a building next door to the meetinghouse. This "People's Hall" was to be a forum where outside speakers and debaters would come. Inside the building, over the platform where speakers would address the people, was the slogan "Let Truth and Error Grapple," a paraphrase of a famous passage from John Milton's classic anti-censorship work, *Areopagitica:* "And though all the winds of doctrine were let loose to play upon the earth, so Truth be in the field, we do injuriously by licensing and prohibiting to misdoubt her strength. Let her and Falsehood grapple; who ever knew Truth put to the worse in a free and open encounter? Her confuting is the best and surest suppressing." (J. Williams's later account of the founding of People's Hall did not focus on the nearby Friends Meeting, but on the claim that the hall was built after the 1844 expulsion of Ercildoun's Lyceum Association "from the public school-house.")[16]

The new People's Hall was dedicated on August 1, 1845. A poem, written by J. Williams, was read for the occasion. The poem speaks of a "living language" which can be read in nature, the language being "The one unchanging oracle to man," urging "Be free! Be free!" All nature issues this call—"The people heard that voice/And built this free hall." The hall "hath no creed, nor rules by penal laws.... 'Tis free to all the brotherhood of man." Furthermore, "error too is free, too weak to move,/ Much less to bear a chain where truth is free." The poem took shots at "intemperance" which brings "The lingering life decay," and scorned the "worship[]" of "The most successful murderers," while poor murderers were hanged. And "slavery is a cloud that comes between/And blots the book of Nature from our view." J. Williams's hope was that "this free hall/ Was reared with the warm wish and youthful hope/ That Truth's unfettered power might soon dispel/ The slavery clouds that come before our eyes." The "free airs" call on people "to worship a holy God." The poem concluded:

> May we not warmly hope that yet these walls
> In no far future hour, will echo back
> To the free universe its own free voice,
> In one sweet union strain, one joyous song,
> Of all mankind—the world—the world is free![17]

The clashes at Fallowfield Meeting seem to have led to several resignations. The reasons for the resignations were not explained in the

3. Let Truth and Error Grapple

People's Hall, Ercildoun, Chester County, Pennsylvania (Wikimedia Commons).

meeting's minutes, but it could be that the departing members objected to the actions of one side or the other, or both, in the turmoil over outside activities in the meetinghouse.[18]

Abolitionists and reformers from all over the Western Quarterly Meeting assembled at the Friends meetinghouse in Marlborough on several occasions between May and September 1845, to discuss whether they should remain with the Hicksites or break away in protest at the anti-reform element within the denomination. After all this talk, the reformers finally agreed to stick with the Hicksites for the moment.[19]

Amid this local religio-political turmoil, J. Williams Thorne may have been living on his father's farm. But now he established his own farm, and the reason may be guessed. He married fellow Quaker Mary Jones Pusey on March 10, 1846.[20]

Finding a new home for himself and his bride, Thorne took a bold step. On the western edge of Chester County was the township of Sadsbury

Quaker Carpetbagger

(not the Sadsbury in Lancaster County where his mother had attended the Quaker meeting). In Sadsbury there was an abandoned, overgrown piece of property of about one hundred sixty acres. The owners were long gone. Local tradition held that the prior owners had subsisted by selling wood that they gathered on the undeveloped property. First the mother of the household, then the father, had been felled by a disease epidemic. After their mother's death, the sons of the household were supposedly with their horses gathering wood for market when they got word that they had inherited property elsewhere. On hearing this news, they left without even unhitching the horses from the wood sled. Later visitors, chasing a fox onto the property, found the horses' skeletal remains. Such, in any event, was the story attached to the property.[21]

Where others saw abandoned acreage associated with a disturbing and creepy story, Thorne saw opportunity. He managed to find the owners and cheaply purchased the land from them, determined to make a home and farm there. This required backbreaking labor in clearing the land, erecting a house, and generally turning a useless property into a working farm. J. Williams and his new wife stayed in a log cabin on the land while the farmhouse was being built. A man J. Williams hired to erect the barn, as Thorne later recounted it, predicted disaster—the man said the barn "could not be filled in ten years from his farm, if every straw raised upon it were carried in and nothing ever taken out!" The county agricultural society, in a report on Thorne's farm twelve years later, added: "And yet, in less than two years after its completion," the barn "was filled to the roof." Thorne ultimately grew fruit trees, and cultivated fields of wheat, rye, corn oats and Chinese sugar cane, on the supposedly infertile land.[22]

J. Williams was busy building his farm and family. Caleb Pusey Thorne was born on October 13, 1847, at seven in the evening. As later events showed, the precise time seemed to be known by many in the community.[23]

Chester County's Quakers had been accustomed to receiving visiting Friends and reformers from remote places; now the whole population of the county, Quaker and non–Quaker, was increasingly exposed to outside speakers. Local debating societies, and the Lyceum system of bringing paid lecturers into different communities, was hitting its antebellum stride, and the county seat of West Chester, as Douglas Harper puts it, was taking on "the appearance of one big night school."[24]

J. Williams was in the middle of all this activity, as one R.J. Houston later recalled: "He was a complete encyclopaedia of knowledge on almost every subject, and probably did more than any other man in the state to

3. Let Truth and Error Grapple

maintain and popularize the lyceum and debating school in that section" of the country. J. Williams focused his lyceum activities in Lancaster County—his farm abutted or straddled the line between Lancaster and Chester, and Houston recalled that J. Williams "diligently attended all the well-conducted lyceums and debates within a radius of five or six miles from his home, most of them in Lancaster County." Houston described J. Williams as an excellent debater who, once "he got his antagonist in a hole ... took care to keep him in it, but he did it so pleasantly that no one could find fault."[25]

Many of those visiting Chester County were Protestant temperance speakers making vivid warnings about the dangers of drunkenness. But outsiders were not needed to alert reform-minded county resi-

A young J. Williams Thorne, from Thorne family papers (courtesy Nancy Plumley).

dents to the evils of drink. Grand jury reports linked drunkenness and crime, while temperance reformers set up alcohol-free stores and hotels. Chester was one of a group of counties where activists were sufficiently persistent that in 1846, the state legislature allowed local option. Villages and townships could vote themselves dry. Most Chester County townships used their new powers to vote to ban liquor within their boundaries. The state Supreme Court soon held local option unconstitutional, putting the prohibition forces back where they started.[26]

Quaker Carpetbagger

In 1847, the Pennsylvania legislature fashioned a response to the *Prigg* decision. Antislavery groups had lobbied the legislature for a new Personal Liberty Law to protect free blacks and fugitive slaves now that the Act of 1826 had been held unconstitutional. The North was roiled by a debate, sparked the previous year by Pennsylvania Congressman David Wilmot, on the status of slavery in the territories being rapidly conquered by U.S. troops in the war with Mexico. Northerners and Southerners argued over whether slavery would be permitted in these new territories, leading many Pennsylvanians to experience renewed suspicion of Southern intentions.[27]

In Pennsylvania's new Personal Liberty Law, the legislators played a clever legal jiu-jitsu, exploiting the states'-rights potentialities in the seemingly nationalist *Prigg* decision. *Prigg* had held that the federal government, not the states, was responsible for returning fugitive slaves. That being so, the Personal Liberty Law declared that Pennsylvania would leave fugitive slave matters to the federal government, and that the state would not cooperate in the return of fugitive slaves, either by arresting alleged fugitives or by putting them in state prison. *Prigg* had decided that slave-owners had the right to go into free states and seize runaway slaves without trial, but had not authorized the seizure of free blacks, and the Personal Liberty Law affixed penalties to those who kidnapped free blacks in order to enslave them. *Prigg* had held that masters and their agents could seize runaways so long as they did not breach the peace; the Personal Liberty Law provided strict penalties if the seizure of a slave was made in a "violent, tumultuous and unreasonable manner." The right of anyone arrested or imprisoned in Pennsylvania to seek the writ of habeas corpus was reaffirmed. Laws against slave testimony, and a law that permitted masters to bring their slaves temporarily into Pennsylvania, were repealed.[28]

Maryland slave-raiders continued to disregard the new Personal Liberty Law, as well as the distinction between fugitive slaves and free blacks. In April 1848, in Downington township, near the center of Chester County, a raiding party broke into a prominent white magistrate's home, pointed a gun at the homeowner, and seized a sixteen-year-old servant girl whom they claimed to be a fugitive slave. They spirited the girl away to Baltimore to be sold in that city's slave marts, but a Downington doctor, probably representing other whites from the area of the kidnapping, went to Baltimore and ransomed the girl, who soon afterwards fled to Canada with her mother.[29]

3. Let Truth and Error Grapple

Henry S. Evans, editor of a newspaper at the county seat, the West Chester *Village Record*, published an indignant editorial about the "armed ruffians" who had broken into the home of a "peaceable citizen." In Cecil County, Maryland, across the Mason-Dixon line from Chester County, the *Cecil Whig* responded to Evans's editorial. The slave raid in Downington was the fault of Pennsylvania for sheltering fugitive slaves, said the Maryland paper. "Large rewards will prompt fearless men to imminent risks, and they will carry out their plans with a skill and desperation which will laugh at every opposition. Arrests, or *outrages*, if they please to call them so, will follow each other in quick succession, and blood and death may deepen them into fearful tragedies, and for all the consequences the people of Pennsylvania will be held accountable."[30]

Kidnappers struck again in Downington in 1849. This time they took a more subtle approach with Henry Lee Brown, a young free black man. First luring Brown to Philadelphia on pretense of a job offer, they then persuaded him to enter a carriage that would supposedly take him to the job in Delaware. The kidnappers were joined by colleagues who helped divert the carriage to Maryland and brought young Brown to a slave pen in Baltimore. The slave pen was run by Bernard Moore Campbell, who with his brother Walter Lewis Campbell headed a leading slave-trading firm in Baltimore. Affairs were looking up for the Campbell firm in in 1849, as they did a brisk business buying Maryland slaves and shipping them to New Orleans for resale. The Campbells had one business practice that was potentially inconvenient to kidnappers: they advertised that anyone who sold slaves to them must have "good title" to the slaves. When Brown protested that he was free, Bernard contacted the young man's employer in Downington and verified his story. Brown was duly released.[31]

Soon after that, an armed raiding band broke into a house rented by a black man named Tom Mitchell in Unionville, East Marlborough Township, which was to the south of Downington. The band forcibly seized Mitchell and took him to Baltimore, to the pen of a different slave dealer named Wilson. Mitchell's white neighbors followed the kidnapper to Baltimore, and after receiving some legal harassment in the Maryland courts, they paid off Mitchell's alleged master and brought him back to Pennsylvania—Mitchell all the time claiming to be a free man.[32]

In the Henry Lee Brown case, three of the kidnappers were arrested, and two were convicted in Philadelphia for kidnapping a free black man into slavery. Other alleged kidnappers were indicted by the grand jury, but they were back in Maryland. One of Brown's alleged kidnappers, Thomas

Quaker Carpetbagger

McCreary, had also been involved in seizing Tom Mitchell. An indignant meeting in Mitchell's neighborhood deplored the acts of McCreary and others for having "invaded the sovereignty of" Pennsylvania, and demanded the indictment of the perpetrators for riot and other crimes, perhaps having in mind the Personal Liberty Law's provision against breach of the peace by slave-catchers. Unnamed abolitionists in the crowd urged blacks to use force in defense of their community against the raiders. In any case, the Chester County grand jury did not issue an indictment in the Mitchell case (though Maryland authorities thought this had happened, conflating Brown's case with Mitchell's).[33]

As it happened, McCreary was a politically well-connected individual in Maryland, which helped him when the governor of Pennsylvania demanded McCreary's extradition in the Brown case. The governor of Maryland refused to extradite McCreary, leaving him free to continue his depredations. The *Cecil Whig*, professing to have "no sympathy with McCreary," nonetheless taunted Pennsylvanians by saying McCreary "will go into their midst and take negroes from under their very noses until they [Pennsylvanians] learn to respect the laws of Maryland and of the United States."[34]

At some point J. Williams joined the famous Underground Railroad, using his Sadsbury farm as a shelter for fugitives. Dr. R.C. Smedley, the historian of the local Underground Railroad whose book was published shortly after the author's death in in the early 1880s (while Thorne himself was still alive), traces Thorne's involvement in the Underground Railroad back to 1850, shortly after Congress had passed a new Fugitive Slave Act. The new statute was harsher than the version of 1793, and empowered quasi-judicial officers known as commissioners, backed by federal marshals, to arrest alleged fugitives. The commissioners, who were not full judges in the constitutional sense and who acted without juries, would hear the cases of alleged fugitives and order those found to be slaves to be handed over to the people claiming to be their masters. Commissioners received ten dollars in fees for sending an alleged fugitive into slavery, and five dollars in fees if he released the prisoner. The federal marshals who provided the muscle for the new law could call on the aid of local citizens to help capture alleged fugitives.[35]

It was in this context, according to Smedley's account, that Thorne held a debate with fellow abolitionist Thomas Whitson in 1850, in the Lancaster County town of Christiana. Whitson lived in Bart, in eastern Lancaster County. He was a Garrisonian, and as such he rejected political

3. Let Truth and Error Grapple

involvement and condemned the Constitution as a proslavery document. Garrison himself had praised Whitson's speaking skills. Smedley said Whitson "was decidedly original, witty, jocose, one of the most apposite in thought and expression, and had a great faculty for 'splitting hairs' in a close argument." Whitson was a member of the Hicksite Friends meeting in Sadsbury, the Lancaster County counterpart to Chester County's Sadsbury.[36]

Thorne, for his part, according to Smedley, urged abolitionists to vote for the Liberty Party. That organization, never large to begin with, had shrunk considerably since its heyday in the mid–1840s. A large chunk of Liberty Party members had left in 1848 to join another third party, the Free-Soil Party. Political pragmatists under the leadership of an Ohio lawyer named Salmon P. Chase had led the exodus. To Chase and his group, a viable third-party movement should capitalize on Northern opposition to new slave territories in the West. Such a movement would need to disavow any immediate plans to free slaves in the South—considered a radical position which would turn off Northern voters. Politically opportunistic New Yorkers under former President Martin Van Buren were willing to join the Free-Soilers on these terms, and the new party nominated Van Buren for president. The Free-Soil Party platform seemed radical to non-abolitionists, with its call for divorcing the federal government from slavery. This meant the federal government could not maintain slavery in areas under its jurisdiction, such as the territories and the District of Columbia, and that there would be no more slave states. Abolition of slavery was the ultimate goal, but the power of states to allow slavery under their own laws was acknowledged. Van Buren came in third in the 1848 election, but the Free-Soilers kept at it until 1854, when they merged with the Republicans. As if to confirm that his was the pragmatic position, Chase later became governor of Ohio, Secretary of the Treasury, Chief Justice of the United States, and a perennial presidential candidate.[37]

But for the moment, if Smedley's timeline is correct, J. Williams was with the hard core of Liberty Party members, who believed the Free-Soil movement had made too many concessions. After Chase and the others left for the Free-Soil Party, the remnant of the Liberty Party proclaimed that the federal Constitution banned slavery in the states. The whole thrust of the Constitution, from its liberty-affirming preamble to its guarantee of republican government in the states to its protection of fundamental civil liberties, precluded slavery at either the state or federal level, the Liberty Party held. The rump Liberty Party was financially sustained

Quaker Carpetbagger

by Gerrit Smith, a wealthy New York philanthropist who donated to many abolitionist and reform causes. Under Smith's influence, the Liberty Party endorsed other reforms in addition to its uncompromising stance on slavery. To a generally libertarian focus on shrinking the federal government and putting an end to government chartering of corporations, the Liberty Party platform added a temperance plank—another cause of Smith's. Members would, in 1851, be required to deny that either slavery or liquor could have any legal existence. Interestingly—considering the views J. Williams would express about the Bible—a Liberty Party convention in 1849 had endorsed a book by its future presidential nominee, William Goodell, that argued that the Bible was pro-democracy. The convention had even gone so far as to recommend that every Liberty Party member get a copy of Goodell's book. Goodell was a Christian editor and minister of an independent congregation in upstate New York, a congregation based on Biblical, radical abolitionist and temperance principles. Whether Thorne took the Liberty Party's advice and studied Goodell's pro–Christian book is unknown.[38]

In their debate as recounted by Smedley, Whitson challenged Thorne. Whitson had been in the Underground Railroad for at least nine years by this time, and he gave Thorne the following dare: "Would thee be willing, against the pro-slavery clauses of the Constitution to assist fugitives in escaping from bondage?"

Thorne responded: "Yes, there is nothing in the Constitution to prevent it. The very spirit of the preamble commands that I shall do it."

Whitson said: "Thee shall have the opportunity."

"I will be glad of it," declared Thorne, speaking "emphatically," according to Smedley.[39]

4

The Federal Invasion and the Progressive Friends

Dr. Smedley summarized Thorne's Underground Railroad operation:

> Many were sent to him by Thomas Whitson and many others by Lindley Coates, Joshua Brinton, Joseph Moore, Joseph Fulton and James Williams. He sent them in the night to other stations—generally Bonsall's—in a covered wagon in care of trusty colored men. Some remained a few weeks and worked for him, for which he paid them the full customary wages. No case was ever proved to his knowledge of any anti-slavery men employing fugitives for weeks, and then startling them with a report that slaveholders were in the vicinity, and hurrying them off under plea of security, giving them two or three dollars when they owed them much more. This was an accusation commonly and falsely made against the Underground Railroad men by their pro-slavery neighbors.[1]

Despite the proximity of the slave state of Maryland, and the risk of kidnapping, many blacks, including fugitive slaves, still found Southeastern Pennsylvania, and Chester County, to be a congenial area for settlement. But suspicion was rightly rife concerning the omnipresent kidnappers. The ancestors of Pauli Murray lived in Chester County for a time, and a key part of family lore from that period was the need for constant watchfulness. Door to door salesmen might be scouts for kidnappers. Even some members of the black community were under suspicion as potential informers. Murray's ancestors "never went to bed without barring the door heavily and setting a loaded musket within reach. Great-Grandfather Thomas taught each of his sons to shoot straight, for they never knew when they might have to fight for their lives."[2]

Thorne's own summary of the perilous position of the black community at the time, written in 1875, says:

> As the poor slave was wont to look upon this section of country as most likely to afford him protection and assistance, so also the slave hunters of Maryland and Virginia knew well that here they would in all probability strike the trail, and recover their fugitive chattels.... The sanctity of the domestic hearth of freeman—

respected even by semicivilized peoples—was no bar to the incursions of these insolent and overbearing people. Their peace was likely to be disturbed night and by day, and the colored man never knew what it was to possess the greatest of all boons government can vouchsafe to man—personal liberty and personal security. Not only were escaped slaves captured and carried back into slavery but free negroes were very frequently kidnapped, drug from their homes and families by night and hurried off and sold into hopeless slavery....[3]

Local blacks formed a self-defense association to cope with the menace of the kidnappers. The group acted as an intelligence network to give an early warning if slave-hunters were in the area, and to find out who the targets were. At-risk people could be spirited away. On a more militant note, the group, under the leadership of William Parker, would mobilize to defend blacks against being seized, and take reprisals against the slave-hunters' local collaborators, white and black.[4]

William Lloyd Garrison, the abolitionist pacifist, reported in his *Liberator* in October 1850 that "the fugitive slaves and the free colored people" in Pennsylvania "are arming themselves with pistols, bowie knives and rifles, and learning to use them."[5]

Around 1851, Thorne acquired some new in-laws. His younger sister, Caroline, married Washington Hanway, a miller in West Marlborough in Chester County. Both bride and groom were in their early twenties.[6]

Washington's brother Castner, also a miller, lived in Lancaster County near Christiana. Early on September 11, 1851, Castner Hanway heard a commotion in his neighbor's house and rode on his horse to check it out. The house belonged to a Quaker couple, the Pownalls, and was rented by William Parker. Some white men were confronting the armed black men and women holed up in the house. One of the whites, Henry Kline, announced himself to be a federal marshal. The other whites with Kline were Edward Gorsuch, a Maryland slaveholder, accompanied by his son and some others. Kline and Gorsuch, with a warrant from a U.S. Commissioner under the Act of 1850, were in search of four fugitive slaves. The black self-protection society had notice of the Gorsuch party's arrival, and local blacks assembled at the sound of a horn sounded by Parker's wife. Aside from the slave-raiding party, the only whites around were Hanway and another local man, Elijah Lewis, who had also come to see what the noise was about. Matters escalated with an exchange of gunfire, after which Edward Gorsuch was left dead, his son was wounded, and Kline cowered in a cornfield in a most un-marshal-like manner.[7]

Local and federal posses combed the area looking for suspects, taking

4. The Federal Invasion and the Progressive Friends

Zercher's Hotel, where Edward Gorsuch's body was kept briefly in the wake of the "Christiana Massacre" (now generally referred to as the Christiana Resistance). Today the building houses the Christiana Underground Railroad Center. The obelisk commemorating the events at Christiana was built in 1911 and later moved here (Wikimedia Commons).

particular satisfaction in breaking into the homes of black people and arresting them. The local authorities had the aid of Irish railroad workers, while the federal posse included around forty-five marines and many policemen. Hanway and Lewis turned themselves in, while numerous other suspects were arrested on both state and federal charges. While the state grand jury ultimately did not return any indictments—Parker, the main suspect, had fled to Canada—the federal grand jury in eastern Pennsylvania indicted thirty-eight men, including Hanway and Lewis, for treason, under the theory that they had violently resisted a law of the United States, namely the Fugitive Slave Law.[8]

The Christiana events took place in the middle of a heated political campaign. Whig governor William F. Johnston was against the extension of slavery, a supporter of Pennsylvania's Personal Liberty Law, and an opponent of the Fugitive Slave Act of 1850. He thought the Act should be amended so that full-fledged courts, not "commissioners," would decide the alleged fugitives' fate. Democrat William Bigler seized on the

Quaker Carpetbagger

Christiana "riot" in order to blame Johnston for stirring up abolitionists and blacks with his supposedly radical anti-slavery ideas, thus upsetting the delicate North/South Compromise of 1850. State voters bought it and elected Bigler, while awarding the legislature and elected state offices to the Democrats. The voters in Lancaster County were not so impressed, rolling up large Whig majorities. Chester County was near evenly divided but broke for the Whigs.[9]

The federal government selected Castner Hanway to be tried first. Hanway's life was in the balance as teams of lawyers on each side argued to the court and jury over whether Hanway had committed treason. Hanway's defense lawyers, including an antislavery politician named Thaddeus Stevens, argued that Hanway had been a mere innocent bystander who if anything had tried to keep the peace. The defense team also presented evidence of the plague of kidnappings that afflicted blacks in the area. Blacks were being regularly seized and taken south without legal process, and Hanway had initially had no reason to suppose the commotion he heard and came to investigate involved a federal marshal with a duly issued warrant.[10]

U.S. Supreme Court Justice Robert Grier of Pennsylvania was one of the judges presiding at the Christiana trial. A "doughface"—a Northern appeaser of the South—Grier is known today for joining Justice Taney's *Dred Scott* opinion in 1857, after being lobbied by President-elect James Buchanan. Grier supported the fugitive slave law and appointed commissioners to execute it, including Harrisburg's ruthless Richard McAllister. In the Christiana trial of late 1851, Grier denounced abolitionists. Still, Grier was aware that respect for the Fugitive Slave Act might be impaired if legitimate officials serving warrants were to be confused with private kidnappers: "How is anyone to judge when a man carries off a colored man at night, whether it is the master, or his agent, or an absolute kidnapper?"[11]

Elijah Lewis, who was in prison with Castner Hanway, kept a sort of journal listing people who visited him and other defendants while they were in Philadelphia's Moyamensing Prison. The list is filled with the names of local Quakers and antislavery people, but the names of Joseph Williams Thorne and his wife Mary are not included. The list does not cover the prisoners' prior detention in a Lancaster jail through September 25, or Hanway's visitors after November 29, when U.S. Marshal Anthony E. Roberts, with the court's permission, took "Hanway under his particular care in order to provide more comfortable quarters on account of his health." Marshal Roberts showed a great deal of helpfulness to the

4. The Federal Invasion and the Progressive Friends

prisoners, eating with them (and, according to some Southerners, letting some escape). Roberts was politically allied with defense lawyer Thaddeus Stevens, an influential antislavery politician from Adams County (another southeastern Pennsylvania county on the Mason-Dixon line).[12] Thus, Lewis's list does not conclusively exclude the possibility that Thorne visited Castner Hanway in prison, but one can ask if Thorne's work kept him too busy to visit his brother-in-law's brother.

Justice Grier told the jury he didn't think Hanway had committed treason, and the jury acquitted him. The charges against the remaining defendants were dismissed soon thereafter.[13]

Recalling events about twenty-four years later, Thorne said that the Christiana clash "had the effect of opening the eyes of the people of the north to the iniquities of the Fugitive Slave Law…. It also put a stop to slavehunting in that section of the Country, and taught the slaveholders that an animal even so low and vile as a 'nigger' when trampled upon would turn upon it's [sic] persecutor."

Thorne's sweeping statement shows a degree of seeming complacency which Thorne himself in the 1850s probably did not share. Whatever Thorne meant by "that section of the Country," southeastern Pennsylvania in general continued to be plagued by kidnappers, official and unofficial. At the very time that Hanway was being tried and acquitted, the Maryland kidnapper Thomas McCreary and his accomplices were kidnapping two free teenaged black girls in Chester County, Rachel and Elizabeth Parker. Elizabeth, the younger of these two sisters, was seized with her employer's connivance and taken to Campbell's slave pen in Baltimore. Apparently less scrupulous than on previous occasions, Campbell sought to coerce Elizabeth into "admitting" she was a fugitive slave, and he sent her to New Orleans to be sold there.[14]

Then McCreary and his accomplices went to the house of Joseph Miller in the southern part of the county, and seized young Rachel Parker. After trying unsuccessfully to spike the kidnappers' carriage wheels with a fence beam, Miller gave the alarm and led a posse of local whites into Maryland. In Baltimore, the Miller party tracked down Rachel Parker, and Miller filed kidnapping charges against McCreary. The day after that, with a local Quaker merchant assisting Rachel by suing for her freedom, the posse was in a rail car waiting to ride back to Chester County. Miller was eager to return because the Baltimore crowds, riled up at the "abolitionists" who had come into their state so soon after Gorsuch's "murder," seemed very hostile. Miller needed a smoke, though, and he stepped outside the railway car for a tobacco break because he wasn't allowed to smoke inside the train. His friends never saw him alive again. Miller's body was later found hanging from a tree some miles from Baltimore.[15]

Two inquest juries in Maryland attributed Miller's death to suicide, but an inquiry in Chester County found his death was murder. One of McCreary's accomplices later pretended that Miller—despite all outward appearances—was actually an accomplice in Rachel Parker's kidnapping and hanged himself out of guilt, but Miller's neighbors, the people of Chester County, and even many Marylanders accepted the most obvious explanation: proslavery lynchers, either whipped up to a fury at the Gorsuch "murder" or acting at the initiative of McCreary, had hanged Miller for daring to challenge one of slavery's enforcers.[16]

The defense of the Parker sisters was not an exclusively Quaker enterprise. A local Presbyterian minister, John Miller Dickey, helped rally the community in support of freedom for the Parkers. Thanks to the efforts of Dickey and others, many Chester County whites attested to Maryland authorities that the Parkers were longtime free residents, not slaves.[17]

Rachel Parker's freedom suit in Maryland—soon joined by a similar suit by Elizabeth as Campbell was obliged to return her to Baltimore—remained pending throughout 1852, along with McCreary's trial. In the Pennsylvania state capital of Harrisburg, Governor Bigler took steps to conciliate the South. He signed a law allowing the states' jails to be used to hold alleged fugitives, thus watering down the Personal Liberty Law of 1847. Bigler also granted pardons to the infamous Pennsylvania kidnapper George F. Alberti and an accomplice, who in seizing a fugitive slave woman had also seized her freeborn infant child and sent him, too, into a lifetime of bondage. A Pennsylvania court had sentenced Alberti and his crony to prison for enslaving the freeborn infant. Marylanders demanded the release of Alberti and his companion—in the ironic language of one Maryland politician, "to unbolt their prison doors and relieve their sufferings." Bigler complied.[18]

J. Williams Thorne and his wife Mary would at least have been following these events through their subscription to the abolitionist *Pennsylvania Freeman*, if not following it even more closely through their family and antislavery contacts. But Mary omitted these dramatic public events in letters she wrote to her sisters, in the intervals of a fairly busy schedule at the Thorne home, known as Fountain Hill. She acknowledged her sister Sarah's letter "which was quite satisfactory particularly on Bloomerism"— Amelia Bloomer was a reformer famous for her campaign for women to

4. The Federal Invasion and the Progressive Friends

be more comfortably dressed—but Sarah's letter should have contained more family news. Mary had another child, Anna Emma, born in 1850. Mary hadn't written letters recently: "[I]ndeed I wonder sometimes what was the use in learning to write or anything else but nurse babies or keep house." There had been two barn-burnings in the area, one with the culprit(s) unknown, and one where the offender was "a black man who robed [sic] the house of one thousand dollars whilst it was burning." Mary's husband was quite busy, and the prices for his wheat and rye were not as high as he would have wished. J. Williams ("Williams") had been at a wedding recently—"Williams just now read the definition of marriage in a new paper which is 'imprisonment for life' that is to the wife I infer, well for myself I can say my prison is my palace, and my world too, and I know you'll all try it girls and see for yourselves as aunt Hetty says." The "new paper" may have been circulated at one of the Lyceum meetings.[19]

As it happens, 1852 was a prolific year for discussion of marriage. A radical Fourierist (socialist) named Marx Edgeworth Lazarus published a free-love work called *Love vs. Marriage*, spurring a debate in Horace Greeley's *New York Tribune* over whether the existing marriage laws and customs should be replaced with greater permissiveness.[20]

Issues of women's rights—though not free love—were covered in June 1852 when a national women's rights convention met in West Chester. Leading members of the new feminist movement came to West Chester's Horticultural Hall from throughout the country. As some of the reformers described it in a later history of their movement, "Chester County had long been noted for its reform movements and flourishing schools, in which the women generally took a deep interest." The convention canvassed issues of women's suffrage, freedom to hold jobs traditionally reserved for men, equal pay for equal work, and similar reforms—but not Fourierite attacks on marriage.[21]

Meanwhile, the divisions among the Hicksite Quakers continued and grew more marked. In Ohio, New York and Michigan, groups of "Congregational Friends" or "Progressive Friends" split off from the Hicksites, and the reformist elements in Chester County's numerous Hicksite Quaker meetings wanted to recognize these new brothers and sisters. The faction that wanted to abstain from unbridled reformism objected to any recognition. This broke the delicate balance between factions that had existed in meetings. In the Kennett Monthly Meeting in Longwood, in southern Chester County, the dispute led to a schism. The members of the meeting could not agree on whether to recognize the memberships of a couple of migrants from a Progressive Friends Meeting in Ohio. The two factions in Kennett, one recognizing and the other not recognizing the new arrivals, each claimed to be the legitimate Kennett Monthly Meeting. The Hicksite Yearly Meeting in Philadelphia recognized the faction opposing the reformists as the true meeting.[22]

Then came the women's rights convention, when an announcement declared that the New England–born Garrisonian abolitionist Oliver Johnson would be speaking at the Marlborough Monthly Meeting. Progressives and anti-reformists both claimed control over the Marlborough Meeting, and the Philadelphia Yearly Meeting had just recognized the non-reformists' claims. The secular authorities also recognized the non-reformists as legitimate, and had Johnson arrested for disrupting a religious assembly when he came with some friends to speak at the meetinghouse during what the anti-reformists claimed was the appointed hour for their separate worship. Some of Johnson's friends were arrested as well, including Dr. Bartholomew Fussell of later women's medical college fame. The Progressive Friends held their quarterly meeting in the Kennett meeting house near the end of July.[23]

If J. Williams or Mary Thorne attended the women's rights convention or were involved in the intra–Quaker battles in the aftermath, Mary gave no indication in her next letter, an undated response to a letter of July 30 from her sister Sally. Sally wanted to know the news since her last visit to Mary: "Oh! How I wish we had a telegraph by which we could communicate together dayly [sic]," Mary said. Lacking such a device, Sally had shared some family news, including brief news of Washington Hanway. In her reply, Mary mentioned her "large, busy, bustling family" (another baby, Eugene, would be born in September) and contrasted it to her unmarried sisters' presumably "lonely" situation. It seems J. Williams had promised to review some of the sister's poetry but had not had the opportunity, being busy with the oat harvest.[24]

Mary added, "I have been snatching a little time now and then to read Uncle Tom I find it exceedingly fascinating. the characters are so full and so well delineated it seems like a true picture." The Thornes lived in the middle of very dramatic events in the struggle between slavery and freedom, and reading a novel about slavery may seem insignificant. Harriett Beecher Stowe, however, would cite the case of the Parker sisters when her novel *Uncle Tom's Cabin* was accused of exaggerating the problems of slavery. A final verdict in the sisters' freedom suit had still not come from the Maryland courts.[25]

4. The Federal Invasion and the Progressive Friends

In the fall of 1852, a young black man who had been raised in Chester County's Kennett Square left to seek his fortune in Philadelphia. James Walker Hood was from a very religious family, tenants and close associates of a local Quaker family, and himself felt a calling to the ministry. Meanwhile, he took secular jobs in Philadelphia.[26]

In October 1852, the People's Hall in Ercildoun showed its commitment to free discussion when it opened itself to a local meeting of the slavery-appeasing Democratic Party. Also in October, the Progressive Friends held a Quarterly Meeting and decided it was time to form their own Yearly Meeting, independent of the Hicksites. Several noted local Progressives, but not J. Williams, signed the call for the new Meeting, which was to be held in May 1853. Signatories included Dr. Bartholomew Fussell, Oliver Johnson, and an antislavery Delawarean, Thomas Garrett. Garrett had been subject to crippling damages in federal court for his Underground Railroad activity, but famously replied when the U.S. Marshal suggested that now Garrett wouldn't help any more fugitives: "I am now past sixty and have not a dollar to my name, but be that as it may, if anyone knows of a poor slave who needs shelter and a breakfast, send him to me."[27] Indeed, many abolitionists and Underground Railroad operators would gravitate to the Progressive Friends.

Also signing the call was Castner Hanway. He had not been a Quaker before—a report by the Sadsbury (Lancaster County) Monthly Meeting said that "Castner Hanway is not a member of the Society of Friends"— but the expericnce of his prosecution seems to have made him a Quaker. (Hanway moved to Wilber, Nebraska, in 1878, but he left instructions that he was to be buried in Longwood, and his body was brought there for interment after his death in 1893.[28])

The call for the new Yearly Meeting began with a ringing declaration: "The various religious denominations in the land are arrayed against the progressive spirit of the age," suppressing "freedom of speech and of conscience" and "requiring a slavish conformity in matters of abstract faith and sectarian discipline." Many Quakers shared this repressive, sectarian attitude, seeking "ecclesiastical domination." Quaker meetings had disowned reformers "whose lives are without blemish ... and [who] are seeking to know and do the will of God at every sacrifice." The call summoned "all those who feel the want of social and religious co-operation, and believe that a Society may be formed, recognizing the Progressive Element which will divorce Religion from Technical Theology."[29]

While many of the country's leading reformers, and local Quakers

Quaker Carpetbagger

like J. Williams and Mary Thorne, prepared for the forthcoming meeting, McCreary was cleared of Maryland criminal charges in the Parker case. In early 1853, the Parkers' civil-court freedom trial was concluded in Maryland, with the state of Pennsylvania providing the Parker sisters with lawyers to defend their claims to freedom. After numerous witnesses from Chester County attested to Rachel Parker's free status, and her would-be "master" brought unconvincing testimony identifying the sisters as slaves who had run away in 1847, the proceedings were concluded by a compromise. James Campbell, the attorney general of Pennsylvania and one of the Parker legal team, worked out a deal with the "master" to accept a jury verdict in favor of freedom for Rachel and Elizabeth, in exchange for not filing kidnapping charges against McCreary in Pennsylvania.[30]

After the Parker sisters returned to Chester County, a local grand jury disregarded the agreement and indicted McCreary for kidnapping. Governor Bigler, ignoring his attorney general, demanded McCreary's extradition from Maryland, which Maryland's governor refused to grant. Bigler was trying to juggle many balls—he was a Northern Democrat trying to appease the South and promote the presidential candidacy of James Buchanan, an elderly and ambitious Lancaster County statesman now serving as an ambassador abroad. Keeping the South sympathetic to Buchanan's claims, while reassuring Pennsylvania voters that he would maintain a bright line between "illegal" kidnaping of free blacks and "legal" renditions of alleged fugitive slaves, Bigler had to observe considerable caution.[31]

In an undated poem, which was written at some point in the antebellum period, Mary Thorne gave vent to her—and presumably her husband's—views on the kind of proslavery politics practiced by Bigler and Buchanan. Frequently during the 1850s, including the aftermath of the Christiana events, Northern politicians like these spoke of the need to conciliate the South, and uphold the Compromise of 1850 including the Fugitive Slave Law of that year. Such conciliation was needed to preserve the Union, was the refrain. Mary Thorne rebutted these attitudes in her verses:

> Must we ply the lash for tyrants,
> Must we bend the servile knee,
> Must we bow down to slavery,
> To make us great and free?
> While on blood we rear our altars,
> While we build our house on wrong,

4. The Federal Invasion and the Progressive Friends

> While justice weakly falters,
> Can we be proud and strong?[32]

A reference to "No safety for a brother/ Who seeks a Southern clime/ Though his guilt may be no other/ Than that *'cruelty is crime'*" may well have meant Joseph Miller, who sought a "Southern clime" to fight "cruelty," only to lose his life in the attempt.[33]

The Pennsylvania Antislavery Society held its annual meeting in West Chester's Horticultural Hall at the end of October 1852. With William Lloyd Garrison in attendance, the Society affirmed its Garrisonian opposition to the Constitution, while affirming Garrisonian disunion principles. The meeting also denounced the Christiana treason prosecutions, the Parker sisters' kidnapping, and Miller's murder.[34]

J. Williams Thorne, who was such a notable member of the Progressive Friends in later years, was probably (with Mary) at the founding meeting of the Progressive Friends, which met at the Old Kennett Meetinghouse on Sunday, May 22, 1853, when the Yearly Meeting of the Progressive Friends began. The meeting was to last for four days, but the Thornes would have had no shortage of lodging, even if they didn't know anyone in the area (which they probably did). The later reminiscences of Emma Worrall were of extensive hospitality: "The invited speakers and other strangers were expected to remain during all the sessions of the meeting, the lovely homes of the neighborhood being hospitably thrown open to them, and also to the transient visitors from adjacent communities." Historian Albert J. Wahl says that "the dusty roads leading to Old Kennett were crowded with buggies and carriages, and that the house was filled to overflowing when William Barnard, the temporary chairman, rapped for order."[35]

Castner Hanway and Sojourner Truth, an abolitionist former slave visiting the meeting, were on a committee to help prepare the meeting's testimony on slavery, one of many testimonies to be issued to the world to indicate the contours of the changes the Progressive Friends sought. Local and national celebrities, in addition to Truth and Hanway, included feminist Ernestine Rose, black abolitionist Robert Purvis, and influential Philadelphia Hicksite Quaker Lucretia Mott. Topics covered, in addition to slavery, included drink, women's rights, peace, capital punishment, and tobacco—the debate over tobacco proving more contentious than the other subjects of discussion. Another difficult topic was introduced by two of the guests: Sidney Jones and Fannie Lee Townshend spoke in favor of free love, much to the consternation of those members whose progressivism had not progressed quite that far.³⁶

The atmosphere outside the meetinghouse is captured by Albert J. Wahl:

> [L]atecomers to the scene would find something of a carnival atmosphere, with sutlers' wagons and stands doing a thriving business, and a veritable potpourri of humanity milling around the grounds. Sometimes the crowd outside the hall was so large that Progressive leaders felt impelled to mount the steps and address the throng. Earnest-faced Quakers were there, clad in plain brown coats and broad-brimmed hats, with their women in "casing" bonnets. There were also men with beards and long hair, and bob-haired women who supported Amelia Bloomer.

In the evening, the visitors would be invited to attend gatherings at the house of one of the host families for "social mingling and interchange." Given the Progressive Yearly Meeting's testimony on temperance, these were probably sober gatherings, but if a celebrity was present, (s)he could enliven the proceedings with a talk or a story.³⁷

Of the statements issued by the meeting, there was, of course, a testimony against slavery. This was the declaration that Sojourner Truth and Castner Hanway had helped draft. The declaration called slavery "the master crime of our country and of the age." The testimony celebrated the immediate-emancipation movement for raising an urgent issue on which the public had previously been silent, or where such antislavery zeal as existed had been "turned into the foul channel of Colonization." The testimony denounced "the indifference of the Church to this avalanche of human woe" and found it appalling that slavery "should find apologists and defenders in men aspiring to the rank of statesmen, or claiming to be the ministers of Him who came to preach deliverance to the captives, and the opening of the prison to them that are bound."³⁸

A testimony on temperance advocated total abstinence from alcohol. "We feel perfectly assured that sottishness of the very worst kind, with all its horrors, will continue to a greater or less extent, so long as the custom of using alcoholic beverages is continued; and that a generation of temperate drinkers without drunkards is an impossibility." The testimony praised temperance lecturers in terms that paralleled Progressive Friends' reaction to their former Hicksite brethren who had balked at the association of Quakers with reform activists: "Now we are so presumptuous as to maintain, in opposition to the dictum of such Friends, and regardless of the elevation of the seats on which they sit"—probably referring to the literal high seats in the galleries where a Hicksite meeting's leaders oversaw

4. The Federal Invasion and the Progressive Friends

Quaker services and rebuked reformers—"that every human being has an undoubted right to think and speak on any subject involving human welfare." Though recognizing that some members of the Progressive Friends were anarchists who questioned the validity of any kind of government, the testimony proclaimed that *if* the government had any legitimate functions, those functions should include legal prohibition of alcohol: "If governments of force have any rightful authority whatever, we do not see how they can be justified in protecting, or even permitting a traffic so destructive to the dearest interests of society. If they have not power to suppress the grand cause of three-fourths of the pauperism and crime existing in the community, surely it were worse than folly to pretend that they have a right to lay the strong arm of power upon any transgressor, however flagrant may be his offences."[39]

A testimony on the "Rights, Wrongs and Duties of Woman" said that woman must have "equality before the law.... She must also be secured an equal remuneration for labor performed, and allowed equal voice and representation in the government and legislation of the country." Men's monopoly on politics had exacerbated "[t]he abuses of government, which have become so glaring in our country." If women had equal political rights, "it is not too much to expect that her moral influence and refinement would prevent those scenes which have hitherto disgraced our national councils, and made election days occasions of riotous disturbances and vice."[40]

The much-discussed testimony on tobacco said that "the widely-prevalent use of Tobacco" was one of "the worst evils of our day." Citing medical and economic authorities, the testimony said tobacco was addictive, that it harmed the brain, and that its cost harmed the pocketbook.[41]

The Progressive Friends approved a petition to the Pennsylvania legislature seeking the abolition of the death penalty. The petition alleged the "entire inefficiency" of capital punishment for murder, and asked for abolition for the sake of "the poor misguided murderer" and also "for the good of the whole people." The legislature should replace the death penalty with "some means of prevention more in accordance with the Christian precepts, and the advancing spirit of the age."[42]

Their energies still not exhausted, the new Yearly Meeting sent a petition to Congress asking that the Army and Navy be abolished, together with federal military academies, and that "an arrangement be entered into to settle all disputations with Foreign Powers, by reference to an Arbitration of Nations."[43]

Quaker Carpetbagger

The Progressive Friends also issued an "Exposition of Sentiments" defending their defection from the alleged tyranny of the Hicksite Friends, and their rejection of all forms of sectarian domination. "The Romish Church sets up for herself a claim of absolute infallibility, and the various Protestant sects, professing to deride her pretensions, yet tax our credulity scarcely less.... Even the Quaker regards the decision of his Yearly Meeting with a superstitious reverence scarcely inferior to that which the Catholic awards to the decrees of the Pope and the Cardinals." Against this the Progressive Friends set "the whole genius and spirit of Christianity as exhibited in the life and teachings of Jesus" as well as "the writings of the Apostles and primitive Christians." The meeting proclaimed: "We have set forth no forms nor ceremonies; nor have we sought to impose upon ourselves or others a system of doctrinal belief. Such matters we have left where Jesus left them, with the conscience and common sense of the individual."[44]

Thorne was probably at this inaugural meeting of the Progressive Friends, and we know he was at subsequent meetings, as they gathered each year in May or June to consider the needs of reformist religion.

There was a continued need for vigilance to protect fugitive slaves and free blacks. A gang of criminals in eastern Lancaster County, near Chester County, were willing for a price to help seize blacks as slaves. The Gap Gang ran diversified criminal enterprises, from counterfeiting to fencing stolen goods to horse theft, and they did not scruple to add slave-raiding to their repertoire. They could use their knowledge of the local area to their advantage. When some of the gang's key people, feeling the heat, fled to Maryland in 1854, there was premature speculation on the demise of the criminal traffickers.[45]

5

Reform, Slave Raid, War

In the winter of 1853–1854, a man based in Ohio lectured in the Philadelphia area, criticizing Christianity. Joseph Barker was an Englishman who had grown up as a Methodist, showing great promise as a Methodist minister as he attracted large audiences. When he left organized Christianity and became an anti–Christian polemicist, abolitionist and all-around reformer, he continued to attract a fan base in England. Later trying his fortune in America, he associated with Garrison and other abolitionist leaders. In a series of well-attended January debates with Dutch Reformed minister Joseph Berg, the ex–Christian Barker laid out for Philadelphians and visitors a Deist case against Christianity and the Bible. The Bible, alleged Barker, supported slavery and polygamy. The "Bible men" had "reigned supreme" for "ten hundred years that are known as *the dark ages.*" Christian doctrines allowing last-minute repentance for sinners encouraged immoral behavior, contended Barker, who also had some choice words for the defenders of Biblical Christianity: "The deceitfulness and dishonesty of leading believers, and distinguished writers in defense of the Bible and Orthodox forms of theology, destroyed my faith in them."[1] Thorne may well have attended some of Barker's lectures, perhaps noting Barker's arguments for future use.

In 1854, the Progressive Friends held their second annual meeting. They met in the Kennett Monthly Meeting's house of worship, but some members of the anti-reformist faction at that meeting raised a disturbance. Not sure if they could any longer rely on the shaky agreement between Kennett's factions to share the meetinghouse, the Progressives adjourned to the town of Hamorton, where another hall was prepared for the meeting. Castner Hanway was again on a committee to prepare another testimony against slavery.[2]

Operating in what was technically a different religious sphere than the Progressive Friends, the Chester County Presbyterian minister John Miller Dickey was at this time beginning an initiative of his own.

Quaker Carpetbagger

Galvanized by the affair of the Parker sisters, whom he had helped rescue from slavery, Dickey grappled with the plight of America's free blacks. Dickey was a colonizationist—part of the movement denounced by the Progressive Friends for proposing to settle free blacks in Liberia. Different colonizationists had different motives, with some of them seeing the movement as a chance to get rid of a free population that endangered slavery. Dickey, on the other hand, had in mind the welfare of the oppressed black American population, and the spiritual welfare of the black African population. It was (incorrectly) believed at the time that American blacks were more resistant than whites to the diseases of Africa that took such a toll on white missionaries. Colonization, to Dickey, would therefore both uplift American blacks by giving them a homeland and uplift black Africans by bringing them the Gospel through evangelists of their own race from America. Desiring to set up an institution to provide potential black missionaries the extensive learning Presbyterians insisted on for their ministers, Dickey decided to found a black college in Chester County. Dickey's Old School Presbyterian denomination approved the idea of such a college to train Liberian missionaries and ministers for black congregations. Dickey's Quaker brother-in-law provided funds, while the Pennsylvania legislature provided a charter for the new Ashmun Institute, which was to be located in the Oxford area in Chester County (many key legislators were former schoolmates of Dickey—the Presbyterians were known for their schools). Oxford was a black township and not far from the Mason-Dixon line.[3]

Thorne's farm remained a refuge for fugitive slaves, particularly large parties of fugitives who could not be accommodated in the regular Underground Railroad route. The likely explanation for this is that Thorne probably had a good number of laborers, black and white, on his farm, so there would have been nothing inherently suspicious about parties of black people on the Thorne place. Thorne also owned at least one building that he rented to laborers—a house across the Lancaster County side of the line.

The Chester County Agricultural Society gave Thorne an award in 1854 for "the best and greatest number of choice varieties of Peaches." The Society noticed "with much pleasure many promising seedling Apples, of Pennsylvania origin. Among these we will mention the People's Choice, from J.W. Thorne, of Chester county."[4]

The prohibitionist, or "Maine Law" movement—so called after a pioneering law in Maine banning the manufacture or sale of liquor—reached

5. Reform, Slave Raid, War

a prewar peak in Pennsylvania in 1854. A prohibitionist gathering called for an alcohol ban, threatening to run an independent Prohibitionist ticket if the legislature did not pass a law. Instead, the legislature called for an advisory referendum on prohibition, which was held in October along with the state elections. The prohibitionists lost by what Thorne would have seen as a tantalizingly close margin.[5]

Some good news—from the perspective of prohibitionists like Thorne—was that the new legislature, heavily infiltrated by anti-immigrant "Know Nothings" who linked alcohol and its concomitant abuses to Irish whiskey and German beer, passed a liquor-by-the-drink ban limiting the sale of alcohol in small quantities. This would soon be repealed as prohibitionism faded into the background amid growing controversies over tariffs and slavery.[6]

The Progressives had begun building a meetinghouse of their own, to be used for their annual meetings and to host speakers and events during the rest of the year. The May 1855 gathering of the Progressive Friends was the first in the new hall, and the first in which Thorne is noted in the records as taking part in the proceedings. Whether this was his first appearance at the Progressive Friends or not, he certainly made up for any previous silence by taking part in a discussion of a proposed testimony on proper amusements. Debate on the matter was to be continued in the 1856 meeting.[7]

The World Alliance for Human Happiness (American branch) was an organization dedicated to fighting "superstition" as the greatest barrier to "human development." The Alliance sent a memorial to the 1855 Progressive meeting, presented by one of the signatories, Thomas Curtis, who was also put on the committee to draw up a response. The memorial was in favor of education, peaceful settlement of international differences, and other good causes, all advanced in the name of the "Religion of Noble Deeds" which was praised as superior to the "creed(s)" promoted by the clergy of every religion. Signers included people familiar to the meeting, including Lucretia Mott, Theodore Parker (who had given the dedication address to the Progressive Friends' new building), and Joseph Barker of Ohio. The Progressive Friends adopted a friendly but vague resolution promising to work with the Alliance when "appropriate."[8] As for Barker, his spiritual odyssey was not over, and Thorne would hear from him again.

The annual meetings were the highlight of the Longwood Meeting's life. The rest of the year the building could be used as a lyceum—the lecture system popular in Chester County—where visitors could, for a quarter, hear speakers on many subjects.[9]

Quaker Carpetbagger

Political developments in 1855 included the founding of what became Pennsylvania's Republican Party. For the office of Canal Commissioner, on the ballot in this off-year election, the state Republican convention nominated Passmore Williamson, a Quaker who was in prison by order of a federal judge for his role in liberating an alleged slave whose putative master had been taking her through Pennsylvania. Williamson was the kind of candidate who could rally abolitionists, though for other voters this "single issue" candidate had less appeal.[10]

In the 1856 Progressive Friends meeting, the assistant clerk, Oliver Johnson, suggested a change to the report on amusements. The proposed amendment denounced most existing forms of theatrical entertainment. With that modification, the report was approved. According to the report, friends and families ought to engage in wholesome entertainment—especially in intergenerational groups. This would avoid the extremes of unwholesome entertainments (like the theater) on the one hand, and the alleged evils of fun-killing asceticism on the other. Asceticism was denounced as leading to cruelty by ascetics, and the alienation of the young from religion as they rejected the latter in favor of indiscriminate and dubious forms of entertainment. Music, many forms of dancing, and libraries also met with approval.[11]

Politically, Pennsylvania with its decisive electoral votes added to those of Southern states, helped choose the slavery-sympathizing James Buchanan, of Lancaster County, for president. The Republicans, who had pledged to oppose the spread of slavery, lost despite much support in the North.[12]

Thorne established a boarding school near his farm in 1856. He would keep this school running for ten years, teaching the children French, Latin, history, English and astronomy.[13]

The same year, J. Williams's father Joseph decided to move to Illinois and farm there. Joseph brought with him two of his daughters and their husbands—Ann Eliza Thorne Underwood and her husband Jeremiah Underwood; and Carolina Thorne Hanway and her husband Washington Hanway. The pioneers moved to Ottawa, Illinois, which in 1858 was the site of the first of the famous Lincoln/Douglas debates. Joseph and his daughters' household may not have heard the debate, since they returned to Pennsylvania that year. Washington Hanway died in February 1858 from typhoid he had contracted in Illinois. Joseph went back to Illinois to arrange the sale of his land, but whether he was there in August to hear Lincoln and Douglas, or whether he spared the time if he could have attended, is not clear. Joseph would come back to Pennsylvania in 1860.[14]

5. Reform, Slave Raid, War

In 1857, Joseph Barker was back in Philadelphia, giving weekly sermons to a secularist congregation. Barker returned to Nebraska (his new home base) and in 1858 announced his conversion from Deism to atheism.[15]

Meanwhile, Thorne's new school did not mean that Thorne was neglecting his farm. The Chester County Agricultural Society's Committee on Farms conducted an inquiry in 1858 to find the best-cultivated farm. It visited five farms, including Thorne's in Sadsbury. The committee said Thorne "is, no doubt, the largest and most successful fruit grower in the country." Thorne cultivated strawberries, raspberries, gooseberries, peaches, pears and apples in the formerly neglected acres he owned. This was in addition to wheat, oats, rye, "and one half acre of Chinese sugar cane." He also raised sweet potatoes, and in livestock had cows, horses and sheep. While the award and the second prize went to two of the other farmers, Thorne and the two remaining competitors were each designated a "country gentleman" in this "friendly competition."[16]

Prizes which Thorne *did* win included recognition by the county agricultural society for the best syrup from the Chinese sugar cane, best quarter peck of peaches, best tomatoes and best cider, as well as a third-place showing for his watermelon. At an agricultural exhibition held in Philadelphia in September and October 1859, he got an award for his peaches and for his Chinese sugar cane molasses.[17]

The October 1858 meeting of the Pennsylvania Anti-Slavery Society had taken place in West Chester's Horticultural Hall. The meeting blamed both Democrats and Republicans for federal cooperation with slavery, echoing Garrison in saying that for the slaves, the Constitution was "a covenant with death and an agreement with hell." Early in 1859, opponents of slavery in the Pennsylvania state legislature introduced a bill—based on a law in Massachusetts—by which anyone held as a fugitive slave could have the benefit of the writ of habeas corpus and a jury trial, with the alleged master having the burden of proof and the decision of the jury being final. This bill did not get considered in the Democratic-majority House. In October 1859, while Thorne was winning agricultural prizes in Philadelphia, the white abolitionist John Brown conducted an unsuccessful slave-liberation raid into Virginia, causing considerable stir. Brown was caught and hanged, and Esther Kent, who was teaching at J. Williams's school, wrote a poem to honor the militant abolitionist. Calling Brown a "martyr to the cause of truth," the poem called on Brown's "spirit" to "Nerve, nerve our spirits, give us strength/ To follow where thy feet have trod:/ Guided by thee, 'twill surely lead,/ Nearer unto the throne of God."[18]

J. Williams was not involved with the abolitionist John Brown, but he had a chance to strike his own blow against slavery by coming to the rescue of a black tenant of the same name. This John Brown, a laborer, lived in a tenant house on Thorne's property in Lancaster County, just to the west of Sadsbury. Brown often worked for Thorne, but on Friday, March 2, 1860, Brown had spent the day working at a rock quarry. On his way back home, he met a white man, Gilmer Hull, who invited him to a "game of raffles." Brown declined.[19]

Soon after Brown got home, Hull and a man named Frank Wilson were observed near Brown's house, talking about how a party was being held there. The whites forced themselves into Brown's house and suggested a party was going on. Brown said that this was not the case. Then some more whites came to say Brown was under arrest for robbery. Brown denied his guilt but agreed to go along with his captors in a carriage. Brown's wife witnessed these events.[20]

So did some local black people, who observed the white men with Brown in a carriage. They followed the carriage some distance and then broke off pursuit. Either they were not fast enough, or perhaps they slowed because they were approaching Maryland and knew that free blacks who came into the state from the North could be arrested or even enslaved.[21]

Of course, the white men who had seized Brown were not law officers, but kidnappers, seeking to bring Brown into Maryland to be sold to the slave dealers there. The criminals reached a tavern, where they tried to ply Brown with liquor. Brown would not open his mouth, so the liquor poured down onto his chest.[22]

Thorne and others got together a search party but at first couldn't catch up with Brown. They did find two alleged kidnappers, thanks in part to the testimony of Brown's wife. Gilmer Hull and Frank Wilson were ordered held for trial. Two other defendants, Sylvester Gordon and Franklin Bostick, were later charged, as was another alleged kidnapper named Edward Mackay.[23]

In Baltimore, the kidnappers lodged Brown with the slave-dealer Joseph Donovan. This gentleman had been in the news ten years previously, when he went to Washington, D.C., and brought the enslaved family of William Williams, a free black man, back to the Baltimore slave pen. Williams, who had been a coachman to three presidents, used his connections to raise the considerable money needed to buy the freedom of his family.

5. Reform, Slave Raid, War

John Brown's rescuers found Brown in Donovan's premises, and a white man named William Bond came from Pennsylvania to the slave dealership to attest to Brown's free status. There was no need to pay Donovan this time—Donovan acknowledged Brown's freedom, and allowed him to go back to Pennsylvania.[24]

During the Progressive Friends meeting of 1860, Thorne contributed to two discussions. One proposed resolution was in favor to kindness to animals. Thorne participated in the debate, and the resulting report said: "Particularly would we call attention to the care and comfort of those domestic animals in common use—the horse, so noble, spirited and valuable to man; the ox, patient, meek, and strong, teaching his master many lessons of honest industry and endurance; the cow, when humanely treated, so gentle and useful, and affording one of the most valued necessaries of life; and the minor animals, the dog and cat, so companionable and tractable."[25]

Thorne was a convinced vegetarian and even had his dog on a vegetarian diet. He insisted that this made his dog smarter than the neighbors' dogs. One story says that when his son killed a chicken, the elder Thorne was annoyed that "[e]very time someone gets hungry around here we have to kill something." This suggests that he was bemoaning his family's meat-loving tendencies rather than forbidding them altogether. Still, a sympathy for chickens as well as snakes indicates which side Thorne would take in the Progressive Friends' debate on animals.[26]

The slavery issue also prompted a vigorous debate in the June 1860 meeting, and here it would have been helpful if the Meeting had kept more detailed records. We know that Thorne took part in the debate, but we do not know which side he took on what turned out to be the debate's most contentious issue. The difficulty was that Abraham Lincoln, recently nominated for president by the Republicans, had supported the idea of a federal fugitive slave law in his debates with Senator Douglas in 1858. Also, as Wendell Phillips would argue in the *Liberator* at the end of the month, Lincoln as a congressman had proposed to extend the Fugitive Slave Act to the District of Columbia (as part of a D.C. emancipation bill). This, to Phillips, made Lincoln the "Slave Hound of Illinois." But many of the Progressive Friends had by this time become supporters of the new Republican Party as the best defense against the "Slave Power" in the country, and as the closest thing to abolitionism that practical politics allowed. The Republicans disavowed any power in the federal government to interfere with slavery in the states, but they promised to keep slavery out of the rapidly growing West, and any other federal territories.[27]

Quaker Carpetbagger

As written, the proposed antislavery testimony seemed to advise a vote against Lincoln: "The Fugitive Slave law of this land we regard as infamous, and therefore not to be justified, or even excused, by any plea of constitutional obligation; and we call upon the friends of freedom everywhere to be careful that they do not, by their votes or otherwise, countenance those who, whether as magistrates or citizens, would aid in its enforcement." The meeting took a formal vote and decided, 53 to 23, to keep the controversial language. The minutes of the meeting do not indicate who voted which way, so we don't know whether Thorne was uncompromising or pragmatic on the question of a pro–Lincoln vote. The matter probably did not affect anyone's vote at the election, since the Progressive Friends insisted on respecting their members' individual consciences.[28]

The 1860 census listed Thorne and his family as black. The census taker, a local physician named Latta, probably thought he was playing a good joke on these vocal abolitionists by classifying them with the disenfranchised race they defended.[29]

This was not the worst harassment Thorne was subjected to that year because of his antislavery activities. On October 20, 1860, Thorne's barn burned down. His home was at risk of being engulfed in the conflagration, but Thorne's exertions (and probably those of his neighbors) kept the house from sharing the barn's fate.[30]

The next day, Thorne found a man's tracks in the cornfield, going to the barn and then leaving. The tracks led to a part of the fence to which a horse had been tied. Horse tracks, which Thorne followed, led to the Mt. Vernon Hotel and finally to the home of Frank Wilson, one of the defendants awaiting trial on the charge of kidnapping John Brown. Thorne went to a justice of the peace to swear out a warrant against Wilson for arson—or rather, to affirm out a warrant; Quakers generally made affirmations in lieu of oaths, and Thorne was no exception. At the time Pennsylvania followed the common-law rule that witnesses in court, in order for their testimony to be received, had to believe in the existence of a God who punished falsehood. No objection seems to have been made to J. Williams giving his testimony.[31]

The *National Anti-Slavery Standard*, to which Thorne was a subscriber (and perhaps a source for the *Standard*'s story), reported the arson and Wilson's arrest. The paper suggested that Thorne's neighbors should help him make good his losses, since the insurance company's payment had allegedly come $2,000 short of the value of the destroyed barn.[32] The

5. Reform, Slave Raid, War

paper added: "Mr. Thorne belongs to the class of men who call themselves 'infidels' [non–Christians] (a class usually as hostile to the anti-slavery movement as the sectarians represented by *The New York Observer*), but if the ministers and Churches in his neighborhood possessed as much of the Christian spirit as is manifested by him in his daily life, there would be little danger of anyone there being kidnapped and sold into slavery." (The *New York Observer* was edited by Presbyterian laymen of the Old School denomination, and focused its coverage on religious issues.[33])

It is worth noting that the editor of the *Anti-Slavery Standard*, Oliver Johnson, was one of the founders of the Progressive Friends Meeting at Longwood and was familiar with the members and the neighborhood. He would thus be in a position to know about Thorne's religious views.[34]

The John Brown kidnapping case went to trial in November 1860. Gordon and Bostick had absconded after giving bail, but Frank Wilson and Gilmer Hull showed up to defend themselves (Wilson was presumably also awaiting trial—perhaps on bail—on the arson charge). Brown, his wife, and local black residents testified to the incidents of the kidnapping, while local whites showed that Brown was a free man who had lived for a long time in the community. John Richardson, one of the black witnesses, said Wilson had offered $20 for Richardson to swear Wilson was at home at the time of the kidnapping. Wilson and Hull defended themselves by trying to cast doubt on the witnesses who had identified them, but to no avail. The jury found Wilson and Hull guilty, while eleven of the jurors recommended a sentence that took into account the supposed good character of Wilson and Hull before the kidnapping. The judge gave sentences of five years and three months to each defendant, plus a $200 fine for each man, half of each fine to go to Brown.[35]

Also in November 1860, Abraham Lincoln won Pennsylvania and other Northern states, who outvoted the South to make Lincoln the president-elect. During the ensuing secession crisis, some Keystone State advocates of compromise urged the legislature to get rid of most of the Personal Liberty Law of 1847 (except the ban on kidnapping free blacks). This suggestion was rejected and Pennsylvania kept its law.[36]

When the Civil War broke out, the Longwood Meeting canceled its annual gathering scheduled for 1861. Edward Mackay, one of the defendants in the Brown kidnapping case, was also put on trial in the Civil War's first year and received a five-year sentence. As reported in the *Lancaster Examiner and Herald*, Mackay "asked permission of the Court to make some revelations relative to the stealing of this negro, but as the prisoner had offered nothing in extenuation of the offence during the progress of the trial, the Court refused to hear him."[37]

Northern Quakers were divided over the war, with some holding to their traditional testimony against war and others endorsing the North's war effort for the sake of extirpating slavery. Where Thorne stood on the question is not fully certain. In a generally favorable article in 1875, professedly based on knowledge of J. Williams, Henry Ward Beecher's *Christian Union* said without elaboration that Thorne "acted on the non-resistant teachings of Jesus." However, Thorne's name does not appear on the list of "Chester County Militia Fines and Exonerations" maintained at the County Archives' Web site, and one would expect a nonresistant Quaker to have been on such a list of persons fined or excused for failing to serve in the militia, as a strict nonresistant would have done. A clue can be found in a manuscript essay Thorne's wife Mary submitted to the *Alma*, the newsletter of the local Lyceum.[38]

The essay started fairly cheerfully, describing the author listening to the birds outside her window. Among the birds "there were philosophers, and poets, and orators.... Many of them were fresh from the South, but for all that they were strong for Union[.] Union seemed to be the general topic, not one secesh [Secessionist] among them."[39]

"One of the fellows," Mary Thorne wrote, "who had spent many winters down in Carolina, kept calling on Linkum, Linkum, Abe Linkum, Lick-um, Lick-um, Lick-um." Many other birds expressed similar sentiments, including "a stately old robbin [sic]" who "was for bullets, bullets, bullets for the ribbels, bullets for the ribbels." Such were Mary's sentiments, and if her husband thought differently, he does not appear to have left a record of it.[40]

War news also crept into a letter Mary wrote to her daughter Anna, who was staying with Mary's mother Eliza. While Mary had found time one day to spend time with some of Anna's young friends—"playing little girl"—there were reminders of the ongoing war. Mary worked with many of the local women to make shirts for the soldiers, and she had also visited the camp at West Chester to give the soldiers "grapes and peaches and apples." Mary listed some local young men who had joined the army. (The Thornes' sons, Caleb and Eugene, were around 12 and 9 at the time, too young to serve.) Mary added: "The colored people are holding a camp meeting about a mile from here over the pike. I should like to go one day but do not expect to be able to find time to go."[41]

The annual meeting of the Progressive Friends was coming in June

5. Reform, Slave Raid, War

1862, but meanwhile Thorne had not forgotten the burning of his barn, and he wrote William Darlington, a prominent lawyer who apparently was representing the insurer in the incident. Thorne said that a key witness against Frank Wilson in the arson case, a local resident named William Nethry, was seriously ill with "no hope of his recovery," and his testimony should be officially taken as soon as possible. "There is no time to lose," Thorne insisted. "I am likely to have evidence," he predicted, "of the intention of the kidnapping party to burn my barn in case they could not get clear of the [kidnapping] prosecution in any other way. They were advised to take that course by two men in this neighborhood, who told them that it had, in former times, proved successful."[42]

It is not clear if Wilson was ever prosecuted for the arson. Editor Edward B. Moore of the West Chester *Republican* wrote in 1869 that the "incendiary ... was caught and sentenced to several years in prison, where he died before he had served the full term which had been allotted to him as a punishment for his iniquity." It is possible that the editor was thinking about Wilson's conviction for kidnapping, for which he had already been caught and sent to prison. In any case, Wilson's death while imprisoned put an end to his criminal career.[43]

As the Progressive Friends began their meeting in 1862, a great deal had been happening to disappoint abolitionists who had hoped that the Lincoln administration would fight a war against slavery as part of the war against the Confederacy. The year before, General John C. Fremont had issued a proclamation freeing the slaves of Confederate sympathizers in Missouri, but Lincoln had overruled the general. Fremont became something of an abolitionist hero as a result, while Lincoln was condemned. More recently, General David Hunter had issued a proclamation to free the slaves in Georgia, Florida and South Carolina, but President Lincoln promptly overruled that order.[44]

A couple of weeks before the Progressive Friends' Meeting's June 6 opening date, abolitionists had been stirred to indignation by events in North Carolina. Federal forces had seized some of the coastal areas of the state from the Confederates, and President Lincoln appointed a former North Carolina politician, Edward Stanly, to serve as Unionist governor of the state. Leaving from California, Stanly, who wanted to conciliate North Carolina whites and cultivate Unionist sentiment among them, arrived at federally occupied New Bern on May 26 and immediately caused an outcry. He sought to have a "loyal" slave-owner "persuade" a fugitive slave within federal lines to return to servitude. He also talked to Vincent

Quaker Carpetbagger

Colyer, the federal forces' Superintendent of the Poor, to suggest that a school Colyer had set up for some of the fugitive slaves violated North Carolina law against educating the slaves. Colyer took this as an order to close the school, which he did. A Quaker who had belonged to New York's Young Men's Christian Association (which later turned out not to be J. Williams's favorite organization), and who helped found the Christian Commission (an interdenominational Protestant aid group), Colyer used his connections to whip up opposition to Stanly's actions.[45]

John Hickman, the congressman whose district included Chester County, took up the crusade against Stanly. Hickman had left the Democrats over the previous few years and carved out an independent course that now brought him into alignment with the Republicans, his combative attitude angering established politicians and delighting his constituents. By June 2, Hickman had rushed a resolution through the House demanding that the administration provide information on whether Stanly had suppressed "the education of children, white or black," and by what authority this had been done. Soon, Stanly clarified that the school could reopen and Colyer suggested he had exaggerated Stanly's actions.[46]

As the Progressive Friends met for the first time since the outbreak of war, one of their activists, Alfred Love, asked the body to reaffirm the traditional Quaker Peace Testimony—the rejection of war. Love, a woolens merchant, had passed over the chance of rich contracts by refusing to sell to the Army. He was developing into a Garrisonian advocate of nonresistance after Garrison himself had become a supporter of the war. Love's resolution, passed "by an almost unanimous vote," declared that the "rejection" of Quaker peace principles "has involved our nation in the present conflict of blood, and that their adoption would forever render slavery and war impossible."[47]

There was less to this resolution than met the eye. Before passing their peace resolution, the Meeting took two steps that could reasonably be said to undercut Love's unconditional peace principles. Urged on by Garrison—who was present—and by Theodore Tilton, editor of an abolitionist paper in New York City, the Meeting adopted a Testimony calling on the Lincoln administration "TO ABOLISH SLAVERY WITHOUT DELAY." The Confederacy was said to be "the monstrous offspring of slaveholding despotism," at war with the principles of the Declaration of Independence. The federal "government—measuring it by its constitutional obligations—had no alternative but to seek to suppress this treasonable outbreak by all the means and forces at its disposal, or else to betray

5. Reform, Slave Raid, War

the sacred trusts committed to it by the people; and therefore, throughout this fearful struggle, it has had our sympathy, and desire for its success." According to the resolution, there was no conflict here with traditional Quaker peace principles, though in reality the Meeting had come quite some distance from its previous advocacy of peace and disarmament.[48]

The resolution deplored Lincoln's revocation of the Fremont and Hunter proclamations, the return of fugitive slaves from military camps, and the actions by Governor Stanly relating to fugitives and black education. The resolution also saw some hopeful signs in the abolition of slavery in the District of Columbia and other steps the government was taking in an antislavery direction. The Meeting now awaited "one great comprehensive decree" to abolish slavery and racial discrimination.[49]

To make sure this message was heard in the right places, the Meeting approved a message to President Lincoln, and took up a collection to defray the expenses of delegates who would go to Washington to bring the message in person. The resolution said that "this sanguinary rebellion finds its cause, purpose, and combustible materials, in that most unchristian and barbarous system of slavery." Thus, "the nation, in its official organization, should lose no time in proclaiming immediate and universal emancipation, so that the present frightful effusion of blood may cease, liberty be established, and a permanent reconciliation effected by the removal of the sole cause of these divisions." If Lincoln did not avail himself of this opportunity, "fiery judgments" might be "poured out" on the country.[50]

With the help of Pennsylvania Senator David Wilmot, the delegation—including the clerk, Oliver Johnson, and the self-sacrificing abolitionist Thomas Garrett—had a meeting with the president. Lincoln with his trademark humor said he was relieved the delegates were not seeking office for themselves. During the conversation, Lincoln remained noncommittal on whether he would issue a proclamation against slavery, but he declared he had "sometimes thought that he might be an instrument in God's hands of accomplishing a great work."[51]

That harvest season, Thorne probably felt the shortage of farm laborers caused by the absence of many young men in the army. This amounted to about 3,000 men from seventeen to forty-five as of September 1862, the time of the Preliminary Emancipation Proclamation. That was about a fourth of those in that age group. The Proclamation itself could have comforted Thorne amidst private problems with labor costs.[52]

Sylvester Gordon, one of the kidnapping defendants in the John

Quaker Carpetbagger

Brown kidnapping case, finally showed up in court and went to trial on April 22, 1863. For whatever reasons—innocence, or the absence of important witnesses in the wartime confusion—the jury acquitted Gordon.[53]

The Progressive Friends met in 1863 from June 4 through the 6th. Over the weekend there was such a demand for attendance that a special excursion rail car brought people from West Chester to the area. In addition to discussion of wartime issues and the future status of the freed slaves, the Meeting debated a resolution on "Religious Associations," a debate in which Thorne joined, though again the minutes do not record what he said. The resolution, which passed unanimously, said that the Longwood Meeting was striving to live up to the principle "the truest and best bond of union for a Religious Society is not assent to any form of theological belief, nor zeal for external observances and rites, but a common love of God and humanity, a common aspiration for moral excellence, oneness of spirit and purpose in respect to the practical duties of life, the communion of soul with soul in a common thirst for truth, and a common desire and purpose to labor for the redemption of the human race from ignorance, superstition, and sin."[54]

Alfred Love again offered a resolution on peace. This one was apparently more pointed than the boilerplate language of the previous year, instead explicitly endorsing the pacifist principle of nonresistance. The meeting minutes recorded that "for want of time to give the subject" of the resolution, "the consideration due to its importance, it was, with [Love's] concurrence and by general consent, laid upon the table."[55]

No sooner had the Progressive Friends Meeting broken up in 1863 than the people of Chester and Lancaster Counties heard of another incursion by somewhat less welcome visitors. The bells in the churches and the courthouse in West Chester rang out on June 16, and "farmers came rushing in just as they had left the field," reported the local *Village Record*. The authorities, based on the limited information they had, announced that Lee's Confederate army had invaded Pennsylvania.[56]

Inhabitants of Chester County buried their valuables, or sent them to safety. Some friends of Thorne, Joseph and Rebecca Taylor, whose son Bayard Taylor was a globetrotting travel writer, novelist and poet, buried Taylor's manuscripts as a safeguard against literary theft. The manuscripts survived, but another Taylor son, Fred, would die at Gettysburg. Refugees fled before the Confederates, including fugitive slaves and free blacks who feared (accurately enough) that the Confederates might capture and enslave them. Virginia troops in the invading forces seized and

5. Reform, Slave Raid, War

enslaved numerous black people and could have been expected to continue these depredations if they reached Lancaster and Chester counties.[57] The Northern victory at the Battle of Gettysburg relieved the fears that the Confederate army would resume the work of prewar slave-kidnappers in Thorne's neighborhood.

On December 3 and 4, 1863 (or at least part of that time), Thorne went to Philadelphia to attend the 30th anniversary commemoration of the American Anti Slavery Society. What a change since 1833, when the Society was suspect in the North as well as the South, and many Northerners considered mob violence a legitimate tool against the enemies of slavery.[58]

In November 1864, Thorne's old debate partner Thomas Whitson, who had persuaded him to get into Underground Railroad work, died. Whitson's funeral was attended by "an immense concourse of loving and admiring friends," white and black. Thorne would probably have been in this mourning crowd.[59]

The Progressive Friends met in 1864 and in June 1865, after the end of the war and the assassination of Lincoln. In their 1865 Meeting the Progressive Friends debated many testimonies, but Thorne's contribution came during the discussion on temperance. Again, the minutes do not record the content of Thorne's two contributions to the debate, but the final resolution was probably to his taste. The Meeting supported full abstinence—"the moderate use of intoxicating drinks is the downhill road to drunkenness." The demoralization of war, and the bad example set by respectable people who served alcohol as social hosts (even if they'd taken the temperance pledge), contributed to the alcohol problem. "[T]he peace, health, virtue and prosperity of the country" were at stake in the total-abstinence struggle. Medicinal alcohol was denounced as a fraud; such "preparations are made rather with reference to pecuniary gain and the gratification of an appetite for stimulants than to give relief in sickness or distress."[60]

In March 1866, Joseph Thorne died, and J. Williams was entrusted with administering his father's estate. After expenses, the proceeds of the estate were distributed among Thorne and his surviving siblings, all sisters: Mary Dubree Thorne Bond, Lydia Ann Thorne Mewes, the widowed Ann Eliza Thorne Underwood, and Caroline Thorne Hanway, widow of Washington Hanway. The five children received $546.68 each. Joseph Thorne was buried in the Ercildoun Friends Burial ground.[61]

In the same year, Thorne closed his school, bringing his ten-year educational enterprise to an end.⁶² Now in his fiftieth year, Thorne had seen a great deal of life without having to leave his own community. Now he began to consider moving to a new community where things promised to be no less exciting. If such were his hopes, he would not be disappointed.

6

Keystone Stater and Tar Heel

In an obituary notice J. Williams wrote for the July 4, 1868, *Anti-Slavery Standard*, he praised his late friend James Fulton, who had been an Underground Railroad conductor. "The poor fugitive from the Southern prison-house of bondage" always got Fulton's aid. "All the great reforms of the age found in him a warm and zealous helper.... [H]e bore faithful testimony against those great national sins, Slavery and Intemperance, when both Church and State were alike dead to them.... He labored not for praise or fame, not that he might win a useless and selfish immortality of blissful existence; but he did simply for the love of man those good deeds which are necessarily immortal in their influence and power over human nature."[1] The reference to "useless and selfish immortality" shows Thorne's anti–Christian opinions, which the *Anti-Slavery Standard* had noted back in 1860.

At that time, many states such as Pennsylvania held their local and state elections at different times from their November federal elections. In 1868, the earlier election date was October 13. This happened to be the twenty-first birthday of Thorne's son Caleb Pusey. Twenty-one was the voting age in those days, so it seemed that the proud father would have the chance to see his son make the smooth transition to his civic responsibilities by casting his first ballot that day.

A Democratic Party polling official had other ideas. Determined not to allow any Republican votes that he might challenge—and the Thornes seem to have been reliably Republican—the official made what he clearly thought was a clever point to exclude Caleb Pusey from voting. The official knew (it seems it was hard to keep secrets in these small communities) that twenty-one years earlier, Caleb had been born at 7 p.m., so, the official triumphantly proclaimed, he would not be 21 until that time, when the polls would be closed.

Quaker Carpetbagger

J. Williams Thorne had not been an astronomy instructor for nothing. He debated the Democrat, calculating that Caleb had gone through several leap years in his young life, adding up over his lifespan to just over 21 years when the calculations were done properly. The Democrat didn't know how to rebut the elder Thorne, though he kept insisting that Caleb should not be allowed to vote. The Republican official finally put Caleb's ballot in the box when the time came to around 7. This story was reported in several newspapers throughout the country, introducing what Thorne's neighbors were already aware of—his remarkable persistence as a debater.[2]

Also on the voting front, John Hickman, the Chester County ex-congressman who was now a member of the Pennsylvania legislature, sought to change the state constitution to extend the vote to adult men regardless of race, which would remove Pennsylvania's constitutional provision for a whites-only franchise. The legislature, though Republican, was unwilling to move on the issue, even though black suffrage had already been established in the South. But soon a proposed federal constitutional amendment, the Fifteenth, forbade race discrimination in voting in any state, North or South. As good partisans, the Pennsylvania legislators ratified the amendment, which would become law in 1870.[3]

In its edition of March 3, 1869, the Wilmington, Delaware *Daily Commercial* included this item among the notices on its front page: "J. Williams Thorne, of Sadsbury Township, Chester County, has recently been on a visit to the state of North Carolina, where he purchased 1,700 acres of land. It is located on the Choccoe [Shocco] Creek, near what is known as the Ridgeway settlement, and within nine miles of the village of Ridgeway, on the Raleigh and Gaston Railroad. His son will take charge of the property and proposes to raise grain, instead of tobacco." (Recall that the Progressive Friends had adopted a testimony against the tobacco habit.)

J. Williams at some point decided that he would move himself and several family members and friends to settle in North Carolina, setting up a "colony." In 1928, D.T. Smithwick, whose sister married Mary Thorne's nephew Evan Pusey, would write that the Thorne party "came South originally more to aid and contribute in a constructive way to upbuilding the South after the war." The migrants "brought Car loads of the most beautiful household goods and furniture."[4] These may have been a subtle response to the "carpetbagger" slur directed by embittered white Southerners against postwar migrants to the South, which implied that these migrants were penniless adventurers, all of whose goods fit in a small

6. Keystone Stater and Tar Heel

"carpetbag" suitcase. The seeming implication of such attacks was that the "carpetbaggers" planned on enriching themselves at the expense of the war-ravaged South.

In a speech to Antietam veterans in 1868, General Daniel Sickles challenged this derogatory conception of carpetbaggers. A former Democratic politician, Sickles had lost a leg at Gettysburg, grown more militant during the war and Reconstruction, and served as military governor of North and South Carolina until removed by former President Andrew Johnson. Sickles's speech tried to reclaim the term "carpetbaggers" by applying it to the settlers of the American West, the *Mayflower* pilgrims, and (more provocatively, from the Southern perspective) William the Conqueror's Normans. "Our carpet-baggers," said Sickles, "carry intelligence and civilization and enterprise wherever they go, and they are not to be barred out or excluded from the South at rebel dictation."[5]

On August 2, 1869, shortly before his departure, J. Williams entertained Edward B. Moore, editor of the *West Chester American Republican*. Major Moore wrote a highly complimentary description of his visit to J. Williams's farm, combining praise for the family's hospitality with a description of the farm's produce and a disquisition on J. Williams's dietary habits. Moore, at least in the version of the article reprinted in the *Lancaster Evening Express*, did not mention J. Williams's forthcoming Southern venture.[6]

Soon after arriving at the farmhouse around 3:30, Major Moore was

> enjoying a dinner such as only farmer's wives and daughters can set before their guests. We will state, *en passant*, that Mr. Thorne is, to a great extent, a disciple of the hygienic or health-reform school, and has raised his family of children largely in accordance with the teachings of its acknowledged leaders. He has not eaten meat for *twenty-five* years, and his table is always supplied with the different varieties of fruits and the best vegetables, which in connection with the *unbolted* wheat-meal bread, he considers the most healthful and natural diet of man; his guests and helpers, however, are liberally supplied with meat and white bread if they desire them.... Mr. Thorne attributes his strong and vigorous condition of body, as well as the excellent health enjoyed by his family, to their manner and habit of living, together with their entire abstinence from alcoholic beverages. He also eschews the use of drugs or medicines, relying entirely upon the curative powers of nature and good nursing in cases of sickness.

J. Williams's barn, which Frank Wilson had burned, had been "replaced by another one of very large dimensions, and it is now probably one of the finest in the neighborhood." Major Moore rhapsodized about

Quaker Carpetbagger

J. Williams's apple trees, blackberries, and oats, sorghum crop, and "good, substantial mill" for making syrup.

Most of the farm was on the Chester County side of the line, with some on the Lancaster County side. "The view from the dividing ridge between Chester and Lancaster counties, on this farm, embraced a wide range of the celebrated Pequea Valley, in the latter county, and of the Welsh Mountain in the distance, which forms the northwestern boundary of Chester, is most beautiful and picturesque; after enjoying it for a long time, we found ourselves quite loath to turn our gaze away."

But J. Williams and family were turning their gaze away—toward the south.

The North Carolina government at the time wanted more "carpetbaggers." Republican Governor William Holden and his allies had set up the North Carolina Land Company to lure migrants from the North and Europe. A booklet published by the company boasted: "The world does not possess any where a more quiet, peaceable, honest and frugal population, than the people of this State. Notwithstanding the devastation, ruin and demoralization of the late civil war, our people are rapidly returning to their old customs and labors. A more law-abiding people cannot be found." In a promotional letter of his own, Holden declared that "the State is now thoroughly reconstructed politically and civilly."[7]

The land company booklet set forth the advantages of each county. Warren County, an inland county on the Virginia border in the northeast of North Carolina, was Thorne's choice as a place to settle. The booklet presented the county in appealing terms: "This county is considered one of the best in the State. The people are intelligent and hospitable. Lands are fertile, rich and productive." Yearly production included "wheat, 125,000 bushels; corn, 500,000 bushels; oats, 98,000 bushels; tobacco, 6,150,000 pounds; cotton 500 bales." One downside from Thorne's point of view was that the booklet said Warren contained three distilleries.[8]

One might imagine that a Quaker settler in North Carolina would move to the "Quaker belt" in the central Piedmont, around Greensboro and several surrounding counties. The war had left many North Carolina Quakers impoverished and considering emigration from the state. Many Northern Quakers established the Baltimore Association to help Southern Quakers out. In North Carolina, this translated into relief, schools, and instruction in the latest methods of agriculture. For the latter purpose, the Baltimore Association set up a model farm on the border of Guilford and Randolph Counties. Allen Jay, a Quaker and Baltimore Association

6. Keystone Stater and Tar Heel

worker, said that "several farmers from Maryland and Pennsylvania"—no names mentioned—examined this model farm to see that it was set up properly.[9]

Counting against the possibility of Thorne's coming to North Carolina under Quaker philanthropist auspices is that Warren County was quite removed from the "Quaker belt." Also, if Quaker organizations had inspired Thorne to move to Warren, one would expect Thorne to meet up with other Quaker-inspired migrants. Yet two teachers who had worked under the auspices of a Philadelphia-based Quaker association "for the Relief of Colored Freed men," and who then moved to Warrenton, the Warren County seat, to teach black students in a public school, did not leave evidence of having met Thorne. Elizabeth Pennock was a Quaker; Margaret Newbold Thorpe had a Quaker mother and made notes of her life in Warrenton in the 1869–71 period. Margaret Thorpe makes no express reference to meeting with the Thornes. A visit to the Thorne farm, or Thorne's calling on the teachers when visiting Warrenton, would probably have been sufficiently worthy of remark to be preserved in Margaret Thorpe's notes, yet such encounters are not mentioned.[10]

Whether or not Thorne was involved with the work of the Baltimore Association or other Quaker groups, he would not necessarily have been interested in moving to the Quaker parts of the state. North Carolina Quakers were far closer to evangelical Christianity than to Thorne's "infidelity"—they were Orthodox, with that Quaker denomination's focus on evangelical-style spirituality and belief in the authority of the Bible. Religiously, they were far from the wide-ranging spiritually inspired reformism Thorne had grown accustomed to at the Progressive Friends meeting in Longwood. Their Orthodox affiliation hadn't protected Tar Heel Quakers from enduring extra suffering during the war due to their opposition to conscription and the public suspicion against their traditional antislavery orientation.[11]

Some parts of Warren County's history Thorne would need to find out from other sources than the North Carolina Land Company's booklet. Before the war, Warren was one of the few Tar Heel counties where a majority of the population were black slaves. Wealthy whites in the prewar years held knightly-style jousting tournaments, while well-off residents and visitors came to the alleged healing baths of Shocco Springs and Jones Springs. There, in the words of historian Manly Wade Wellman, "Crinoline skirts and low-necked bodices made the girls lovely, and many a sidewhiskered, ruffle-shirted cavalier found that he had lost his heart." On the other end of the social scale, as a former slave told Margaret Thorpe, "every few days she would see or hear the bloodhounds after a run-away, and many a time she had seen the poor things brought home bleeding and torn." Another former slave told Margaret Thorpe about her son who ran away twice, the second time burning to death in the Great Dismal Swamp to the east.[12]

Upon the outbreak of war, a Warren County mob had threatened a local jeweler, a former Pennsylvanian who had taught his slave janitor, John Hyman, how to read. The mob was opposed to literate slaves, and yielding to the pressure, the jeweler sold Hyman down south to Alabama.[13]

The war in Warren County was not as bad as in many other areas of the South. The county's sons went forth to fight for the Confederacy, while the civilian population suffered the general shortage of consumer goods. The Confederate-leaning inhabitants could point with pride to two Warren County–born Confederate figures: General Braxton Bragg and his brother, Confederate Attorney General Thomas Bragg. But the county was not a seat of war—no battles were fought there, and the Confederates were not driven out until the war was over and the Northern occupiers spread throughout the South.[14]

Now that Congress, and the Republicans who had taken over the state, had enfranchised black men, the black majority in Warren was capable of influencing the destinies of the county. The county elected a new state senator—John Hyman, who had returned from his wartime exile in Alabama to set up a store and organize politically among the former slaves. Hyman built up his influence as he helped put together a deal with the white Democratic minority—black voters elected Democrats as sheriff, local treasurer, and superior court clerk, while the whites supported blacks for many other offices.[15] To someone like J. Williams, such cooperation with racist Democrats may have seemed unnatural; there is certainly no evidence that J. Williams was associated with the Hyman faction, and much evidence to the contrary.

With the new opportunities provided by freedom, a significant minority of slaves became small landowning farmers. Certainly they were not all paupers. Margaret Newbold Thorpe wrote: "Our two hundred pupils are comfortably dressed, some of the families employ servants, *have sewing machines* and keep horses and carriages." She also, however, noticed a pauper pupil whom she provided with proper food and clothes. Most of the black population worked either as farm tenants or as hired

6. Keystone Stater and Tar Heel

farmhands—the tenants worked under the emerging sharecropping system, while the farmhands got what work they could.[16]

Other than Quaker connections and Holden's emigrant appeals, there are a couple of other possible guesses we can make about how Thorne chose Warren County as the location for his colony. A black poet named Frances Ellen Watkins Harper had been on a tour of the South and had spoken in the vicinity of Warren County, at least speaking in nearby Edgecombe and earning some grudging respect from a paper in Tarboro. The following year she was speaking in Chester and Lancaster County. A letter from J. Williams, published on December 15, 1868, in the *Philadelphia Press*, described the "fit audience, though few," who had greeted Harper at Coatesville, Compassville and Christiana, suggesting that but for "our absurd prejudices against color," Mrs. Harper would have had a much bigger audience. Thorne invited *Press* readers to come to Concert Hall in Philadelphia on the 17th, when Harper would read from her poem "Moses," concerning the biblical hero who renounced a privileged Egyptian life to lead his people from slavery. Whatever reservations Thorne may have had about Harper's Christian beliefs and affiliations, he praised the poem as "a work of great genius."[17] Information from Harper's earlier tour may have interested Thorne in the possibilities of settling down South.

There is another, more far-fetched possibility as to how J. Williams learned about Warren County—this is a highly speculative scenario, but worth at least noting. J. Williams maintained an interest in educational affairs, even after closing his Chester County school in 1866. When the Pennsylvania State Teachers' Association met in Lancaster in August 1870, J. Williams was listed as attending what the *Pennsylvania School Journal* estimated as the second-largest such gathering in the organization's history. Thorne's associations with Pennsylvania educators raise the possibility that he may have met three sisters—Rosa, Laura and Miriam Mordecai—who ran a girls' school in Philadelphia. If he met the Mordecai sisters, Thorne would probably have been intrigued by the history of the Mordecai family. At the turn of the century, the Mordecais had run a school for girls in Warren County, an important and respected institution among the (white) population. For a time, one of the teachers at Philadelphia's Misses Mordecai's School for Young Ladies was the principals' father Alfred, an Army engineer who had resigned from the military and from war work to avoid choosing sides in the Civil War between his largely Southern family and his devotion to the Union. The sisters' cousin was Marx Edgeworth Lazarus, the Fourierist reformer who in 1852 (shortly before his own marriage) had written the free-love tract that inspired so much debate that year (a year in which J. Williams read a Lyceum paper calling marriage a prison for women). These suggestive connections, geographical and ideological, indicate a possible way Thorne may have learned about Warren County—but there is no proof of such a scenario.[18]

Either when he first went South, or when he returned there in 1870, J. Williams prompted his widowed sister, Ann Eliza Underwood, to write a sad poem bemoaning his departure (Ann had previous experience with moving out of state, with her father's ill-starred settlement in Ottawa, Illinois).

> Dear brother is it so
> That thou wilt leave thy home
> Where thou hast toiled from youth & age
> Where thy children too have grown
>
> The home thy mother looked upon,
> And smiled and blessed thee too,
> And canst thou now for sunnier clime
> Say unto all Adieu
>
> Does the sun shine more brightly there
> And [lovelier?] flowers bloom?
> Than thou hast tended and looked upon
> Around thy own dear home.
>
> Trees thou hast planted here stately grown
> Under thy fostering care
> All things are lovely and endeared
> For thou hast reared them there.
>
> Thou knowest Brother what is best
> Far better than I know,
> And in thy choice I trustingly
> Will hope it wise to go.
>
> But Oh 'tis to realize
> To know thou art not near
> To lend a helping hand in need,
> To those whom thou art dear.[19]

J. Williams's daughter Annie was falling in love with a Pennsylvania Mennonite lad, Peter Hershey. They had met at Millwood Lyceum, and as they corresponded over the debates and business of the Lyceum, their letters grew into a more personal conversation. In April 1869, Annie wrote Peter about her father, mother and others and their move to Warren County: "We have heard from them several times since they went South and they are all highly pleased with it. I suppose in a year or less time

6. Keystone Stater and Tar Heel

perhaps will find all our family in North Carolina. I shall be sorry to leave my native place but I hope it will turn out for the best."[20]

J. Williams, as Smithwick later recalled of the Thornes' adventures in Warren County, "bought the Brodin estate and much other land near Jones Springs." The Thornes acquired a farm called Oak Grove, and there J. Williams, or his family during his absences in Pennsylvania, grew cotton, apples, peaches, and scuppernong grapes, and even raised some pigs (presumably not for vegetarian purposes) and chickens.

In a letter of August 1869 to her children Annie and Eugene, still in Pennsylvania, J. Williams's wife Mary sang the praises of their new home. Mary didn't have to do any washing, because "three of our colored women" did the washing for three of the local families. This left Mary time to sew and look out the window at the "grove of grand towering oaks that surrounds our [great?] substantial old mansion." Life could be good in the South, where "labor" was "a blessing instead of the proverbial curse it ever must be where people are burdened with debt and extravagant wages." Whether Mary was alluding to the "extravagant wages" her family had to pay their farm workers in Pennsylvania, or whether she was simply singing the praises of a simple life, is not clear. She liked watching "the little darkie boys" playing around the plantation as if they "owned" it, "for I do not believe great possessions make people happy." Mary announced, "I have seen our Southern home and am very certain I shall like to spend the remnant of my days here very happily if you [Eugene and Annie] were both here."[21]

In Pennsylvania, Annie and Peter's romance blossomed. By January 1870, Annie was telling Peter about Eugene's moving to Warren County, where her brother Pusey and her cousin (on her mother's side) Alfred were already there.[22]

Annie and Peter set a wedding for mid–August, to be held at the farmhouse in Fountain Hill, Chester County. J. Williams and Mary Thorne were there to preside over the festivities, while Caleb Pusey was back in Oak Grove. Mary's unmarried sister Ann Pusey was there as well, writing Annie before the wedding to share her felicitations—and to warn that not all was going well in Warren County. "I do not want to make you unhappy, but you would not believe that gambling for money is carried on at the store," and "I know [Caleb] Pusey and Alfred gamble for I heard them at it. They gamble with the black people." The neighbor, Joseph Jones, had complained about such goings-on and warned that J. Williams would be ruined if his son Pusey kept gambling. "I should not right [sic] such a sad letter as this," said Anne, "if I did not think it my duty to let Pa [J. Williams] know how things are going here."²³

The wedding came off on August 16, and Annie and Peter embarked on their honeymoon. J. Williams left for Warren County and either brought the newlyweds with him or received them later. He wrote: "This morning [September 5] Peter & Annie and our other Northern folks will leave for the North. It has been very pleasant to have them with us. They all seem very much pleased with Warren County." He reported, "We have a good deal of very good cotton," and that "the rest of our Colony" had a "fine growth" of the staple. J. Williams seems to have been alerted to his sister-in-law's concerns about gambling, since he seems to have done a quick investigation. "There is not a particle of card playing on the Plantation, nor had there been for some time before I came here. I can not learn that there had been playing for money to any extent."²⁴ Still, such reports about gambling on his plantation would recur later.

J. Williams also wrote his wife and his son Eugene about getting agricultural supplies from Chester County to Warren County. He was hopeful that John Hershey, apparently one of the Hershey relatives, would buy one of his farm properties in Pennsylvania—"the Thompson farm." He hoped to have the Fountain Hill and Thompson farms rented out, unless John Hershey could agree to buy the Thompson farm.²⁵

By November, J. Williams was advertising his Fountain Hill farm for sale in the *Lancaster Examiner and Herald*. "This is a superior farm in all respects," boasted the ad, enumerating the orchard, the barn, the farmhouse, the sorghum mill and the tenant houses: "Is highly improved and in good order." Eugene would show potential purchasers around.²⁶ From subsequent references to the family's correspondence, it didn't sell at this time.

Political developments in North Carolina in 1870 showed that the promises about a "law abiding" population were somewhat exaggerated. White terrorists, calling themselves the Ku Klux Klan or other names, used assault, intimidation and murder to "punish" black challengers to white supremacy, and to suppress the Republican vote (white and black) in favor of the white-supremacist Conservative party (which caucused with the national Democrats). The Klan terror was primarily wielded in counties such as those in the central Piedmont, where there was a close balance between whites and blacks, and between Republicans and Conservatives. Though there was a Klan presence in Warren County, the terrorists seemingly didn't think it practicable to keep down the massive Republican vote

6. Keystone Stater and Tar Heel

associated with the black majority. At any rate, Margaret Thorpe had written in 1869: "We are most thankful that the K.K.K. does not infest this part of the state." The terror in other counties, however, was enough to affect the state elections and bring the state legislature into Conservative hands. The new legislature's first action was to impeach Governor Holden for violating the civil liberties of Klan suspects when he sent troops and made an unsuccessful attempt to subject the suspects to martial law. Holden was removed from office and the Republican Lieutenant Governor, Tod Caldwell, became the new governor of the state. Racial violence infected the Pennsylvania elections in October 1871 as well, as white mobs in Philadelphia attacked newly enfranchised black voters, and black leader Octavius Catto was murdered.[27]

The federal government finally bestirred itself against the Klan, with President Grant declaring martial law in two North Carolina counties in response to a resurgence of the group's violence. After trials, about twenty-five Klan members went to prison. These incidents had the effect of excluding a leading Conservative figure, Zebulon Vance, from the United States Senate. The former Confederate Civil War governor had been elected to the Senate by the North Carolina legislature, but to take his seat, he would have to persuade Congress to remove the political disqualifications he labored under as an ex–Confederate. Concerned about Klan violence and Vance's seeming tolerance of it, the Republican Congress retained Vance's disqualifications, obliging Vance to resign his Senate seat in favor of a new candidate. Though Vance's political rights were restored in 1872, embittered Conservatives probably resented and remembered how the Republicans had excluded Vance.[28]

J. Williams continued to keep a foot in two states, trying to manage both his Warren County and Chester County farms or at least supervise the latter when he went north to Pennsylvania in the winter. He also kept up with political developments. A news item from 1872 announced that on June 30, there had been a meeting of "The Colored Republicans, Chester and Lancaster counties." This meeting was held in the "wood of J.D. Pownell, of Christiana." Speakers included William Parker, hero of the Christiana resistance of 1851, who was going to give the commencement address at Lincoln University (the former Ashmun Institute). Another of the many speakers was J. Williams, who according to the article made a "first-rate speech of about twenty minutes duration," though the content of the speeches was not described.[29]

The affairs of both his northern and southern properties kept J. Williams's attention at this time. He postponed his return to North Carolina so that he could negotiate the sale of the Thompson farm, for which, he wrote his wife, he believed he had found a buyer. His wife in Warren County had sent him some bad news, that some of his creditors had complained about missed payments on his notes. J. Williams assured Mary that this was due to "an informality in the making of a note, which delayed the discounting of it for near a week. You may assure all the parties concerned that the checks will all be made right in a few days." Indeed, "I am determined to settle up my financial affairs so that they will give me no further trouble." He added, "I have reason to believe that I will soon have them all right."[30]

Problems persisted with at least one creditor, Benjamin W. Jones, since Jones went to court to have the Chester County sheriff seize the Fountain Hill and other Chester County property belonging to J. Williams, in order to pay off a debt J. Williams owed to Jones. Since J. Williams continued to hold onto the Fountain Hill property after this, it is likely that he settled matters with Jones.[31]

Peter Hershey stayed at Fountain Hill in Chester County while a lonely Annie Thorne Hershey stayed in Warren County. Peter was J. Williams's tenant while J. Williams looked for a buyer. In several letters in September 1872, Annie vacillated over where she would prefer to live. J. Williams's sister Caroline—widow of Washington Hanway—had taken a second husband, Barclay H. Lippincott of New Jersey, and the couple had become part of Thorne's "colony." Annie noted that the Lippincotts' daughter Emma, who had been born in New Jersey, "has the Southern dialect—talks just like the darkies. I would not like to see children raised down here." Annie noted in a letter of September 26 that "Papa [J. Williams] caught two darkies at his scuppernong vine last night. They think nothing of lying or stealing down here." In an addendum to the letter the next day, Annie said, "I like NC better than I did—it has improved very much since I was here." Perhaps two days later Annie noted that it was a lonely Sunday without Peter (with nothing to do, since apparently the family did not go to church). Annie was uncertain if she would end up living with Peter on the Fountain Hill property or in Warren County.[32]

Early in 1873, Thorne again encountered the Englishman Joseph Barker, who was once more making a lecture tour of the Philadelphia area as in 1853–54. This time, however, Barker was speaking as a Christian, denouncing his former "infidel" colleagues in England and America. Back in 1860, having developed to the point of full atheism, Barker had left the United States to return to England, where he began drifting back into the

6. Keystone Stater and Tar Heel

Christian camp. In 1863, Barker announced his re-conversion and once again became a Methodist. The American abolitionists with whom he had once had an uneasy alliance were now, to him, evildoers and fanatics—especially those like Garrison who, like Barker at an earlier time, had opposed the Bible and organized Christianity. Now Barker not only defended his renewed faith, he took part in English debates over the American Civil War, defending the Confederacy—not on proslavery grounds, he insisted, but because the Confederates were resisting Lincoln's supposedly wicked effort to solve the slavery problem by violence and bloodshed. The Confederates were simply standing for their rights vis-à-vis the North, defending themselves from Northern aggression and offering low-tariff cotton to trade with England. The Confederates could be trusted to deal with slavery. When Lincoln was shot, Barker believed the American president had gotten what was coming to him.[33]

Though believing that the wrong side had won the American Civil War, Barker came to the United States again to return to his former Nebraska home. From this base he proposed to lecture in favor of Christianity and against the "infidelity" he used to preach. Thus it was fitting that he planned a return to the Philadelphia area, where he proposed to argue the opposite side of the positions he had argued two decades before. In testy exchanges with a freethinking paper, the *Boston Investigator*, Barker indicated that he might be interested in engaging in a debate with an "infidel" opponent, but militating against it were his age and health—he had recently suffered blood loss due to an attack of "violent gastralgia, brought on by excess of mental labor. Still, if a debate be demanded, I will use what strength I have in defense of Christianity."[34]

This commitment was put to the test when Barker lectured in Coatesville, Chester County, Thorne's stomping ground, when Thorne was in the county in January. Thorne attended one of Barker's three Coatesville lectures, and after Barker spoke, Thorne proposed a debate between the two of them: "We should discuss," as Thorne later summarized his proposal, "before the people of Coatesville, the great question regarding the fate of Christianity, as a religion, the '*Divine Authority of the Bible.*'"[35]

Thorne reported that Barker gave the same explanation he had given the *Investigator* for fearing a debate—claiming, J. Williams said, that "exciting discussion" was inadvisable given a "hemorrhage of blood" Barker had recently had. "Besides," according to J. Williams's summary, "since his conversion to the religion of Christianity, his life had become too valuable to the world to run such risk of losing it."[36]

Quaker Carpetbagger

Barker declined to hold the debate in the presumably less stressful setting of "Mr. [Thomas] Windle's or Mr. Roberts' parlor." J. Williams left it to Windle to see if the latter could still arrange a debate. Even after J. Williams went back to Warren County two weeks after the lecture, he would be willing, he later said, to come back to Pennsylvania to debate Barker if terms could be arranged. But the terms Barker offered—to let J. Williams or other members of the public ask him questions after a proposed lecture of February 4—were not an adequate substitute for a real debate, from J. Williams's standpoint. J. Williams could have submitted to such terms if he were still in Chester County on February 4, but he'd be in North Carolina and wouldn't make a special trip back north just to take part in a question-and-answer period after a Barker speech.[37]

Despite all this, the Young Men's Christian Association advertised Barker's February 4 speech, scheduled for the Market Hall in Coatesville, at which Barker would "*devote three fourths of an hour with* [J. Williams] *or others for discussion.*" This wasn't "a fair acceptance of my challenge," so instead of returning to Chester County to attend Barker's February lecture, J. Williams prepared an essay for publication in "one or more papers of Chester County," giving a rebuttal to Barker. Because the rebuttal turned out to be fairly long—it ended up as twelve pages—J. Williams decided not to submit it to the newspapers, but to print it as a pamphlet, presumably for circulation among people in Chester County.[38]

As to the argument J. Williams was rebutting, here is J. Williams's summary of Barker: It is difficult to find morality among non–Christians ("infidels"); the radicals Barker used to hang out with were rarely very good people; and his radical Ohio neighbors cared more about their own liberty than anyone else's, prompting Barker to move to Nebraska, where he began the process of self-examination that ended up bringing him back to Christianity.

J. Williams proceeded to defend "Infidels," or "Liberals or radicals in religion," as he also called them, against Barker's attacks. Proposing to test Christianity by the Biblical test that "By their fruits ye shall note them," J. Williams began with Barker himself, contrasting Barker when he was a "Liberal" with how he was as a Christian. The Liberal Barker had been antislavery, supported an English Republic, and defended the "common people" of England. As a Christian, Barker had supported Confederate independence, defended the "oppressive aristocracy" of England, and joined England's state church, the Church of England, making himself responsible for the wrongs of the English government (Barker had actually become

6. Keystone Stater and Tar Heel

a Methodist, by now an independent denomination, so J. Williams was mistaken here.[39])

J. Williams proceeded to defend "the moral character of liberals." He said: "In the neighborhood of Longwood, Chester County, Pa., where liberals most abound and give character to the community, there is no where a more temperate, a more moral and orderly people." J. Williams mentioned the "Hicksite Quakers and Unitarians" who denied Jesus' divinity and "have a world-wide fame for temperance, honesty, and a philanthropy that includes the whole human race." Christian Puritans' arrival "was death to the Indian," while "the half-infidel Quakers" had brought "peace and joy" to the Indians. It was liberals and not Evangelical Christians who led "the great Anti-slavery and Temperance movements." If "the evangelical Churches preached human justice and human morals, instead of the mystical superstition of the Trinity, and Resurrection, there would have been neither occasion nor need of the great Reform associations."[40]

J. Williams took a swipe at the Young Men's Christian Association, presumably because of their sponsorship of Barker's Coatesville speech. A New York City YMCA official named Anthony Comstock ran a group called the New York Society for the Suppression of Vice. An avowed crusader for morality, Comstock had helped arrest the famous free-love radical Victoria Woodhull and her sister on obscenity charges after an issue of the sisters' newspaper ran articles alleging immorality in high society. The prosecution was goaded on by supporters of one of the prominent people attacked in the paper—influential minister Henry Ward Beecher. For the first time, the Woodhull article publicized the scandal of the alleged adultery between Beecher and the wife of an old associate, the religious journalist Theodore Tilton. Tilton often played a role in the annual Meeting of the Progressive Friends, so J. Williams's sympathies may have been with the wronged husband. In any case he intended to use the affair to show that Christians had a lower level of morality than the "Liberals." He also wanted to use the case of the wealthy eccentric George Francis Train, who in sympathy with Woodhull had published a compilation of allegedly obscene passages from the Bible and had duly been arrested at Comstock's initiative.[41]

J. Williams declared that while the YMCA was putting Train in jail for his Bible quotes, it was "sending forth" the Bible "to the people, and to the heathen of every land as the holiest and best of all books." As for Woodhull, she had published her revelations "not in a slandering spirit, but for the purification of a gross social atmosphere." The YMCA were "sunk ... deep in the bottomless pit of hypocritical piety" and "never raised a finger" to address the problems Woodhull exposed. J. Williams was somewhat overgenerous to Woodhull's purity of motive—she was a more complicated figure, never free from the taint of scandal or even charlatanism—though these particular revelations of hers turned out to be quite accurate. (J. Williams said that though Woodhull's charges "remain unanswered," Beecher was "more popular in his church than ever."[42])

J. Williams wrote: "It is a rare sight to see an Infidel in jail, except when placed there by religious bigotry, on account of his opinions. Persons convicted of murder and other high crimes, are almost always found to be firm believers in the Bible."[43]

J. Williams warmed even more to his general thesis of the inferior morality of Christianity: "As the Christian Church rose in power and influence, civilization declined. And now, civilization is advancing in exact proportion as the Church loses its power and influence among men.... The Church has no positive influence against injustice or wrong. It never, knowingly, does any good thing that is unpopular.... The Evangelical Church has almost always defended a popular wrong and opposed an unpopular right. This course is reversed by the unbelieving Infidel or Liberal."[44]

Slavery in "Mahommedan countries" was more humane than slavery in Christian countries, according to J. Williams.

J. Williams was probably aware of the Chester County Presbyterian John Miller Dickey's efforts on behalf of free blacks before the war, including the founding of what was now Lincoln University as an institution of higher learning dedicated to the education of black people. This made it all the more regrettable that J. Williams did not even mention Dickey's risky and expensive championship of black education and opposition to kidnappers. J. Williams preferred instead to picture Christians as opposing evils such as slavery and caste oppression only when it was easy to do so.

Now J. Williams's pamphlet turned to the old standby of anti–Christian argument—the behavior of God and the patriarchs and kings in the Old Testament. J. Williams touched all bases—the "exterminating merciless war" waged by the Israelites against the Canaanites, the willingness of Abraham to sacrifice Isaac, Jephthah's vow (in the book of Judges, Jephthah kills his daughter in fulfillment of a vow to kill the first being that comes to greet him on his way home from a victory), David's adultery and the murder of Uriah, David's killing of prisoners of war, Biblical figures practicing polygamy and keeping concubines. "There is little in the

6. Keystone Stater and Tar Heel

history of the Jewish nation that a good man could wish to imitate," J. Williams claimed. David was "a man of cruelty and blood," but the Bible called David someone "after God's own heart." The Old Testament God was indeed like David, said J. Williams, bloody and cruel. The YMCA had rejected the adultery charges against Beecher, proclaiming these charges "exceedingly disgraceful if true" (J. Williams's paraphrase), but such concubinage was nothing more than what the great Biblical figures had done. "If [the YMCA] had Solomon himself in New York, he would fare no better at their hands than Victoria C. Woodhull or Brigham Young."[45]

As for Jesus, during his ministry on earth, "[a]ll around him were the evils of Slavery and Intemperance, but he took no notice of them, and bore no direct testimony against them.... It did not matter much, if men did suffer, in this life, from poverty, oppression, or slavery.... Man's present happiness is almost entirely ignored." To J. Williams, "the Ga[d]erene '*stock growers*'" and the owner of the withered fig tree had legitimate complaints against Jesus for harming their livelihoods.[46]

Jesus' advice to take no thought for the morrow would "make one great '*poor house*' of the world." The doctrine that a wicked person could repent at the last minute and be saved "must operate as an encouragement to crime." (This latter argument, like the alleged Christian approval of polygamy and slavery, echoed Barker's own arguments from 1854.[47])

Under Christian doctrine, as summarized by J. Williams, "God is represented as an omnipotent despot, who created millions of human beings for no other purpose, but, that he might drink in their flattery and homage forever. Or, if they withheld this servile adoration they had the alternative of eternal damnation.... Can Heaven be Heaven to that parent who knows that his children are suffering the intensest torments of an everlasting hell?... The few [God] saves, he saves not out of kindness to them, but only to please his Son."[48]

God, said J. Williams, could prevent the evils of the world but did not, and human beings are not allowed to be so "impertinent" as to question this, lest God "call down further vengeance on our heads.... The pious Despot feels himself at ease; His oppressed people are all going to Heaven by that purest of all ways—poverty and suffering.... We spend time in absurd forms of worship, which ought to be devoted to mental and physical education.... Let us make the present life good with good works, and there need be no fear for the future."[49]

J. Williams added that he was not against "devotional feelings," he merely wanted "a more rational devotion and use of" these feelings. "The best we can do, is to worship our highest ideal of truth and good; still striving with unceasing effort, in the great life movement, to make it higher and higher.... That we are naturally devotional, is no good reason why we should devote ourselves to the worship of an unworthy, ignorant and wicked God."[50] Then the peroration:

> When the great Christian Church has sufficient confidence in its own principles to establish a free platform; and when it not only does not fear, but invites the fullest and freest discussion of those principles on that free platform; then, loosed from the bonds of a false, despotic religion, it will become a source of light and knowledge that cannot fail to bless the world, as it has never yet been blessed[.] It would, indeed, be well for the world, if the Christian Church were thus free, instead of being as now, the great Bastile [sic] of the human mind; the greatest extinguisher of reason, the mightiest engine of darkness that the spirit of superstition has ever invented for the humiliation of man.[51]

A financial panic and depression hit the whole country by the end of 1873. Industry and agriculture both suffered. A farmer would soon write the *Warrenton Gazette:* "Our houses and fences are rotting; our fields are becoming more and more impoverished and our low grounds, for the lack of ditching and keeping the streams open, have been partially given up to briars, bushes and cess pools, which have converted one of the healthiest counties in the State into a malarial district." The *Gazette* editorialized against "many of our best young men, those who are industrious and ambitious," who were migrating to other states due to "[b]ad crops, poor weather, and inefficient labor" in Warren County. The *Gazette* doggedly urged those who were dissatisfied not to leave, but to marry local girls and "settle down near the old homestead and be contented."[52]

In November 1873, J. Williams and his wife and sons were in Warren County; Annie and Peter were in Chester County, apparently at Fountain Hill. Mary wrote Annie: "It will now but be a short time until Papa [J. Williams] will leave us for the north. It is hard to part with him. If he has to find a tenant for the farm [Fountain Hill] he will be longer away." Mary hoped Peter would stay at Fountain Hill another year. Peter had apparently had a difficult year: "The first year is always the hardest, having to stock the farm and get fixed. And then times may change for the better, everything now is so uncertain." Mary hoped Annie and Peter would come to North Carolina: "Peter would not have to work so hard nor you either." Mary was suffering from "erysipelas" but had good news about J. Williams and "Genie" (Eugene). "Genie weighs 170 lb and Papa soon will if he continues to have so good an appetite." Basically, "we all make out to get enough to

6. Keystone Stater and Tar Heel

eat and are content." She wrote: "I like home too well to go visiting much and papa and Genie are just the same way."[53]

Caleb Pusey married Elizabeth Davis, daughter of another member of the Northern "colony" in Warren County. The Thorne family correspondence suggests she was a sickly young woman who often took to her room. The local white community as a whole may not have welcomed the Thornes fully into respectable society. D.T. Smithwick claimed the Thornes received a chilly reception: "Even with all their deep piety and Christian spirit they were not received with any tolerance by the Warren Co. people." The experience of Elizabeth Pennock and Margaret Thorpe in Warrenton indicated the isolation that radical Yankees could endure. At first, local white women would not call on the two teachers, their black landlord and the mayor had to drive off two white men giving them unwanted attention, and otherwise the only chance they got to associate with the whites was by attending the Episcopal church on Sunday. After a few months, Margaret Thorpe wrote: "Our social status is slowly improving although we yet number amongst our acquaintances more maids than their mistresses, more valets than their masters. Still the proportion is better than it was before our trouble with those two men."[54]

Caleb Pusey Thorne, about 1885 (courtesy Nancy Plumley).

By January, J. Williams was back in Pennsylvania and Mary hoped Peter would buy the Fountain Hill farm if it went up for sale. Although Mary said "the cotton picking is going on now finely" and would soon be complete, weather permitting, Eugene had been obliged to throw out some cotton after a fire in the cotton gin that "scared him."[55]

Quaker Carpetbagger

By June 1874, the time of the Progressive Friends meeting in Longwood, Thorne for once was missing. He left a letter to be read to the members; the minutes called him "J. Williams Thorne, of North Carolina."[56]

A political opportunity soon opened up that interested J. Williams. John Hyman, the state senator from Warren County, began turning his attention to running for Congress. Like Warren County itself, the Second Congressional District—of which Warren was a part—was majority-black, and a candidate backed by a united Republican Party would win an election, just like in Warren County. Hyman won the Republican nomination for Congress on May 14 at a district convention. A week before that, on the 6th, was the Warren County Republican convention, at which time Hyman may or may not have made up his mind to leave the state Senate. In any case, Thorne planned to run for Hyman's state Senate office, and he presented himself as a candidate on that occasion.[57]

During his remarks, as he reconstructed them later in response to attacks from the *Warrenton Gazette*, Thorne advocated the racial integration of "our white schools and colleges," just as legislative bodies were now integrated by race. He mentioned Oberlin, West Point, and Chester County's own Lincoln University as examples of successful integrated institutions. Thorne's remarks came as the U.S. Senate was about to pass a civil rights bill that included school integration.[58]

Someone in the audience asked if J. Williams believed in a God—it seems that some reports to the contrary were circulating. Judging by his later letter to the *Gazette*, J. Williams may have replied that he believed in "an unknown and unknowable mysterious Infinite ... the quick spirit that sustains and gives life to all things."[59]

J. Williams's speech at the county Republican gathering included denunciation of liquor, even for medicinal or sacramental purposes, and a call for total abstinence. As J. Williams was "leaving the platform," Hyman, not yet having obtained the congressional nomination, may have been seeking to preserve his state Senate seat, and the sitting senator interjected that J. Williams manufactured wine for sale. Staying on the platform to answer Hyman's charge, J. Williams basically replied that he made scuppernong grapes into grape juice, "utterly destitute of alcohol," and so reliable as a temperance beverage that "the most *ultra* temperance people" in Chester County used this sort of drink.[60]

The *Gazette* reported J. Williams's speech to the Republicans, giving as bad a coloration to Thorne's controversial views as possible. The paper reported charges by Alfred Christmas, a black laborer who had apparently

6. Keystone Stater and Tar Heel

worked on J. Williams's farm for eighteen months. According to Christmas, Thorne "invariably weighed out his rations a pound short," and on Sundays J. Williams played cards for money with Christmas, winning back the wages he'd paid Christmas the previous day.[61]

Thorne published a handbill answering the *Gazette*'s charges. He denied short-rationing anyone, saying that the dealing out of rations was done by "one or the other of my two sons," in whose honesty J. Williams—and local blacks—trusted. As for card-playing, J. Williams indignantly said he had "never played a game of cards in my life.... I despise gambling in every form it can assume. Betting, lotteries and stock gambling have ever had my most intense and steadfast abhorrence." Gambling was almost as bad as "the vice of drunkenness." It is interesting, of course, that J. Williams's sister-in-law had once charged his son Pusey and nephew Alfred with similar gambling behavior. This indicates that perhaps Christmas's charge could have accurately applied to these particular branches of J. Williams's line. In any case, J. Williams's flyer said that his home township of Shocco supported his senatorial nomination, which they would not do for a short-changer.[62]

J. Williams denied the *Gazette*'s report that he had said believers in God were fools, or that "man is a spontaneous production of the earth," though he avowed his belief in "the theory proposed by Mr. Darwin of the origin of the species." Answering a taunting question by the *Gazette* as to why he had not run for office back in Chester County, J. Williams fell back on a distinction common among many nineteenth-century politicians: He was not *running* for office, he was *standing* for state Senate, willing to accept the position if the people gave it to him.[63]

To establish his political *bona fides*, J. Williams included in his flyer a letter of commendation from E.W. Baily, a Republican in the Pennsylvania House of Representatives. Baily called J. Williams "my friend and co-laborer in the cause of Republican principles, for the last twenty-five years," and vouched for J. Williams's "early and continued efforts in behalf of the rights of *all men* ... no colored man will ever have cause to regret his action" if he voted for J. Williams for State Senator. J. Williams said he also had a letter of recommendation from Chester County's congressional representative, Washington Townsend, but that there was no time to arrange for its publication in the flyer because the letter "is now in the hands of a friend in the River District."[64]

The Republicans decided not to nominate Thorne, giving the nomination—and hence Warren County's state Senate seat—to a black candidate,

Quaker Carpetbagger

John M. Paschall. William H. Williams, another black candidate, was newly elected from Warren to the state House of Representatives (as the former House of Commons had been renamed). Warren was one of a few Republican pockets in North Carolina; most of the state House and Senate went to the Conservatives (Democrats).[65]

The death of young William H. Williams on December 18 necessitated a special election. Thorne was a candidate for the unexpected vacancy in the state House. His opponents were William S. Ransom, patriarch of a prominent Conservative family, and a Republican, Richard Falkener.[66]

J. Williams won this special election. He was on the way to the state capital.

7

Cast Out

At the time of J. Williams's election in a special election on January 14, 1875, the mood in the Democratic-dominated legislature was militant. The federal elections of 1874 had returned a Democratic majority to the U.S. House of Representatives for the first time since the Civil War. In addition to the bad economy, the Congressional Civil Rights bill was said by both sides to be a factor in turning Northern voters against the Republicans. The Senate version of the bill had provided for integrated public schools, and white voters all over the country rejected such an idea. In North Carolina, the Conservative-dominated legislature bubbled over with delight at the victory of the Democrats (with whom the Conservatives caucused on the federal level) and passed a post-election resolution saying so. The legislature cheered "the great political victories achieved by our sister states." The resolution rebuked the Civil Rights bill as based on "bad motives," endangering the public schools, and threatening "ruin and disaster" to both races. Republicans on both the state and federal levels backed off from their endorsement of integrated schools, believing the issue to be electoral poison. The Civil Rights bill continued to proceed through Congress, but without the school provision—though its provisions for integrating theaters and inns were in themselves provocative to North Carolina whites.[1]

When Thorne entered the legislative chamber and took his affirmation of office on January 19, the Democratic majority was 38–12 in the state Senate and 93–27 in the state House, which he was joining. J. Williams was the only "carpetbagger" in either chamber. Apart from J. Williams, the Republican minority was made up of blacks and Southern-born whites. This made Thorne the only Northern-born white Republican legislator who had come South after the war. J.G. de Roulhac Hamilton, a Democratic-sympathizing historian of North Carolina's Reconstruction, wrote that if J. Williams were "a Democrat or even a native Republican," his colleagues would not have put him through the ordeal he was about to undergo. All that was needed to ignite against Thorne the House's distrust of anything Northern and radical was a good excuse.²

In some way, members of the legislature got hold of the pamphlet J. Williams had published in 1873 against Joseph Barker. How the solons got this information is unclear, but there is a suspect, and it is someone in J. Williams's own household. Jacob C. Davis had moved to Warren County along with Thorne. Davis, a New Jerseyite, had married Martha Lippincott, whose brother Barclay Lippincott had married J. Williams's sister Caroline (Washington Hanway's widow). After Jacob and Martha had moved South, their daughter Eliza married J. Williams's son Caleb Pusey. Thus, Jacob Davis and J. Williams seemed tied by strong family bonds. Yet Davis was very angry at J. Williams.³

"I find," wrote Davis, "that you are Still Striving to Stop me from Selling Liquor."

Davis believed that J. Williams was trying "to Stop me individually" from engaging in the liquor traffic, rather than act to ban liquor "all over the Country"—which Davis would support. But singling Davis out, as J. Williams was supposedly doing, struck Davis as a gesture of self-interest, based on fear that Davis "will get a Dollar or So that you might get in your Shop."⁴

Davis did not specify how J. Williams was trying to stop Davis's liquor-dealing, but it is possible that Thorne had been trying to get the Warren County Commissioners to deny Davis a liquor license—by state law, county commissioners had broad discretion to reject applicants. Whatever the case, the anti-liquor movement was making some progress in the Tar Heel State, with local option and with the beginning of a trend of local laws banning liquor in particular communities. Prohibition and liquor regulation were the subject of more petitions to the North Carolina legislature than other subjects.⁵

Davis's indignant letter declared:

> You have already got every Dollar you can from me & my Family and now you are trying every means to prevent me from making a little for to Balance losses We have met with.... I think it a low selfish act. So does a great many others think But as you are trying so hard to prevent me from getting along well, I will do my best to return the Favor
>
> Will be pleased to hear from you...
>
> PS Your own Representatives are the worst drinkers I have. If I did not keep it they would walk until they got where it is. [T]he way I look at [it,] they will have it anyhow.

7. Cast Out

Davis had both the motive and (through his legislative customers) the opportunity to acquaint the legislators with J. Williams's anti–Christian Barker pamphlet. This does not prove Davis was responsible, but it makes him a possible source of the legislators' information.

However they learned of it, Thorne had only been a representative for three days when Paul B. Means, a representative from Cabarrus County, moved to order an investigation into Thorne's qualifications to hold his seat. Under the state Constitution, "any person who shall deny the being of Almighty God" was disqualified from public office, and the question was whether this disqualification applied to Thorne. The motion was adopted, and the matter was dropped in the lap of the Committee on Privileges and Elections.[6]

J. Williams wrote to the Committee on February 4, sending them the circular announcing his candidacy for state Senate the previous year, "containing my latest public declaration of my religious faith." The circular also expressed his support for the racial integration of the schools, though perhaps J. Williams hoped the committee could rise above its prejudices and overlook that part. He made a solemn averment that he had never denied the being of God, which he hoped would spare him the expense of calling "a thousand witnesses in a distant state."[7]

J. Williams obtained a leave of absence from the House on the 5th, to last until Wednesday the 10th. This was probably to give him the chance to prepare for the Committee's hearing on the 9th. When the Committee convened, J. Williams admitted his authorship of the Barker pamphlet and testified under affirmation, again offering his campaign circular of the previous year.[8]

The Committee members examined J. Williams on whether he believed "the Bible entire" as God's word and whether he believed in "the God of the Bible." Thorne replied that he believed "largely" in the Bible, but did "not believe in it entire." He disagreed with "many of the characteristics ascribed to" God in the Bible, but he believed in "a Supreme, self-existent God" who was the same deity mentioned in the Bible.[9]

Richard Montgomery Norment, a Republican from Robeson County, sought to bring the questions in a different direction. Dr. Norment was a physician and Confederate veteran (and a Mexican War veteran as well) who had cared for the afflicted in a smallpox epidemic in his home county when others had fled. He had also offered an abortive peace plan for the Lowry rebellion in Robeson County a few years previously, even though the Lowrys had killed his brother. Now the doctor zeroed in with surgical precision on the main issue of the case: "Did you ever deny the existence of a God?" To which Thorne's answer was: "If I ever have, directly or by implication, I hereby solemnly repudiate such sentiment."[10]

J. Williams presented three witnesses who had come down from Pennsylvania to deny his atheism. Annie Pusey—presumably his unmarried sister-in-law who had expressed concerns about gambling—during about thirty years of knowing J. Williams, had never heard him deny the existence of God, but had heard him avow belief "in a Supreme Ruler of the Universe" and knew that he belonged to the Progressive Friends, "which is a religious society." Lizzie Walton affirmed the same, based on a year of knowing J. Williams closely and having known him "by reputation, all my life." Barclay H. Lippincott—J. Williams's brother-in-law—said the same, based on ten years of knowledge.[11]

Then J. Williams was back on the stand. He faced a new question: "Do you believe in a state of future rewards and punishments?" As in Pennsylvania, North Carolina's common-law rules would not let anyone testify in court unless he believed in a God who punishes falsehood—and could someone who was religiously disqualified from giving evidence be allowed to hold office? But Thorne replied that he believed in future rewards and punishments, in the sense that "punishments always follow crime, either here or hereafter." The state Supreme Court had been satisfied with witnesses who believed in divine punishment in this life, so it remained to be seen if the House would be satisfied, too. A final question was whether J. Williams believed in Almighty God, to which he replied, "I do as firmly as I believe in my own existence or that of the Universe."[12]

The Committee on Privileges and Elections gave its report on Wednesday the 17th. Taking no position, the Committee, through chairman John M. Moring, asked to be discharged.

The following day—the 18th—J. Williams may have sealed his political fate in the House. Earlier that month, a bill had been received from the Senate to amend the apprenticeship laws and forbid white children being bound out to black masters or mistresses. Wasting little time, the House now had the bill up for consideration. The bill passed easily, 87 to 12, and since the Republican governor of North Carolina, Curtis Brogden, lacked veto power, the bill went right into the statute books. Of the twelve House dissenters, eleven were black, including Hanson Hughes and Thorne's colleague from Warren, Hawkins W. Carter. The only white dissenting vote was cast by Thorne. Denounced the next day by the Democratic *Raleigh News*, Thorne wrote a reply that the paper refused to publish, explaining

7. Cast Out

that he would have been happy to support a racially neutral law against this "species of child-slavery." A racially discriminatory law, he observed, not only violated the Golden Rule, but "in the present mixed condition of the races," it would often be difficult to differentiate between black and white.[13] He instead had his reply published in a Republican paper.

The House considered Thorne's case again on Saturday, the 20th (after the Education Committee, in an unrelated development, recommended against a bill for Bible-reading in the public schools). The clerk read the testimony and Thorne's pamphlet. Hezekiah A. Gudger moved to discharge the indecisive Committee so the House could consider Thorne's case, and this motion was approved. Gudger was a Democrat who had won election in traditionally Republican Madison County (he later became a Republican and served as consul-general in Panama and chief justice of the Panama Canal Zone high court).[14]

A black representative, Hanson T. Hughes, moved to expel Thorne for having "advocated and promulgated a most sacrilegious doctrine, subversive of the principles of the Constitution of the State of North Carolina and the Constitution of the United States." Hughes was a Republican representative from Granville County, which adjoined Warren County on the west. Hughes, who may have been a slave before the Civil War, was a barber who by 1870 had accumulated $250 in personal property and $1,000 in land. He had become a leader in the black community, which does not seem to have pleased Granville's Democratic leadership. Around the time of the Thorne controversy, Hughes was fighting charges of rioting for leading a procession in the town of Oxford, the county seat, celebrating the anniversary of the Emancipation Proclamation. Both the local Superior Court and the state Supreme Court held that the procession had been perfectly legal.[15]

Gudger proposed a friendly amendment to Hughes's resolution to delete the reference to the federal Constitution. Hughes accepted. As a proposed substitute motion, Democrat Platt D. Walker of Richmond County (a future state Supreme Court justice) offered a substitute motion to expel Thorne on the grounds that he "denies the being of Almighty God, and entertains religious views at variance with those which should control the action of a representative." On Dr. Norment's motion, both proposed resolutions were postponed until noon on Tuesday, February 23.[16]

When high noon on Tuesday the 23rd arrived, Walker was allowed to withdraw his motion, and the House took up an expulsion resolution by Moring as a substitute for Hughes's resolution. Moring's resolution, like Walker's, accused Thorne of denying God, apparently under the theory that denying the Biblical account of God was equivalent to denying God altogether. Thorne spoke in his own defense. Comparing himself to St. Paul and to Daniel in the den of lions ("I have no fear that the magnanimous lions will either tear or bite me"), Thorne mentioned affidavits he had procured in Pennsylvania from people who knew he wasn't an atheist. There were many ideas of God—even, Thorne provocatively added (as if he could not help himself), in the Bible itself, "from Anthropomorphism all the way to Pantheism." One can certainly question whether Thorne was doing himself any favors with these rhetorical thrusts.

Then Thorne took a more promising line of defense, looking at the development of the state constitution's provision on religious tests for office. Originally, only believers in the principles of the "Protestant religion" had been qualified (though, as Thorne could have mentioned, the Catholic William Gaston had been allowed to serve as a legislator and on the state Supreme Court during this time). In the 1835 Constitution, officeholding rights were broadened to Christians generally, and in the Reconstruction Constitution of 1868, officeholding privileges were extended to anyone but atheists. Thorne listed eminent antebellum North Carolinians—including Gaston and the powerful Warren County statesman Nathaniel Macon—who had wanted religious disabilities removed. "I will not believe," commented Thorne, "that a state, once so fruitful in the growth of free minded men, is barren of them now." Thorne said he was not required to believe in any particular conception of God. Thorne then offered the first of the thirty-nine Anglican articles of faith as a true expression of his concept of God: "There is but one living and true God; everlasting, without body, parts or passions; of infinite power, wisdom and goodness; the maker of all things visible and invisible."[17]

While Thorne was explaining that his "'Barker' pamphlet was written to arouse the churches to the necessity of preaching a more humanitarian religion," someone interrupted to ask if he believed in the soul's immortality. Thorne said, "I am not absolutely sure of it," but that spiritualists claimed to have conversed with the souls of the dead, and "I shall be glad to see and make their acquaintance." Asked if he believed in rewards and punishments in an afterlife, Thorne reiterated his view that "punishment always follows crime, both here and hereafter." Walker asked, "Where is Hell?" and Thorne answered that he did not know, but that if the Kingdom of Heaven could be within a person, the same could be true of Hell. Thorne concluded by saying that God surely had not appointed "his weak creature man to assist him in punishing his enemies."[18]

7. Cast Out

Nathaniel Macon, whose Warren County house is shown here, was an antebellum defender of religious freedom in North Carolina (National Park Service).

The House adjourned until 7:30 that evening.[19]

When the debate resumed, Thorne had been advised not to give another speech—a decision he later regretted, but which may have come as a relief to his supporters. But Thorne did interrupt Guilford County representative John N. Staples, who said that denying any part of the Bible was equivalent to denying God. Thorne asked Staples about "the Jews and Martin Luther," presumably based on the former's denial of the New Testament and the latter's denial of the epistle of James. Gudger and Walker gave speeches against Thorne. The future appeals court judges impressed the *Raleigh News*, not by their legal but by their theological learning: "We have frequently heard the first efforts of theological graduates that would not begin to compare with the speeches of these young barristers last night in the way of a sermon." The *News* did not, however, give a summary of the arguments of Gudger and Walker, or of other speakers.[20]

The powerful Democratic paper, the *Raleigh Daily Sentinel*, did not give much coverage to the speeches against Thorne, though it summarized many of the speeches in his favor. This was not part of any favoritism toward Thorne. Instead, the *Sentinel* thought it could make the case against Thorne by quoting juicy extracts from his pamphlet. The editors overcame their reticence against publishing the "worse than blasphemous pamphlet" of the "carpetbag member" Thorne; apparently the *Sentinel* published the excerpts under advice from the representatives who planned to vote for expulsion. The *Sentinel* agreed to publish the pamphlet ("The wickedness of the paper defies comprehension") in order to show that expulsion would be justified.[21]

Nereus Mendenhall, a Republican who was the colleague of Thorne's opponent John Staples from Guilford County, was one of Thorne's defenders. Mendenhall—the grandson of a Quaker who moved to North Carolina from Chester County—was also one of the most prominent Quakers in North Carolina's public affairs. A prosperous businessman, he had run the New Garden Boarding School, a Quaker institution that later became Guilford College. During the Civil War, Mendenhall, though he disliked the Confederacy, had achieved some success interceding with Confederate authorities on behalf of Quakers who had been drafted contrary to their pacifist consciences.[22] Knowing that the state's Quakers were at a disadvantage with the Democratic establishment due to their history of pacifism and antislavery, Mendenhall faced an extra burden in defending Thorne's right to serve in office. From Mendenhall's point of view, it was necessary that the evangelical Quakerism of traditional North Carolina Friends not be confused with J. Williams's radical, anti–Christian variety of Quakerism.

In his speech, Mendenhall made clear that Friends in North Carolina traditionally revered the Bible and instructed their children in its precepts. This was an important point to establish, since Thorne "was looked upon as a leper" and his defenders could be tarred with the same *"odium theologicum."* Reviewing the matter strictly as a constitutional question, Mendenhall traced the increasing liberalization of the state Constitution's religious test for office. Mendenhall, like Thorne, name-dropped Nathaniel Macon and William Gaston and their unsuccessful antebellum defense of religious freedom for non–Christians. In doing so, Mendenhall probably meant to remind legislators that prominent members of the prewar elite had stood up for the rights of non–Christians, and that such rights were not simply an invention of the Republicans' Reconstruction Constitution of seven years before. Macon had been willing to accept a "Hindoo" if the people elected such a person, Mendenhall said. Under the 1868 constitution even "Mahomet" or Voltaire—both of whom, though not Christian, believed in a God—could serve in the state House if otherwise qualified, Mendenhall proclaimed.[23]

If the God mentioned in the state Constitution was confined to the God of the Bible, then Mendenhall said that the definition would open

7. Cast Out

quite a can of worms, because of all the different ways in which different people had traditionally interpreted the Biblical God. Mendenhall made sure to mention Stonewall Jackson and Robert E. Lee (than whom no Civil War soldier had a "truer and nobler heart"), apparently to warn that even these revered figures might not be safe if everyone's Biblical orthodoxy was open to examination.[24]

J.H. Foote of Wilkes County and John A. Spears of Harnett County offered alternative resolutions, but both were rejected. Hanson Hughes obtained an indefinite leave of absence "on account of sickness in his family." The timing of Hughes's exit raises the possibility that his alleged grounds were a pretext for ducking out of the Thorne debate, but on the other hand, Hughes's expulsion motion had been replaced by a new one, so Hughes may have felt no particular interest in remaining for the debate. Having sat for four hours, the House (on Dr. Norment's motion) adjourned a half hour before midnight, to meet at 10 the following morning.[25]

The morning of the 24th, the House handled some other business and granted leaves of absence to five more members (whether related to their squeamishness about the Thorne case or not). The House adjourned until 7:30 that evening. It is likely that many of the Democrats caucused at some point before the evening session and dealt with the scruples of some members who were convinced Thorne believed in God and hence did not want to expel him for atheism. In any case, when the House reconvened that evening, Montraville Patton, a prominent citizen of Buncombe County and a three-term House member from the 1830s and 1840s, offered a substitute motion to expel Thorne for his pamphlet alone, without accusing him of atheism. Dr. Norment tried to commit or postpone the resolutions, but was voted down.[26]

Defenders of Thorne objected to the substitution of Patton's resolution for the original Moring resolution. Then Patton, probably by prearrangement with other Democrats, made another suggestion: Patton would drop his resolution, since the other side had fussed about it, and he proposed to reinstate Rep. Hanson Hughes's original resolution. Unlike Moring's resolution, Hughes's resolution did not accuse Thorne of atheism, but focused solely on the objectionable content of the Barker pamphlet. Also, the fact that the absent Hughes was black and Republican probably struck the Democrats as a clever trick to pull on Thorne's supporters. The House agreed to debate the Hughes resolution instead of the Moring resolution, taking the accusation of atheism off the table and giving the proceedings against Thorne both a bipartisan and a biracial flavor.[27]

Quaker Carpetbagger

The maneuver also took some pressure off Rep. Patton. That very day the United States Senate had received a favorable report on a bill, previously approved by the U.S. House, to compensate Patton for hay that Union forces in 1865 had taken but not paid for. Patton's previous attempt at relief had somehow disappeared into the Congressional abyss, but he was finally on the verge of receiving a belated payment of $130. Patton was probably glad not to risk provoking the Republicans in the U.S. Senate by having his name on a motion aimed at a Southern Republican. (Patton's claim would ultimately be approved on March 3, just before the end of the lame-duck session of Congress).[28]

To at least one Democratic member of the North Carolina House, Patton's parliamentary maneuver was a salve to the conscience, permitting him to vote to expel Thorne. Sidney M. Finger of Catawba County was a Confederate veteran who had lost three brothers in the war. He was also an educator (he would end up as the state's Superintendent of Public Instruction). Major Finger (he was often addressed by his Confederate rank) told his legislative colleagues that he was glad the Moring resolution, accusing Thorne of atheism, had been set aside. Now the only issue was whether the author of such blasphemy as the Barker pamphlet was fit to serve in the legislature. Finger thought not, and the new resolution was worded such that he could conscientiously vote for Thorne's expulsion.[29]

A motion to send the whole question to the Judiciary Committee lost, with only sixteen votes in favor. Now the House voted on the expulsion resolution, and the black Republican W.H. Crews, the absent Hanson Hughes's colleague from Granville County, asked for the yeas and nays. The expulsion resolution received 47 votes to 30 votes in opposition. Then Thomas S. Harrison, a Republican member for Caswell County who had voted to expel, changed his vote to nay, saying that given the existence of a doubt he would give Thorne the benefit of it. Thus the final vote to expel was 46 to 31. However, one of the "yea" votes was from Dr. Norment, who explained that he had voted "yea" strategically—anyone on the winning side of a vote gets to move for reconsideration. Almost every Democrat had voted to expel and virtually all Republicans voted against expulsion. The next day, 5 additional members were allowed to be recorded on the "yea" side and three on the "nay" side.[30]

Dr. Norment did not have a chance to use his planned parliamentary maneuver, since Rep. Gudger promptly moved for reconsideration and the House voted to lay that motion on the table, killing it. Norment, of course, voted against tabling, but strangely, so did two others who had voted for

7. Cast Out

expulsion: Democrats Thomas L. Gash of Transylvania County (member of a prominent political family) and John A. Spears of Harnett County. Perhaps Spears and Gash, during the cut and thrust of debate, had not been fully convinced of the merits of the resolution and wanted to discuss it some more.[31]

With reconsideration ruled out, Speaker James Lowrie Robinson of Macon County announced that Thorne's seat was vacant and that Thorne should collect his pay up to the time of his expulsion and no further.[32]

The final wording of Hughes's resolution, as tweaked by amendments, was:

> WHEREAS, J.W. Thorne, the member from Warren county, has advocated and promulgated a most blasphemous document, subversive of the principles of the Constitution of North Carolina, and of sound morality; therefore,
> BE IT RESOLVED, That the said J.W. Thorne be and he is hereby expelled from a seat on this floor.

The following day, Dr. Norment made an unsuccessful point of order against Thorne's expulsion. Dr. Norment also sought to file a protest against the expulsion, on Norment's own behalf and on behalf of eleven other members (including W.H. Crews of Granville, Hughes's colleague) who sought to exercise their state constitutional right, as dissenting legislators, to record in the legislative journal their protest against measures they oppose. Speaker Robinson had some unspecified objection to the language—perhaps it reflected too harshly on the House—so the protest was recorded only after some modifications were made. The protesters said that "this action of the House is susceptable [sic] of being construed as indicative of a spirit of religious bigotry and persecution." Thorne's "moral character is irreproachable and unimpeachable, and while we most emphatically condemn his criticisms of certain portions of the Scriptures, yet cannot see how they are subversive of the principles of constitutional liberty or sound morality, and we believe his expulsion by this House, for causes alleged in the resolution, will do infinitely more harm than any publication of J. Williams Thorne could possibly make."[33]

J. Williams stayed in Raleigh for another month—he "remained at my post," as he later put it—"and endeavored to serve my constituents as best I could." He left only when the legislature adjourned on March 22. By then the legislators had approved $16.10 for each of the three witnesses J. Williams had brought from Pennsylvania.[34]

The *Raleigh Daily Times* triumphantly declared that Thorne's much-discussed trial had "ended ... just as the public desired that it should end." Noting the demand for Thorne's pamphlet, the *Times* claimed only twenty-five copies had been sold, and "some one should hunt them up and cremate them." Thorne was worse than Thomas Paine and Voltaire, because unlike those famous, deceased anti–Christian authors, Thorne was "the acknowledged leader of 2,500 ignorant Warren county negroes," for whose sake, as well as that of "our young men and boys," the pamphlets should be "used as fuel to cremate the author."[35]

Thorne's case came at a time of great public interest in church/state issues. The public interest had been roiled by controversies over reading from the King James Bible in public schools—Catholics objected to the use of a Protestant Bible, while religious "liberals" objected to any use of the Bible as a breach of the separation of church and state. Many evangelical Protestants (though not all) wanted the King James taught, or at least read from, as a defense against the Catholics and the infidels. There was also a backlash against state aid to Catholic parochial schools, which was also denounced as a breach of church/state separation—though those who wanted public schools to have a monopoly of government aid differed on what, if any, degree of Protestant religious activity could be allowed in these putatively nonsectarian institutions.[36]

The Republican *Tribune* in Chicago used Thorne's case to riff on the insidious influences of those who tried to introduce God into politics. "It is doubtful," said the newspaper, "whether a Jew, or Unitarian, or even a Universalist, could pass muster in the North Carolina Legislature." It was "better to keep creeds out of constitutions and out of politics."[37]

The *West Chester Republican*, in an item reprinted in the *New York Times*, the Chicago *Tribune*, and perhaps other national publications, printed a letter from Thorne promising a fuller account of his experiences. The editor of the *Republican* published an accompanying note saying that they had previously stopped publishing Thorne's letters on religious subjects, which had now brought him into trouble. At the same time, the *Republican* called Thorne "a great deal better man" than most of those who expelled him, and called the expulsion a "Democratic expedient" to eliminate Thorne after he had "become quite a power in the district in which he lives."[38]

The Napa (California) *Register* was "at a loss to understand" Thorne's expulsion. His declaration that he only believed parts of the Bible sounded to the editors like what many Christian preachers and many professedly "enlightened and orthodox Christians" believed. Thorne's religious views were probably "only made a pretext" by the Democrats to get rid of him.[39]

7. Cast Out

Henry Ward Beecher's *Christian Union* came out against Thorne's expulsion. The scandal about Beecher's alleged adultery with Theodore Tilton's wife—a scandal whose early stages had prompted Thorne's snide comments about Biblical concubinage in his Barker pamphlet—had led to a trial that took up the first half of 1875. Meanwhile, Beecher continued his ministry and published an editorial calling Thorne's ouster "a great mistake" that would "wear the appearance of persecution, and thus bring the cause of Christ into reproach." The affair would also give unwarranted publicity to Thorne's pamphlet. The editorial gave a brief account of Thorne's career in Pennsylvania, commenting on his persistent anti–Christian attacks: "Voluble in speech, and of unbounded self-conceit, he could be demolished a dozen times in argument, and never know or suspect it!" Nonetheless, "upon every moral and social question, not distinctively theological," Thorne always "stood shoulder to shoulder with his most intelligent Christian neighbors" in seeking "to elevate the standard of public morals." The probability was that his religious views were simply the "ostensible" reason for the North Carolina House's action against him, with his opposition to "legislative dishonesties" being the true reason. The *Christian Union* hoped other religious papers would defend Thorne's right to religious dissent.[40]

One "infidel" paper that took up Thorne's case was D.M. Bennett's *The Truth Seeker*, published in New York City. A former Shaker, Bennett had been a pharmacist and an entrepreneur in various ventures before turning to full-time editorship of his journal. A private letter indicates that Bennett was probably an atheist—in any case, he devoted *The Truth Seeker* to attacks on Christianity, Christians, and their supposed sinister influence.[41]

Soon after J. Williams's expulsion, *The Truth Seeker* noticed the case, regretting that "the resolution [of expulsion] was offered by one of the newly enfranchised citizens of the African persuasion." In any case, situations like this would soon be historical curiosities, because in a few years "a man who doubts the existence of the Jewish Jehovah will be as much respected as he who disbelieves in Brahma, Vishnu, Fot [?] or Jupiter."[42]

Another paper, the *Index*, also focused on "Liberal" or "infidel" agitation. The *Index* was edited by a former Unitarian minister named Francis Ellingwood Abbot. Abbot and other former Unitarians who found the denomination too Christian had formed a Free Religious Association, and Abbot had started the *Index* to spread a message of radical secularism. Abbot, a deist, moved his *Index* to Boston where he tried to rally opponents of Christian influence in public life, while sometimes quarreling with those whose anti–Christian views were of a different flavor from his own. Former abolitionists William Lloyd Garrison and Wendell Phillips, as well as Reform Rabbi Isaac M. Wise, were among the distinguished personalities who lent their endorsement to the *Index*. Cleverly using the National Reform Association—a small group of Christians who wanted to amend the Constitution to include recognition of Jesus Christ—as a foil, Abbot mobilized a petition drive to push the constitution in another direction.[43]

Abbot promoted the formation of Liberal Leagues in American communities to push "Nine Demands," including taxation of church property, abolition of government-paid chaplaincies, no government aid to religious institutions, no judicial oaths, no Sunday laws, and no legal "enforcement of 'Christian' morality." To achieve some of these objectives, Abbott organized a petition campaign in Massachusetts for a secular amendment to the federal Constitution. This amendment would prohibit any religious discrimination or favoritism by either the state or federal governments, while forbidding religious tests for officeholding or voting. A congressional committee rejected the proposed amendment in 1874, but Abbot had achieved the goal of putting his issues before the public.[44]

When first addressing Thorne's case in March, the *Index* didn't seem to have full information on Thorne. A contributor named "A." (perhaps Abbot) said Thorne was an atheist and had been expelled as such, setting a precedent for proscribing unpopular types of religious people. By March 25, the *Index* realized that the charge of atheism against Thorne was false, and that Thorne had been expelled for being a deist who rejected the God of the Bible. The case, argued the *Index*, showed the need for the Religious Freedom Amendment: under present law, each legislature was the exclusive judge of the qualifications of its own members, and a constitutional ban on religious tests was needed to prevent cases like Thorne's in the future. Thorne's case allegedly illustrated that "superstition lets rationalism do the talking, while it stands ready to act on short notice in case of emergency."[45]

There was some press comment against Thorne. The *Cincinnati Times and Chronicle* said that "[p]olitically speaking" Thorne "digged his own grave; and it is no more than right that he should be put into it, and securely covered up." The *Times and Chronicle* quoted the Raleigh *News* to illustrate Democratic and press hostility towards him—"a carpet-bag civil-righter and a miscegenatist."[46]

The *Christian Statesman*, the organ of the National Reform Association,

7. Cast Out

approved Thorne's expulsion as in accord with the state Constitution and the "law of God" and reiterated the Association's support for a Christian Amendment on the federal level: "Christian men must blush to think that a man expelled from the Legislature of North Carolina could sit without question in the halls of Congress. No appeal could be made to the National Constitution against his presence."[47]

The *Christian Statesman*'s editorial prompted a response from a Chicago Spiritualist paper, *The Spiritualist at Work*. The Spiritualist movement believed in communing with the souls of the dead—Thorne had alluded to them in his remarks on the soul. Spiritualists were part of America's secularist coalition, influencing ostensibly secular reformers and aiding the fight against Christian influence. *The Spiritualist at Work* cited the *Christian Statesman* editorial to illustrate the dangers of putting God in the Constitution, and it reprinted much of Thorne's Barker pamphlet for the edification of Spiritualist readers.[48]

As he had promised the *West Chester Republican*, Thorne put out a pamphlet about his case, available for twenty-five cents, titled *North Carolina in the 19th Century: The Great Ecclesiastical Trial of J. Williams Thorne, Representative from Warren County, who was expelled for opinion sake, by the House of Representatives of North Carolina, on February 24, 1875*. The pamphlet was noted in the *Index* among the books, pamphlets and periodicals it had received. *The Truth Seeker* also announced the availability of the pamphlet, which Thorne had sent: "Thousands who have heard of this case will be glad to read the account in detail, and also to learn Mr. Thorne's theological views. Such can be accommodated." Readers could write *The Truth Seeker*, or Thorne himself, to order copies.[49]

The pamphlet included a copy of Thorne's earlier pamphlet against Barker—for which he had been expelled—as well as Thorne's February 16 affirmation of his belief in God. There were letters, mainly from individuals in Pennsylvania and especially Chester County, testifying to his integrity and denying any atheism on his part. These testimonials included a brief letter from W.Y.P. Noble, of Philadelphia, of a somewhat provocative nature, which said in part that "if Southerners are bent on driving northern emigrants, by hook or crook, on one pretext or another, out of politics, in their adopted States, the late Democratic victories will be speedily reversed." Though Noble had voted for Democratic candidates since the Greeley/Grant contest of 1872, "when we see attacks made on emigrants from our own neighborhood, whom we know *not to be carpet-baggers*, but settlers in good faith, who on their visits to the North make every effort to put Southern character and society in a favorable light, (as we all know *you did*,) we begin to feel that the South is 'joined to her idols,'—learning nothing, forgetting nothing. We look wistfully again toward Grant and Sheridan, and hunt up the telegram about 'banditti.'" This latter reference had to do with unrest in Louisiana the previous January, when General Philip H. Sheridan, commanding in Louisiana, had deployed federal troops to defend the Republican legislature against armed Democratic forces known as the White League. Sheridan had sent a telegram to President Grant suggesting that, if authorized, Sheridan would treat the White League forces as "banditti"—bandits.[50]

Thorne's final character witness was Samuel D. Moore of Adrian, Michigan, who had looked at Thorne's allegedly atheist pamphlet and found in it no denial of God. "Your criticism of the professed Christian Church, and its religious text book, certainly was fair and bore evidence of its having been written in a good spirit. Then your closing remarks savored much of a high order of inspiration, and is worthy of the careful consideration of every intelligent mind." Moore signed the letter, "Yours as ever in the cause of human progress." Thorne did not discuss Moore's background, but the latter was a religious liberal and reader of *The Truth Seeker*.[51]

In his own voice, Thorne connected his expulsion to his support of "the '*Golden Rule*,' as embodied in the '*Civil Rights Bill*,'" and his support for the principles of the Declaration of Independence. He denied being a "Miscegenatist," and took aim at the Democrats for being the real offenders in this regard: "In Warren county I am acquainted with many persons of mixed blood, and I do not know of one who does not trace his lightness of color to Democratic fatherhood." Thorne added a story from Delaware about a Republican candidate who, faced with the charge of miscegenation, said he was the sole non–Democratic miscegenationist in the area, adding, "I assumed this relationship when I was a Democrat." If miscegenation was an evil, Democrats were to blame; and probably with some sarcasm, Thorne called on his opponents to join the Republican Party, "the only pure race party on the continent."[52]

Thorne sought to turn the tables on his Democratic adversaries in the legislature—and perhaps rally sentiment in Warren County—by contrasting his affirmation to support the state and federal constitutions with the oaths the Democratic legislators had taken on the Bible to do the same thing. The Democrats had violated their oaths, Thorne said, by passing "municipal gerrymandering" bills for New Bern, Raleigh and Wilmington

7. Cast Out

that replaced "republican government" with "a moneyed oligarchy" and "effectually robbed" black citizens "of their political and civil rights." He continued, "Like the Pharisees of old they talk much about their religion and their 'sound morality.' But it is 'by their fruits you shall know them.' ... They are indeed practical Atheists." By their own Christian principles, the "religious bigots" who had oppressed black citizens had incurred the punishments of Hell: "[I]t is a judgment of their own choosing" under the parable of the sheep and the goats. Thorne "was expelled not because I was not, but because I was a Christian."[53]

Far from subverting *"sound morality"* in his Barker pamphlet, J. Williams wrote, he had defended sound morality against the slurs against God contained in the Bible. And "the House of Representatives of North Carolina have shown by their action against me that they endorse and believe all the false and wicked characterizations of the ever-living and just God, found in the Bible." Thus, J. Williams concluded, "I arraign them before the bar of civilized world, and in the sacred cause of truth, justice, freedom and a pure and undefiled worship of the ever living and Infinite God, I ask and calmly await its sure judgment against them."

Thorne also included suitable quotes from Macon and other sources in defense of religious freedom. He also included some of his poetry—including a verse summary of a sermon by Quaker minister Jesse Kersey—to rebut the charge of atheism. In the poem, Thorne/Kersey said in part:

> Do not the gales that round us breathe
>   Fresh fragrance as they rove—
> The flowers that careless flow beneath,
>   And the blue Heavens above—
>
> The rivers as they ceaseless run,
>   The restless Ocean's flow—
> And the still burning quenchless sun
>   Their Heavenly Author show?
>
> Do not the stars that shine so bright,
>   In the deep wilds of space,
> Seem as the Maker's guiding light,
>   To our last resting place?
>
> And while we in these orbs of fire
>   His holy hand descry
> Do they not tender hopes inspire
>   Of immortality?

In a report published April 21, a correspondent for the *Philadelphia Times* found "Friend Thorne, of the North Carolina legislature" in "the place of meeting of the Radical Club and of the Citizen's Suffrage Association, No. 333 Walnut Street," along with many other radical figures whom the correspondent enumerated.[54]

Beecher's *Christian Union* did a brief follow-up on Thorne, claiming to have learned by letter that Thorne's "constituents ... are sure to reëlect him ... by the largest majority ever given to any candidate in Warren County." "The almost unanimous condemnation" of the North Carolina House's action in the press "has had a wholesome influence in North Carolina." The *Union* rejoiced at what it considered Thorne's impending re-election.[55]

When the Progressive Friends met in June, Thorne was there, as active as ever, if not more so, in the discussions. During a discussion prompted by the deaths of six Friends in the past year, Thorne was one of those who took part in expressing "[s]erious and hopeful views of human life, death and destiny ... and along with a discussion of the grounds of our hope of future existence, something was said of the sanctity of 'the life that now is,'" though who made that latter remark is not mentioned. During debate on a proposed testimony on Religion, "J.W. Thorne explained why he wished the pulpit to disappear: that all men might stand on an equality in considering questions which equally concern all. The voice of the people can never be the voice of God till it is the voice of *all* the people."[56]

In a Testimony on the "Claims of Woman," the Meeting reaffirmed its longstanding view "that the right of political representation should know no limit of color, race, or sex." In the debate of this Testimony, Thorne said he "believed that age, as well as sex, should be left out of view in settling the question of rights and the qualification of voters," but this idea was not acted on.[57] J. Williams may have been thinking of his son Pusey's trouble in the October election of 1868.

The Meeting supported J. Williams's rights in a Testimony it adopted on the subject of church and state. The Testimony wanted to make the "divorce of the Church from the State" more effective. It criticized the appointment of chaplains by the Pennsylvania legislature and the exemption of church property from taxation in Pennsylvania and other states. The discussion of Thorne's case said: "While we denounce the act of the North Carolina Legislature in expelling a duly chosen representative of the people, for no alleged cause except his religious opinions, as a high-handed outrage against justice, and an indication of the animus of bigotry everywhere, we yet rejoice that it has drawn out the almost unanimous condemnation of the political and religious press, and proved

7. Cast Out

that the American heart is true to the Constitutional principle of impartial religious liberty."⁵⁸

Thorne's greatest concerns, judging from his contributions to discussions in the Meeting, were on matters he deemed at least as important as his own expulsion in North Carolina: the currency and temperance. A Testimony on Public Affairs deplored the harm to currency values that was a legacy of the war, and called on the rich not to exploit the situation lest they exacerbate strife between rich and poor, including labor strikes. Thorne's remedy was more specific, and more radical. As recorded in the minutes, J. Williams "was for exact and equal justice, and no monopoly. Would have government wholly control the currency and withdraw special privileges from banking companies. Three or four great centers draw in three-fourths of all the currency, to the embarrassment and impoverishment of the country. The importance of money has become greatly exaggerated, as society has grown artificial." The economic crisis that had started in 1873 was still going on, and farmers—including J. Williams—were feeling the effects. Beginning with the crisis, more farmers had joined with certain workers' organizations to call for "greenbacks"—currency issued by the government, not by banks, and not backed by specie.⁵⁹

Two competing temperance proposals were before the Meeting—one of which emphasized persuasion to get people sober, the other of which emphasized legal prohibition of alcohol. After a debate in which Thorne participated—though the minutes said that "[n]o adequate report can be given" of the discussion—the Testimony favoring legal prohibition passed "by a large majority." This did not prevent the Pennsylvania legislature, that same year, from repealing the state's local-option law, thus making booze more widely available legally. The Pennsylvania legalization forces, contra J. Williams, blamed the Christian clergy for foisting liquor restrictions on the people.⁶⁰

8

The Carpetbagger and the Carpet Will

In an August fund-raising appeal, *The Truth Seeker* gave itself credit for publicizing Thorne's case "among the people."[1] While the inhabitants of Warren County were probably not rallying around J. Williams's deist ideas and his critique of Christianity, they seemed to appreciate him for having antagonized the Democrats, figuring that anyone who incurred their wrath couldn't be all bad.

J. Williams was soon back in politics, this time in defense of the state Constitution whose principles he had been accused of violating. In the session in which Thorne had been expelled, the legislature had called a constitutional convention. The constitution adopted in 1868 had been written by Republicans and made provision for locally elected officials at the county level. Many of these officials were black, and many were whites with no previous connection to the would-be elites of the Democratic Party (as it was beginning to call itself, casting off the "Conservative" mask). The Democratic-dominated legislature passed an act for the election of a constitutional convention in 1875 whose work would be assessed by the voters in the election of 1876.[2]

J. Williams was duly elected to the constitutional convention. He was optimistic about the statewide results of the convention election, writing Annie: "The State has gone republican by 20,000 on the popular vote. The latest news gives us (8) eight majority in the Constitutional Convention. At the late election several prominent Democrats voted for me." At the same election, Eugene Thorne was elected magistrate.[3]

J. Williams also advised that if his grandson, Annie's baby Carl, "should get sick, do not, as you value his life, send for a Doctor or give him drugs. Have faith in the healing power of Nature." Whether or not Annie took this advice, baby Carl did get sick and died.[4]

Bad news came on the political front, dashing J. Williams's optimistic

8. The Carpetbagger and the Carpet Will

hopes for a Republican majority in the constitutional convention, which met on September 5. Through sharp electoral practices in Robeson County, and maneuvering on the convention floor, the Democrats were able to exclude the Republican delegates from that county, who claimed to have been duly elected. One of the excluded delegates was Dr. Norment, who now found the tables turned: Instead of his trying in vain to defend Thorne's right to a legislative seat, Thorne tried in vain, along with other Republicans, to let Norment take his seat at the Convention. With the support of supposed independent delegates, the Democrats were able to obtain a friendly presiding officer and vote down numerous Republican efforts to adjourn. While the Democrats suffered a setback in the death of an Orange County delegate—the prominent politician William A. Graham—a special election kept Graham's seat in Democratic hands, and the Democrats could proceed to carry out their agenda.

Of the numerous amendments the Convention offered to the Constitution of 1868, the most significant would empower the state legislature to remodel county government. This provision was aimed at eastern counties like Warren, with their black voters and elected black officials—if the amendment were ratified, the Democrats would seek legislation taking the election of many of these county officials out of the people's hands. William Eaton, a lawyer in eastern North Carolina, wrote to Democratic delegate David S. Reid of Rockingham County: "It is absolutely necessary to the salvation of Warren, Halifax, Edgecombe, Craven, and other counties similarly situated, that the county funds be placed beyond the reach of the large negro majorities in those counties."[5]

J. Williams, like other Republicans, opposed the Democrats' local-government measure. He proposed a constitutional provision for "equal and just apportionment of Municipal, Legislative and Congressional Districts." Nothing more seems to have been heard about this proposal, which appears to have died in committee.[6]

One constitutional amendment proposed by the Democrats would mandate that separate schools be maintained for the different races. Like Republicans in the northern states, chastened by the unpopularity of school integration as disclosed by the 1874 election, Republicans in North Carolina had decided to accept segregated schools. Even black Republicans, while resenting the idea that they were unfit to associate with the whites, chose to focus on developing black schools and getting equitable funding, rather than challenging educational segregation.[7]

Thorne's colleague from Warren, John Oliver Crosby, proposed to

Quaker Carpetbagger

guarantee fair treatment for blacks within their separate school system. Black pupils would be given "equal advantages with white children in their vicinage," and funds for the separate public schools would be divided strictly based on the numbers of pupils in the different schools. Crosby was in his mid-twenties and served as Baptist pastor in Warrenton. Born into slavery in South Carolina, the teenage Crosby had been assigned by his master as a servant and drummer in a Confederate camp for Union prisoners. There Crosby aided the prisoners, giving them supplies and helping them evade censorship of letters between them and their Northern loved ones. After the war, Crosby left his family to seek his fortune, being active in South Carolina's Union League (a black Republican organization) before moving to Raleigh to study at Shaw University, a private black college. He graduated in 1874 with a determination to go into the ministry, and the Warrenton church was his first assignment (he later became a prominent educator in North Carolina's segregated system).[8]

After a postponement to deal with other business, the Convention had an unrecorded vote in which it rejected Crosby's amendment. After some tweaking of wording, the final version of the segregation amendment said that "white" and "colored" children would attend "separate public schools," with the seemingly contradictory proviso that there be "no discrimination" for or against either race. The only delegates to vote against this final version were Crosby, Thorne, and F.W. Bell of Bertie County.[9] Thorne probably found this an easy vote, since he tended to speak and vote as he pleased without considering the political context. Rev. Crosby may have been more politically attuned, but could have been expressing his frustration at the willingness of the Convention, in rejecting his amendment, to tolerate an inferior black school system. It is also possible that Crosby did not want to be outflanked by his older, white, non–Christian colleague from Warren on a matter of principle, even a then-impractical principle.

If the issue of school integration was so delicate that the vast majority of North Carolina Republicans voted with the Democrats, the same was true of interracial marriage. The latter question was if anything more politically provocative than the issue of schools. The Democrats liked to accuse supporters of racial equality with supporting the idea of blacks and whites having children together ("miscegenation"). Most Tar Heel Republicans had no wish to record themselves against a proposed amendment making black/white marriages void. This amendment, under consideration by the Convention, would constitutionalize a law that the state legislature had passed in 1830; prior to that date, the solemnization of

8. *The Carpetbagger and the Carpet Will*

interracial marriages had been punishable, but the marriages themselves had been legally recognized.[10]

The Democrats suspended the rules on October 9 to bring the interracial marriage amendment forward for consideration. At first the amendment also banned marriage between whites and Indians, but the convention voted to allow such intermarriages. J.H. Smythe, a black Wilmington lawyer representing New Hanover and Pender Counties, then proposed to delete the word "Negro" just as the word "Indian" had been deleted. Thorne was the only delegate to vote for this, with Smythe voting against his own amendment (four delegates were "paired").

Rather than stand up for the sanctity of interracial marriage, the Republicans in the Convention decided to turn the tables on the Democrats (and make the argument Thorne had made in his *Ecclesiastical Trial* pamphlet): they would portray the Democrats as the *real* promoters of racial mixing. A proposal by James O'Hara of Halifax would supplement the marriage ban by requiring felony penalties for "the cohabitation of white men with black women." O'Hara, an ambitious attorney and chair of the Halifax County board of commissioners, was himself the son of a white father and a black mother. Thorne voted with other Republicans for O'Hara's motion, but the Democratic majority defeated it.

The Democrats also rejected another proposal, offered by a man destined to be the state's most famous carpetbagger, Albion Winegar Tourgée of Guilford County. Tourgée was a Union veteran and a veteran of the 1868 Constitutional Convention whose handiwork was under attack seven years later. Tourgée's proposal required misdemeanor penalties for "any act of illicit sexual intercourse between a white person and a negro." Thorne voted for this unsuccessful proposal as well. In voting down both proposals, the Democrats seemed to confirm the Republicans' point: many black children had come from white Democratic fathers, through unions based on adultery or fornication—so it was matrimony, not "miscegenation," which Democrats truly objected to. On the vote for final passage of the marriage ban, the Republicans voted with the Democrats, making a majority of 96 to two. The only members who voted in opposition were Crosby and Thorne (four delegates were paired; these were the same delegates who had been paired on the Smythe amendment).[11] Thus, the only delegates who openly declared in favor of the sanctity even of unpopular marriages were a Christian minister and an "infidel," both from the same county.

An insult from a Democratic newspaper gave Delegate Thorne the

Quaker Carpetbagger

chance to make a new defense against his adversaries. It started with the orations given by several Convention delegates—including Thorne—on the late William Graham, deceased delegate from Orange County. The *Raleigh Daily News* refused to publish what J. Williams said, calling his remarks "offensive to the living, and disparaging to the dead." The *Daily News* said, "we have not forgotten the transactions of last winter, when the representative from Warren county appeared in so offensive a character. And his defense of the anti-slavery doctrine only makes him the more offensive." J. Williams's attempt to get the *Daily News* to publish a reply was unsuccessful, so as with his comments on the apprenticeship bill, he used the pages of a Republican newspaper—the *Daily Constitution*—to voice his rebuttal. "Is it, at this late day, still unsafe to tread, even with the gentlest step, on the grave of the slavery-lion?" As for the *News*'s reference to his expulsion, the House had failed to prove atheism against him, so at the last minute another resolution was substituted and voted on without giving him a chance to defend himself against the new charges. It was the Democrats, not himself, who had subverted the principles of the state Constitution by seeking "to eliminate from the Constitution its principles of justice and equal civil liberty. Had I been an enemy to the principles of the Constitution, there would have been no expulsion." As for the charge that he had violated the principles of sound morality, J. Williams turned this charge, too, back on the heads of the Democrats, accusing them of violating a key tenet of morality—the Golden Rule. The Democrats had not done unto others as they would be done by; instead, they had voted for discrimination against the black population. This, to J. Williams, reflected class bias more than racial bias: "In the days of slavery, the poor white man and the poor colored man, if free, were alike subjects of their ineffable scorn and contempt." In a "special equality," rich black people in antebellum Charleston and New Orleans had been respected slaveowning citizens. Now the Democrats, with the same sort of "special equality," had scorn for white men like himself who believed that the Golden Rule encompassed "all the different colors and races of mankind."[12]

The Convention adjourned, with both parties looking toward the November 1876 election one year away, when the voters would either accept or reject all the amendments *en bloc*. In other political developments in the country, a former Union general named Rutherford B. Hayes was elected as the Republican governor of Ohio, in a closely watched political race, by emphasizing two issues dear to J. Williams, though not in ways J. Williams would approve. Hayes championed, not the Liberal interpretation

8. The Carpetbagger and the Carpet Will

of separation of church and state, but the Protestant interpretation, capitalizing on anti–Catholic feelings. Hayes also supported returning the country to the gold standard—an event that the lame-duck Republican Congress had scheduled for 1879—and supported the Grant administration's deflationary policies. The Protestant clergy, who supported these hard-money policies, portrayed the currency issue (linked to the issue of repaying the federal Civil War debt) as a matter of morals and keeping public faith, with deflationists and soft-money advocates being essentially branded as thieves. As a soft-money supporter, hater of banks, and opponent of evangelical Protestantism, Thorne had to witness his own party ally itself, as he would have seen it, with two powerful villains: the banks and the Protestant clergy.[13]

The religious Liberals received some encouragement from President Grant. Looking for an issue to revive his administration's flagging popularity amid scandal and economic depression, Grant called for a broad separation of church and state. Grant proposed a constitutional amendment requiring nonsectarian public education, forbidding state or federal support for sectarian education, taxing church property (other than cemeteries and church buildings), and declaring a permanent separation of church and state. Senator and presidential aspirant James G. Blaine (R–Maine) disappointed Liberals when, Hayes-like, he adopted a watered-down, Protestantized version of Grant's position, proposing a constitutional amendment forbidding state aid to private Catholic schools while allowing religious (Protestant) teaching in the public schools. The Blaine Amendment came close to passage (and inspired the passage of some state counterparts), but because the amendment would target only Catholics, and would leave evangelical Protestantism as entrenched as ever, Liberals did not like it.[14]

The various state Liberal Leagues got together in Philadelphia at the time of the 1876 Centennial to form a National Liberal League. Thorne was elected to the executive committee, though at the time and for some time afterwards, League announcements in the *Index* (the periodical that had encouraged the League's formation) gave J. Williams's name as "George William Thorne" of "Warren, NC." A George Thorne of Clearfield, Pennsylvania, is listed as a charter member of the League. League officials may have confused these two different people with each other. By the following year the League finally got J. Williams's name right.[15]

On the strength of his gubernatorial victory in 1875, Hayes received the Republican Party's 1876 presidential nomination. J. Williams, meanwhile, also received the nomination for state Senator from the Warren County area. He had to overcome the resistance of the powerful John Hyman faction to get the Republican nomination, but apparently J. Williams's record of standing up against the Democratic establishment worked in his favor. On the eve of the 1876 election, Mary Thorne wrote Annie in Pennsylvania saying that "everything looks fair for [J. Williams's] election" to the state Senate. Mary said she missed her daughter and wanted "to spend the rest of my life with you but I fear that will never be." Mary mentioned "Ingersoll's great speech," referring to the attorney and lecturer Robert Ingersoll, who spoke frequently in support of Republican candidates and against Christianity (it seems, unsurprisingly, that the family did not attend church, except for Eugene and his wife Unity).[16]

In an addendum to her letter, Mary wrote: "This evening's mail brings news to us of our great defeat. It was very unlooked for to us all and causes serious apprehensions in Republican ranks." This did not refer to J. Williams's race, since he won it. Mary was alluding to the statewide Democratic victories, in which the Democratic constitutional amendments were approved and Democratic candidate Zebulon Vance won the gubernatorial race against Republican Thomas Settle. The Republicans attacked Vance's war record and warned of the dangers to democracy from a Democratic victory, but the Democrats won white support by appealing to racism. Nationwide, the Hayes/Tilden Presidential race was up in the air, with each side claiming victory.[17]

A new party, which came to be known as the Greenback Labor Party, had made an appearance in the election, nominating the wealthy New York reformer Peter Cooper (founder of the Cooper Union Institute). After making the major parties nervous with their soft-money appeal to beleaguered farmers and workers, the Greenbackers ended up getting less than one percent of the vote for Cooper.[18]

Mary wrote at the end of the month to her sister Ann, expressing sorrow not only for the death of baby Carl but for the thoughts on her own situation prompted by this tragedy. Eugene was so focused on the cotton business that "even the necessities of life are sadly neglected," while Mary had to "board three or four men and two boys." After J. Williams left for the state Senate, "so many things go wrong and are neglected that I am out of heart. I intend to go with [J. Williams] when he comes home Christmas."[19]

J. Williams came back to the Raleigh capitol building whence he had been expelled the previous year. Coming to the Senate side of the capitol,

8. The Carpetbagger and the Carpet Will

J. Williams was accepted without challenge as a member on November 20, and a few days later was appointed to the committees on Corporations, Insurance, and Buildings and Grounds.[20]

A bill sponsored by Thorne, in favor of one S.W. Mabry (also spelled "Maberry" in the records), was presumably based on some monetary claim by Mabry since the bill was referred to the Finance Committee. The bill was later postponed from December to January, and in the latter month it was postponed indefinitely.[21]

A defeat for transparency in legislative proceedings elicited a nay vote from J. Williams. On January 9, his old acquaintance from the House, James Robinson, who had moved from his House Speakership and become President of the Senate, moved that the Journal not record the positions taken by Senators in their speeches. This was approved 32 votes to 14, with Thorne as one of the dissenters.[22]

J. Williams had at least one legislative achievement to his credit. A growing movement for alcohol prohibition in North Carolina led to a growing number of bills legally drying up many patches of the state—often areas within a certain radius of some landmark like a school or church. In the nine-year period beginning 1872, the legislature designated 795 schools and one hundred churches, making them the centers of circles with a radius of from one to five miles within which liquor dealing was banned. J. Williams offered a bill of this type, banning the sale or giving away of liquor within a three-mile radius of two sites in Warren County: Shocco Chapel and People's Hall (had J. Williams established a "People's Hall" in Warren County modeled after the People's Hall in Chester County?). After J. Williams offered his bill on December 6, 1876, it moved comparatively quickly toward passage, being added to the statute books on January 11.

How the bill was treated in the interim is not fully clear from the legislative records. Thorne's bill got a favorable committee report, and the Senate approved it. Then, on motion of Wesley Clark Troy, representative from Cumberland County (Fayetteville) and also the son of a legislator, the Senate reconsidered and recommitted the bill. Senator Troy objected to the clause forbidding the "giving away" of liquor in the affected area. A new version of the bill was reported, and presumably passed the Senate, though it is hard to find in the Senate Journal when that happened—the Senate Journal notes that Thorne made an unsuccessful effort to pass his revised bill by suspension of the rules. In any case, the bill was communicated to the House, favorably reported, and passed. In the final version, the title of the bill referred to prohibition within a three-mile radius of the sites mentioned, but the bill's text mentioned two miles. Perhaps the Senate had narrowed the radius by one mile when it modified the bill, but forgot to reflect that change in the title. The final text had also eliminated the reference to "giving away'"—it was now illegal to sell liquor in the affected area or to get compensated for liquor, or to "dispose" of liquor in such a way as to evade the Act.[23]

J. Williams also voted for a successful bill to ban the sale of liquor on Sunday, except for medicinal purposes on a doctor's prescription.[24] Thorne wanted to extend such laws to all days of the week, and to abolish the medical exemption, but he probably thought the legislators had made a start.

The main business of the legislative session was achieved in February, when the Democratic majority used the powers bestowed on them by the new constitutional amendments and remodeled the county governments. The people of the counties were stripped of the right to elect commissioners and justices of the peace—instead, the legislature itself would elect justices of the peace, and in turn the justices of the peace would choose the commissioners. These were the officials who held power over local taxing and spending, so local voters were deprived of their voice in such matters. The new law was aimed at black-run counties like Warren in the eastern part of the state, though it also reduced the power of white voters in other counties.[25]

Thorne spoke vainly against these changes, and published his speech against the local-government bill. The bill "not only proposes to rob the citizen of his money but of that liberty and independence which are far more to him than all the wealth of the world can buy." Challenging claims that elected county governments had led to corruption, especially in black counties, Thorne declared: "In Warren county more than three fourths of the voters are uneducated men mostly of the colored race. And yet, in the whole State, from the seaboard to the mountains, there is no county that has a government more honestly administered." The difference between the two parties, as far as corruption was concerned, was that Republicans stole "money only. The Democrats, both the money and the equal civil rights of the citizen.... Other things being equal, the party that has no conscience against stealing the people's rights, will steal more of their money than the party which conscientiously defends them." The bill would put "the wealthy few" in control over "the many poor." Yet in reality, "the most honest portion of a nation are always its uneducated, hard working people."

8. *The Carpetbagger and the Carpet Will*

If the poor were more likely to be in jail, it was because (quoting the English poet James Beattie) the poor are trapped in laws like "little flies" in cobwebs, while "an insect of renown/ Hornet or beetle, wasp or drone" could escape the cobwebs of the law even if they were "caught in quest of sport or plunder." To Thorne, "The wealthy and educated classes have been all the time straining or breaking the law in order to rob the poor and weak of the fruits of their citizenship."[26]

To illustrate his point more fully, J. Williams indulged himself in an exercise reminiscent of the satires of Benjamin Franklin. First J. Williams introduced a resolution "Declaratory of the equality before the law of the white and colored races." In this resolution, J. Williams framed the racial controversy roiling the state as a phase in the struggle between the poor and the defenders of plutocratic oligarchy. Starting with an assurance that "equality before the law" was not automatically linked to "[s]ocial equality," the resolution went on the offensive by citing the North Carolina Constitution's provision that "all government of right originates in the good of the people ... instituted for the good of the whole." The resolution paraphrased the Declaration of Independence's statement that "all just powers of government are derived from the consent of the governed," and said that "we hereby declare and affirm our determined resolution ... never to give our consent to any form of legislation that has for its object the abridgement of the right of suffrage or the annulment of the voice of any class of our people as a governing power." The resolution would also have committed the legislature to "guard and protect, with jealous watchfulness, the laboring poor, of whatever race or color" in their rights and against "the monopolizing grasp of avaricious power." The resolution defended the voting rights of the "poor and weak"—rights that they needed in order to protect themselves from "encroachment on their rights by the rich and strong." One passage attributed a quote to John C. Calhoun: "[T]hey, who dig the wealth from the soil, have a right to it against the universe." Calhoun, a famous defender of slavery, had probably been a Unitarian, one of those whose "philanthropy" and freedom from superstition J. Williams had praised in his Barker pamphlet. In this context, however, J. Williams was probably not alluding to Calhoun's likely Unitarianism, but invoking his authority as a statesman.[27]

When the legislature predictably killed his resolution, J. Williams introduced another. The new resolution was the reverse of the first, and satirically made the point that the legislature held principles opposite to those of the first resolution. According to this second resolution, the

Quaker Carpetbagger

principle of government by consent of the governed "puts the governing power into the hands of the poor and ignorant many, who are not sufficiently interested in the welfare and happiness of the wealthy and educated few." Jefferson "would have blotted" his Declaration "out of existence" if he had only known of the "unhappy condition of the wealthy and educated classes in the Eastern counties of North Carolina." The resolution sarcastically denounced the Golden Rule, as well as criticizing statements in the Justinian Code and by the English jurist William Blackstone that an unjust law is "null and void." The legislature, under the resolution, promised "to legislate, as far as possible, the governing power of the State, out of the hands of its uneducated and ignorant poor, and into the hands of its wealthy and educated people." In its peroration, the resolution regretted "the rash and hasty separation we made in 1776 from our good old mother country, England," and called for replacing North Carolina's democratic system of county government with a system "modeled closely after our favorite aristocratic English system." The legislature rejected this second resolution also, leading Thorne to comment: "The public will then be able to see how very difficult it is, to adapt resolutions to the fastidious taste of legislators."[28]

Mary seemed to think J. Williams was going to Washington, D.C., to attend President Rutherford B. Hayes's inauguration on March 4. Hayes had, after much controversy, been recognized as the duly elected president, and his withdrawal of military support from the remaining Southern carpetbag regimes presaged a more hands-off attitude toward the South, which in hindsight has been considered the end of Reconstruction. Thorne, though, was not at Hayes's inauguration, but in the state Senate, casting votes. Mary wrote J. Williams a letter on March 4 saying Mason Williams had visited her asking for a government job through Thorne's intercession. Mary marveled: "Who can turn like you, from the drudgery of farming to the drudgery of politics?" She added, "Your friend S.C. Harris said two years ago she felt like calling you St. Will. So now she must hear you are really worthy to be enthroned with the Goddess of Liberty on her triumphal car." Mary teased J. Williams that "as you have been enamored of the Goddess so long I may conclude it was a 'free love' marriage."[29]

J. Williams had some more items of business to attend to in the Senate. First was a formal protest recorded in the Senate Journal against the local-government bill, a protest to which Thorne was one of six signatories. Another signatory was the new senator from Granville County, Hanson Hughes, who in the House had filed the resolution on which Thorne

8. The Carpetbagger and the Carpet Will

was expelled, though Hughes had not stayed for that vote. Now on the same side of an issue, Thorne and Hughes joined their four colleagues and said in part: "The power of the people rests entirely in the right they have to choose the officers who are to exercise the functions of government. They are as much entitled to the choice of these men, who are to levy the taxes they pay, as they are to elect those who make the laws, or the officer who executes them. Why should they have the power to elect Justices of the Supreme Court and Superior Courts, and be deprived of the right to select the magistrates who decide between neighbor and neighbor at their very doors?"[30]

At this time, J. Williams made another legislative effort, a bill to stop doctors "and others" from "prescribing and administering deadly poisons as medicines." A preamble denounced the bad effects of taking poison, and complained that "it is the almost universal practice of physicians to administer to the sick calomel, antimony, arsenic, strychnine, nitre, colchicum and many other more or less destructive poisons." The "wide-spread delusion" as to the "curative power" of these poisons was "materially checking the population," hurting public health, and hurting the "happiness and general prosperity" of North Carolinians. The operative part of the bill prohibited anyone, whether a physician or not, from giving anyone "any drug recognized as poisonous in authoritative works on toxicology." The bill went to the Committee on Corporations, of which J. Williams was a member, and the committee majority gave an unfavorable report. The Senate then defeated the bill by laying it on the table. J. Williams's bill flew in the face of the medical wisdom of the time, which attributed healing properties to properly administered doses of many of the substances listed in the bill. Medicine today allows a much narrower role to the substances J. Williams listed, and the broad role assigned to these substances in nineteenth-century medicine would be deemed improper today.[31]

The Senate adjourned on March 12 and would not meet again until 1879, after the end of J. Williams's current term.[32]

The Senate session being over, J. Williams was back on the farm, but he went to a May Day event at a black school called Coley's Springs. "They spoke pieces and sung and had a nice time," as Mary reported. A few days later, J. Williams was cut by the saw while working on his farm's sawmill. The wound healed in a couple of weeks, and seems to have avoided infection. "He did not grieve for the pain so much," Mary wrote Annie, "as for the loss of time he was doing the work of two men and it was so hard for him to give up work at this time of year."[33]

Quaker Carpetbagger

J. Williams had missed the Progressive Friends Meeting in 1876, leaving a letter for them, but in 1877 he came up to Pennsylvania and attended the Progressive gathering, where he was one of several who "spoke in favor of political action and stringent legislation against the liquor traffic." He brought Annie and his grandson Edgar back with him to the Oak Grove farm in Warren County, where Annie missed her husband but was "glad to be here with Mother and the rest of the home folks." J. Williams and the rest of the family wanted Annie to stay all winter for Edgar's health, a proposition Annie wanted to accept, although she wanted Peter to come down as well. If Peter stayed in Pennsylvania, Annie would be willing to go back north in November when J. Williams went.[34]

Ultimately, Annie and Edgar went back to Pennsylvania with J. Williams, apparently with Peter paying for Annie's ticket, since J. Williams could only afford his own ticket. Before she left North Carolina, Annie wrote Peter some sentiments that she had presumably not shared with her father's constituents. On the much-debated question of whether she and Peter should permanently relocate to North Carolina, Annie said: "The climate is delightful here and the flowers are very beautiful but I think the people are lazy and associate with the negroes a good bit which is not the best company for them.... The Southerners have high ideas of Aristocracy but look at their morals. Yardleys Greens and some others turn up there [sic] noses at Unity [Eugene's wife] and Genie [Eugene] yet Gene would not do such things as Will Yardley does." Annie seemed open to staying in North Carolina if she could move to Greensboro, where "there is quite a settlement of quakers and it is a grass country and the folks are liberal and intelligent. I should not like to raise children here"—presumably meaning Warren County.[35]

Mary, who stayed in North Carolina when J. Williams, Annie and Edgar left, worried that J. Williams would catch cold in Pennsylvania, not having brought his overshoes and not having "a very plentiful supply" of money to buy anything to keep him warm if he took "long walks." Because of his lack of money, J. Williams "need not get me any cotton flannel or anything else." Mary hoped to interest Peter Hershey in getting some land in Warren County to bring the family together.[36]

By 1878, J. Williams was fighting for what he believed was his wife's just inheritance. Mary's aunt, Susanna Pusey Taylor, had died widowed and childless in 1875, with a respectable inheritance. Two people then filed a purported will, dated 1874, with the Orphans' Court, and the will was admitted to probate. Susannah Taylor had supposedly kept this hand-

8. The Carpetbagger and the Carpet Will

written will under her carpet and then arranged to have the will delivered to reliable individuals, sewn up in the lining of her purse. The alleged will provided only one dollar each for Taylor's nieces Mary J. Pusey Thorne and Ann Pusey; without a will, they would have taken a larger share of the inheritance, but under a will, their cousins were preferred over them. Mary, Ann and other Pusey relatives filed a protest against the will "by their attorney (agent) J. Williams Thorne." Ann and Mary both filed suit to get the will declared invalid; Ann lost her suit late in 1877 when the jury, after hearing conflicting witnesses, decided the will was genuine. Mary's suit remained pending.[37]

In January 1878, J. Williams published a two-part article in the *West Chester American Republican* denouncing the jury's decision in the earlier suit. Based on his assessment of the evidence, and his own claims to knowledge of Susanna Taylor and others involved, J. Williams called the purported will a clear forgery, and said the trial judge should have indicated as much in his instructions. This was "a high handed conspiracy to defraud the rightful heirs." For Taylor to so cheat several worthy relatives just before her death would have been inconsistent with her character. Would she have behaved in such an unjust way while "standing on the verge of the grave" and hearing "the very voice of the Eternal,—'For the good and the true there is everlasting beatitude'"? Instead, she had told witnesses that she would not make a will, because "the law" of intestacy "makes the best will." Taylor was also not literate enough to do more than sign her own name, so she could not have handwritten a will. The story of her sewing the will into the lining of a calico bag was "a silly lie." The purported will "might as well have been found in the waste basket, or in the door yard, as under the carpet." The witnesses in favor of the alleged will were either lying or unreliable. Jesse D. Pusey, a witness in favor of the will, had changed his story, and his flexible conscience could be shown by the fact that he had claimed conscientious scruples against bearing arms in "the late war of the rebellion," yet he had taken up arms "against marauding potato thieves." If a court and jury could be fooled into accepting such a plainly phony will, "an amendment of the testamentary law of this state is an urgent necessity."[38]

Since Thorne had his own case still pending about the validity of Taylor's alleged "carpet will," the local district attorney, James H. Bull, took an interest in what he deemed an attempt to influence the jury in that case. The Chester County lawyer Wilmer W. MacElree, later to be district attorney himself, would refer to Bull as "a kindly disposed old man, versed in horticulture, who could prune a grapevine better than he could draw an indictment." Kindly disposed or not, Bull arranged Thorne's arrest for "embracery," a crime that involved improper influence of the courts, because his article exposed potential Chester County jurors to prejudicial publicity about the will case.[39]

J. Williams came back to Warren County, but did not thereby get a break from legal entanglements. The person who had sold them some of their land had purported to sell the same land to a second buyer, and addressing this tangle required consulting with attorneys, who didn't think the second sale was legal. Thorne would be in Pennsylvania court in April to deal with the carpet-will charges; Mary wrote Annie that "he is not yet scared by Judge [William] Butler and his arresting." J. Williams sent word that he would like Peter Hershey to correct an allegedly mistaken article in the *Philadelphia Times* about the arrest. Hershey had mentioned his acquaintanceship with Bull in 1877, though it does not seem to have sufficed to induce Bull to drop the charges.[40]

The *Raleigh Times* took note of Thorne's arrest, adding what Thorne called "some rather harsh comments." J. Williams induced the *Times* to publish his version of events—perhaps the *Times* thought that publishing J. Williams's letter would remind the public of his arrest and publicize legal quarrels up north. "I am engaged," wrote J. Williams, "in a contest against the most gigantic fraud ever known in Chester County." J. Williams explained that Judge Butler had published his jury charge in the earlier case in the *West Chester Local News*. To respond to this, J. Williams had felt called on to publish a rebuttal to such a misleading publication. His arrest was "illegal and utterly causeless.... It was deemed easier to arrest me than to refute me."[41]

On April 23, J. Williams and his Coatesville neighbor, Thomas H. Windle (who had tried to arrange a debate between Thorne and Barker), signed a $500 bond to assure J. Williams's future appearance in Chester County court on the carpet-will charge. Bull worked with William Hayes, the attorney defending the will, to obtain witnesses proving that Thorne wrote the article and that potential jurors had read it. Hayes sent a summary of Thorne's own testimony in the civil case, in which J. Williams admitted sending the article to several people.[42]

J. Williams was actually fortunate that his case took place in Pennsylvania. In some other states, anyone accused of publishing an article to improperly influence a court or jury would have faced a summary form of trial, and would have been denied many of the traditional rights of a

8. The Carpetbagger and the Carpet Will

defendant. Under the doctrine of "contempt by publication" that existed in these other states, the trial judge could have charged Thorne with interference with court proceedings, tried him without a jury, and imposed a punishment. Pennsylvania judges had once tried to proceed in this way, but they had lost that battle. Borrowing ideas from the English jurist William Blackstone (one of Thorne's favorite legal authors in other contexts), judges in Pennsylvania had—on several well-publicized occasions in the late eighteenth and early nineteenth centuries—summarily punished editors who criticized the courts in pending cases. Each instance provoked increasing opposition in the state legislature, culminating in a statute protecting defendants. Under Pennsylvania's statute, courts could not use the summary contempt power to punish critics in the press, or anyone else, unless the alleged contempt was directly tied to court operations. (A Pennsylvania congressman, the future President James Buchanan, tried to transplant this Pennsylvania rule to the federal courts, getting a statute through Congress which for many decades stopped the federal courts from summarily punishing press critics.) Pennsylvania did not recognize an unlimited right to criticize courts in pending cases, but people suspected of prejudicing the courts with their writings would have to be prosecuted in the normal way—with a grand jury indictment, followed by a jury trial—rather than being tried by a judge alone.[43]

Bull therefore labored to compile enough evidence for the grand jury of Chester County. In the August 1878 term of court, Bull brought forward witnesses who had seen J. Williams bring his article to the *American Republican* or who could otherwise link J. Williams to the circulation of his article in the county, where some potential jurors in the pending will case had seen it. Bull's efforts were to no avail: on August 12, the grand jurors refused to indict, and assessed costs against the county.[44]

Meanwhile, J. Williams witnessed, if only at a distance, a split in the country's Liberal movement. This may have reminded him of the prewar divisions in the abolitionist movement, and in any case, he seems to have tried to avoid taking sides in the bitter division.

In an October meeting in Syracuse, New York, the National Liberal League quarreled over obscenity. Specifically, they split over how much attention they should give the obscenity issue and how vigorously they should prioritize the fight against the censor Anthony Comstock and his epigones. While the League had called for reform of the obscenity laws in 1876, the better to protect legitimate speech, some in the League wanted repeal of the federal obscenity laws altogether. D.M. Bennett, editor of

Quaker Carpetbagger

The Truth Seeker, had faced prosecution for alleged obscene works he had published or sold (Bennett was in New York City, Comstock's back yard). Other Liberals had been prosecuted for overly frank discussion of sex and advocacy of more liberal sexual standards. To Francis Abbot, editor of the *Index*—who had helped organize the League in the first place—the Liberal movement could not afford to do anything to confirm the public suspicion that its members, because they opposed Christianity, wanted to subvert morality. At the Syracuse convention, the Bennett forces defeated Abbot and his allies, and the latter walked out and formed their own rival organization, the National Liberal League of America.[45]

J. Williams had experienced something like this before the war, when abolitionists split into mutually antagonistic rival groups, often taking time away from the fight against slavery to fight each other. It may well be that Thorne saw something similar in the acrimonious split of the Liberals. For whatever reason, J. Williams kept a position on the executive committee of both of the rival organizations. This dual membership would provoke at least one purist, who would write to *The Truth Seeker* calling on dual officeholders like Thorne to choose one or the other organization.[46]

J. Williams decided to make a bid for Congress, running (or standing) for the office of U.S. Representative for the Second District in North Carolina, which included Warren County. "Papa will soon be out on another campaign," Mary wrote Annie. "He feels quite confident of success, [illegible]. The prospect looks quite fair for him." Mary reflected: "We may as well *hope* for some thing good even to be in the end disappointed. The tide of fortune does seem to rise a little in our favor now, I hope it will continue to do so."[47]

In the 1876 election, Curtis Brogden had moved from the governor's chair to being elected as representative from the Second District to succeed John Hyman. By 1878, Brogden was losing his political mojo, and the Republicans nominated James O'Hara, the biracial anti-miscegenatist. When it transpired that O'Hara had married a second wife while estranged, though not divorced, from his first wife, the Republicans withdrew their nomination from O'Hara and gave it to James H. Harris, another black legislator. O'Hara stayed in the race, and the white Democratic candidate, William H. "Buck" Kitchin, hoped to benefit from these divisions in the normally reliably Republican "black Second" district.[48]

Throughout the country, still undergoing a depression, the federal government's hard-money policies and the imminent establishment of a gold standard (with only limited concessions to what would prove a

8. The Carpetbagger and the Carpet Will

significant pro-silver movement), followed by violent strikes suppressed by the Hayes administration, all combined to revive the popularity of the Greenback Labor Party and its policy of more widely available currency. Many workers and farmers were interested in the party's ideas for reform, which in the party's platform included various legislative changes but focused on government-backed Greenback currency in place of gold. (The exclusion of Chinese workers, and a federal income tax, were also in the Greenback Party platform.) The Greenback program was popular among workers and farmers in Pennsylvania, and began making significant inroads in the South. Many Southern Democrats, riding the wave to avoid being overwhelmed by it, indicated some sympathy with Greenback policies. Kitchin came out against the gold standard and for the income tax and other items on the Greenback wish list.[49]

Tomb of anti–Christian editor and activist D. M. Bennett, Green Park Cemetery, Brooklyn, NY (Wikimedia Commons).

J. Williams entered the congressional contest as an independent Greenbacker against his three opponents, going around the district debating his two Republican foes (Kitchin seems to have stayed in the background) and preaching the Greenback gospel. The preaching metaphor is apt given the zeal with which J. Williams advocated his version of currency reform. A good idea of the platform he expounded can be found in a lengthy letter he submitted to the *West Chester American Republican* after the campaign. He adopted the ideas of Greenback economic theorists and diagnosed the country's problems as stemming from a money monopoly held by the banks, who unjustly enriched themselves by usurious interest while the hardworking producer classes were impoverished. "The people are suffering a paralysis of their industries," said J. Williams, "not so much because there is too little money, as because that little is chiefly in the hands of a few selfish, monopolizing shylocks."[50]

J. Williams endorsed the "essential monetary principles" of the Greenbackers. His one quarrel with the Greenback financial program was their endorsement of "*fiat* money. I deny the power of government to successfully command or create a currency representing no real value, that shall yet be a true measure of all values." Instead, "[t]he value of a commodity is only measurable by the amount and quality of the labor it takes to produce it." A "National currency" could meet this principle if "government banking agencies" lent out the currency at two percent interest to "all persons who can give such safe security as Congress shall demand." J. Williams did not specify what security Congress should require, or how this vital point of his program was to be protected from political manipulation. The proposed currency would be legal tender (which creditors would have to accept), and it would be convertible at the holder's option into ten-year "Bullion bonds," which would also be issued at two percent interest.[51]

Describing the benefits of the proposed "new National monetary system," J. Williams sounded like a postmillennialist preacher describing the overthrow of Satan and the coming of the Kingdom of God on earth. The existing "money monopolizing Banking system ... is a power mightier for human harm than war, famine, or pestilence ... more than three-fourths of the crime of the world and nearly all its pauperism can be traced to this cause alone." The proposed new system would be "a true and uniform measurer of labor value, and therefore, honest money." With this honest money, "there will be an end to speculative gambling. The 'Bulls' and the 'Bears' will find their occupation gone. That creature of a dishonest money system, the millionaire, will disappear. There will be fewer palaces and the miserable hovel will give way to the comfortable homestead ... money will be accessible to all who can give a safe security at so low a rate of interest as to render failure impossible to any fair average business person." The new currency "will sweep away, as with the touch of a magician's wand, the crime, the poverty, and almost universal financial distress which have so long paralyzed the moral and physical energies of the people."[52]

After all this, J. Williams's other proposals seemed anticlimactic. He

8. *The Carpetbagger and the Carpet Will*

would replace protective tariffs (a key element of Republican policy) with "direct taxation of the unencumbered wealth of the people" (an income tax—a key radical demand). He endorsed free trade, except for "morally contraband" trade (probably referring to the liquor traffic), which "should be prohibited."[53]

Democratic papers exulted in Republican divisions in the Second District, and covered J. Williams as a curious eccentric, not caring that Kitchin was trying to appeal somewhat to the same Greenback sentiment which J. Williams was trying to foment. The *Wilson Advance* greatly enjoyed describing the fireworks at a debate in Kinston among Harris (the regular Republican candidate), George Wassom (O'Hara's brother-in-law, speaking on his relative's behalf), and Thorne. Harris and Wassom exchanged insults and accusations, while Harris accused Wassom and Thorne of being in cahoots, which Wassom denied. The paper spent a few words sarcastically summarizing J. Williams's position: "[H]e would make money so plentiful that it could be borrowed with ease at two per cent." The *Advance* gave even more loving attention to a physical description of Thorne, noting his "white hair, silvered over with the frost of years, a short neck, hump-shoulders, long slender legs, big feet, and arms which extended below his knees."[54] The *Goldsboro Messenger* called J. Williams "intelligent," but said he was "eccentric both in politics and religion," and that his political career was on a downward path.[55]

On election day, O'Hara probably got a plurality of the vote, but the Democrats and anti–O'Hara Republicans contrived to throw out many of O'Hara's votes. The plurality victory was thus awarded to Kitchin, a white Democrat in a majority-black district. Thorne had some support in Warren County, but does not seem to have achieved much support in the other counties of the Second District.[56]

In the adjacent congressional district, the Third, a Greenback candidate was actually elected. Daniel L. Russell, a prominent lawyer and planter based in Wilmington, narrowly defeated the Democratic candidate after the Republican candidate helpfully stepped aside at the last minute.[57] Thorne had had no such good fortune.

9

Returning Home

Soon after his defeat, J. Williams went to Washington, D.C., living on the food he brought with him and renting a room for $5. He probably attended a Greenback convention at the end of November, "not," as his wife explained, "to join them, but to fight them out of some of their foolishness." The "foolishness" may have involved a third-party campaign in the presidential election of 1880. J. Williams also spent some time angling for a federal job from the Hayes administration, so he may have reverted to party regularity at this juncture. He got assurances, or what he interpreted as assurances, that he would be nominated for the post of consul general to Mexico City. On the train back to Warren County, he was delayed by bad weather, arriving on Christmas Eve, later than his family expected, at the station in Ridgeway. He walked home in the dark, but while taking this walk on his sixty-second birthday he had the time to reflect on the chance at a $2,000-a-year position in an even warmer clime than North Carolina.[1]

Mary allowed herself to discuss how she might fare in Mexico, though nothing more seems to have been heard of the promised post. This is not surprising. At the time, President Hayes, in his Southern patronage policy, had shifted away from getting federal jobs for blacks and carpetbaggers and was giving more focus to peeling away wealthy and prominent native-born whites (preferably ex–Whigs) from the Democratic Party. This policy met a setback in the 1878 elections, when Republicans continued their electoral decline (or had their votes stolen by Democrats).[2]

J. Williams learned too late of another vacant office for which he would have liked to apply. Bayard Taylor was perhaps Chester County's most famous son, though not necessarily a favorite son. The globe-trotting Taylor had published many travel books, had written novels and books of poetry, including a translation of Goethe's *Faust*, and had given the Ode at the Centennial, while maintaining a farm in Chester County which he visited when he came home. The more straitlaced among the Quakers—

9. Returning Home

and Taylor was of Quaker parentage—did not like his drinking, and in particular they did not like that his novel *Hannah Thurston* satirized the earnest reformism and alleged provincialism of Quakers around Kennett Square. Taylor was designated minister to Germany in early 1878—his *Faust* translation had made him popular in Teutonic circles—but died at the end of the year, on December 19, at age 53.[3]

J. Williams himself received an appeal for political patronage, after a fashion, indicating that at least in Pennsylvania, Thorne had people following his career. J. Williams had sent a letter to the *Greenback Nationalist* in Huntingdon, describing conditions in North Carolina. The editor, Ben F. Fries, wrote a flattering letter to J. Williams in return. Fries was a committed radical, by his own later account involved in a "secret reform order," the Peers of Kosmos Compact or Industrial Mutualist. Fries's letter to Thorne suggested that Fries was thinking of moving to North Carolina to run or assist in a Greenback paper. Fries wished either for a letter of recommendation to work at the *National*, a recently established Greenback paper in Raleigh run by one Brower, or else for a loan to set up a greenback paper in Warren county—a loan which, of course, Fries said he would pay back promptly. Fries probably didn't get his money—J. Williams was fairly hard-pressed himself—and in any event, Fries was still in Pennsylvania in the 1890s, professing socialism.[4]

By summer 1879, Annie was living in Lancaster, the county seat, with her husband—Peter and Annie now owned the old Thorne farm, Fountain Hill, in Chester County. Mary wished the Hersheys and Thornes could be together either in Pennsylvania or North Carolina. As for J. Williams, Mary wrote, "I often think it strange that so peaceful a man should in his old age, be so entangled in the law…. If I was only blessed with as much hope as he has I could bear it better."[5]

The Progressive Friends met in early June 1879. A memorial to the late Chandler Darlington caused some controversy because it said Darlington did not believe in a future life. There was concern that such a statement in a memorial resolution was false and would give pain to Darlington's family. J. Williams "was in favor of paying respect to his character, independently of his relatives." After some revision, the memorial resolution said of the longstanding Progressive Friends member: "Not attempting to formulate any dogmatic faith in the existence of God, and feeling no positive or express assurance of a life beyond the grave, [Darlington] yet reposed in unbroken trust in the presence and rule everywhere of the infinite Truth, Wisdom and Beneficence."[6]

Quaker Carpetbagger

Another memorial resolution, for Bayard Taylor, provoked objections. Edward M. Davis said Taylor had been a disappointment to "the friends of human freedom." Taylor "became interested in travel, in literature and forgot the slave." J. Williams took part in the ensuing discussion, though the minutes do not state what position he took. He likely agreed with the final resolution, which praised Taylor as a supporter of the Longwood Meeting who did not always agree with the other members.[7]

During a debate on tobacco, J. Williams said that "the churches should be more active in bearing their testimony against the use of tobacco." The Meeting's testimony on the subject denounced "the indecent, unhealthy, wasteful and immoral practice of narcotizing the human body with tobacco.... We also suggest that farmers who cultivate the plant, and merchants who deal in it, are clearly implicated in the results of its use." North Carolina at this time was seeing quite a boom in tobacco farming and manufacturing. Warren County, however, had gone from being the state's top tobacco-producing county in 1860 to not even being in the top 10 in 1880. It was Peter Hershey in Pennsylvania who had four acres used for tobacco cultivation.[8]

A testimony on church and state denounced the efforts of certain Christians who "seek by insidious means to gain greater advantages for themselves at the risk of undermining the dearest rights of the American people." As an example of such encroachment, the testimony cited "the persistency with which the Jewish and Christian Bible is kept in the public schools, seemingly, in defiance of the State [Pennsylvania] Constitution." During the debate on this testimony, J. Williams registered a dissenting voice. He "was in favor of reading the Bible in the public schools. He regarded our opposition to its use an evidence that sectarianism has taken deep hold on us. He would like the children to read all the Bibles with unrestricted comment."[9]

J. Williams came back to North Carolina on July 12. There had been a hot spell, relieved by rain. J. Williams was still concerned about Edgar's health and believed having his grandson in Warren County to eat of the farm's grapes and watermelons would be just the thing. There may have been plans for a school in Warren County like the one formerly at the Pennsylvania farm. Peter Hershey was studying to pass the Pennsylvania bar, which he would do in December.[10]

Annie seems to have taken her father's advice to heart and brought Edgar to Oak Grove, Warren County, for a visit. Edgar had his fill of watermelon, cantaloupes and grapes, and seemed healthier, though Annie

9. Returning Home

herself ate so many she felt sick. Mary Bayard Clarke, a literary woman in New Bern and mother of William E. Clarke, one of J. Williams's former legislative colleagues, sent some sermons by the liberal minister O.B. Frothingham; J. Williams had Annie forward them to Peter.[11]

Annie left early for Pennsylvania to be with Peter (Peter wrote he was "sacrific[ing] my own comfort and feelings" to have Annie away, and he sent her a check to facilitate her coming North as soon as possible). Mary, considering herself too sick to travel, stayed in North Carolina. Before coming North, J. Williams reached a settlement with the rival claimant to the Oak Grove property. The claimant would buy out J. Williams's claim and the Thornes would have some time to live on the Oak Grove property until they found another place. Mary would have preferred to return to Chester County, but J. Williams and Eugene arranged the purchase of a new piece of property in or near Henderson, a town just over the border in Granville County. The new location, which Mary moved into in January, had good garden and orchard land suitable for fruit crops. The area contained many settlers from Canada. Mary wanted her new house to be called "Chester House."[12]

Up north, J. Williams supported the campaign to nominate General Ulysses Grant for a nonconsecutive third term as president. Grant was getting good publicity after a world tour, followed by a trip across the South, where he addressed black audiences at a time when black Americans were restive under President Hayes's comparatively hands-off policy on civil rights. Grant, a reformed drinker, also spoke up for temperance. All this was apparently enough to overcome any scruples J. Williams may have had about the former president's hard-money policies. Mary complained to Annie about J. Williams: "*He* needs help more than Grant, but I fear will not get it, after he is in rags and without a roof. He has helped the world too much for the comfort of himself and family. But I should not murmur while our children are so kind."[13]

J. Williams was in his new North Carolina home in February (he didn't call it "Chester House"), writing some friends, Joshua and Mary Brinton, whom he had failed to meet in Pennsylvania on account of "circumstances, not anticipated." He recommended that the Brintons' sick daughter Callie not take any more "drug treatment," and instead rely on "exercise and fresh air" and "a carefully selected dietive course." J. Williams promised to pay the Brintons some money he owed them when he came north that fall on the "'Will' case, which will be tried at that time."[14]

North Carolina Governor Thomas J. Jarvis (who had become governor when Zebulon Vance resigned to take up a U.S. Senate seat) called the state legislature into special session. Private railroad companies had begun building more track in the state, and Jarvis believed it was time for North Carolina to finally put behind it the old, controversial and scandal-plagued practice of government-built railways. The state-run Western North Carolina Railroad was the last vestige of this policy, and now the state had an offer from some private capitalists to purchase the Western Railroad. Calling the solons together in March 1880, the governor recommended that the legislature approve the proposed sale, which they did.[15]

While the legislature was deliberating on railroad matters, it was persuaded to take up other subjects as well. The liquor industry obtained some tax relief, outraging dry sentiment and adding to pressure for alcohol prohibition. Dr. Norment, again representing Robeson County in the House, made another effort to undo the House's action against Thorne five years before. On March 23, Norment offered a resolution "expunging the record in relation to" Thorne. On Saturday the 27th, the House adopted this expungement resolution. The *Charlotte Democrat*, apparently referring to Thorne's expulsion, called it a "very foolish act from the beginning to the ending." Only four members of the House in 1880 had voted for Thorne's expulsion in 1875, and only three 1880 members had voted against expulsion. While the expungement did not put J. Williams back in the House, it theoretically required the record of the expulsion to be marked "expunged" in the original handwritten House Journal, and for the record to be omitted when the journal was subsequently published.[16]

In a triumphant letter to *The Truth Seeker*, J. Williams described the expungement. He added: "North Carolina is making rapid progress in Liberalism. Some of the most eminent men here are outspoken Liberals. Republicans here are all for Grant. The state will surely go Republican next fall." J. Williams added his congratulations to editor D.M. Bennett, whose prison term on obscenity charges was about to end (Bennett was out by the time J. Williams's letter was published). The Grant boom failed in the face of the two-presidential-term tradition and Grant's unpopular alliance with the Republican Party's anti-reform "Stalwart" faction. James Garfield received the Republican nomination instead.[17]

The legislative expungement did not pay the bills. Eugene was building a cotton gin at the new place, but until the cotton crop came in, the fruit crop does not seem to have been enough to help the family, who could not afford even to buy clothes. J. Williams sought to be elected again to the state Senate, but lost the Republican nomination due to "some trick-

9. Returning Home

ery," as his wife put it. He put his hope in the Republican candidate for Congress, Sheriff Orlando Hubbs of Craven County. Hubbs promised that if he won, he would use his influence to get J. Williams a federal job. Mary commented resignedly to Annie, "[Y]ou know papa never gives up but is still as deep in politics as ever[.] He always has plenty to do when at home and is never discouraged." Contrary to J. Williams's prediction, though Hubbs won the Second District, the Republicans did not take North Carolina, which was part of the "Solid South" vote for Democratic candidate Winfield Scott Hancock. Republican James Garfield, though, won most non–Southern states and captured the presidency. The Greenbackers had a candidate, James B. Weaver, but he was swamped by the other two parties, and his attempt at winning Southern votes was not successful.[18]

After Mary and J. Williams had gone up to Pennsylvania, Columbus Foster, a black laborer on the Thorne place, wrote Mary about an initiative of Eugene's—a general store selling various items (including tobacco and snuff). Eugene wrote Mary that the store was making "good profits." Eugene declared: "The Poor People have a hard time in this country that is the Reason I Struggle so against being poor and dependent—I think I can come through all Right by taking hold of things that pay." As for J. Williams, "[H]e is just throwing away money up there and we have to live very poor in consequence of it—do tell him to have a little sence [sic] and quit squandering money for it is very hard to make." Eugene had decided to "come north," explaining, "I shall never be satisfied for [his children] to pitch their destinies here on this poor soil."[19]

Eugene Thorne, blind in his left eye due to being kicked by horse at a young age, from Thorne family papers (courtesy Nancy Plumley).

While J. Williams

was out of the state, a stirring political development occurred in January in Raleigh—a temperance convention, whose participants and leaders included many Protestant clerics and J. Williams's old adversary from the legislature, Hezekiah Gudger. The convention asked the state legislature for "an absolute and unqualified prohibition law." Although the convention had both black and white support, it couldn't restrain itself from making a racial appeal, raising a lurid possibility in the event of a reduction in the federal liquor tax: "If liquors were 25 cents a gallon" instead of the current 90 cents with the federal tax, "with our mixed population and the passions and prejudices of races, and our small and unprotected families, who can contemplate the probabilities without horror?" The legislature promptly passed a prohibition law, but with an escape hatch—at an election scheduled for August 4, the voters would have the chance to approve or disapprove the law. If adopted, the law would ban the sale of liquor for drinking purposes except as a medicine, and medicinal liquor would have to be imported from other states, since no liquor could be manufactured in North Carolina. This, by "coincidence," would mean there would no longer be any legal distilleries in North Carolina, hence no revenue officers collecting the federal liquor tax—thus depriving Republican presidents of a source of patronage jobs for Tar Heel Republicans.[20]

"What is Papa doing and why don't he write some times?" Eugene wrote his mother in February. "I would like to know whether he intends to live north or south." By March, Columbus Foster had the impression that "mr E[ugene] thorne is about to Stop keeping his Store and close it up trade is Dul now." Be that as it may, Eugene was still running the store at the end of the year.[21]

Eugene wrote to announce in May that J. Williams had "arrived 'Safe and in good Spirits.' ... Columbus trimmed papas hair and I trimmed his beard and took that wild look away he had with all his hair, and made him look civilized once more." Eugene still had dreams of coming back north—perhaps buying some land from Peter Hershey, including the old Thorne place at Fountain Hill. Eugene thought that J. Williams, too, might agree to come back to Pennsylvania. "All Papas colony gradually are getting back north."[22]

Meanwhile, though, J. Williams was back in the thick of political activity. Indicating that his sojourn may have included a trip to the nation's capital, J. Williams wrote his wife not to complain about the quality of ink he had used in his letters: it was obtained "in Washington" and was "recommended as that used in signing important state papers." In North

9. Returning Home

Carolina, J. Williams and other local politicos spoke, in vain, against the proposal for a new county, to be carved out of parts of Warren, Granville and Franklin Counties. These protests were unsuccessful, and the legislature created Vance County. Henderson and the new Thorne place went to the new county.[23]

At the same time, J. Williams contemplated writing another anti–Christian polemic. He still served on the executive committees of both the National Liberal League—which supported the "martyr" Bennett and *The Truth Seeker*—and the rival American Liberal Union (formerly the National Liberal League of America)—associated with Bennett's foes at the *Index*. The American Liberal Union was becoming largely inactive, but the more radical National Liberal League was still trying to rally its troops, printing in *The Truth Seeker* an exhortation to its members and to executive committee members like J. Williams: "Now let every Liberal friend everywhere understand that the committeeman who represents their state is the 'head-center' of the movement in the state or territory, the one to have the general supervision of the work; that he should in fact not only be that, and do that, but should be a 'Liberal lecture bureau' in himself for his state. And our Liberal friends should not ask him to do all this work for nothing and pay his own expenses, but each Liberal of the state should contribute something for his support."[24]

It's not clear how much if anything J. Williams received in donations from North Carolina Liberals as state committeeman, but he saw a potential opportunity to defend the infidel cause. The *North American Review* had published one of Robert Ingersoll's denunciations of Christianity, followed by a rebuttal from the prominent Pennsylvania lawyer Jeremiah S. Black. Though it received some praise at the time, Black's article disappointed some Christians—indeed, from the Christian standpoint, it might seem that with friends like Black, the faith scarcely needed enemies. Styling himself a theological "policeman" opposing Ingersoll's atheism, Black made some of the standard points in defense of Christianity, but added other points that hardly represented a unanimous Christian consensus. Ingersoll had criticized the barbarity of the Old Testament wars against the Canaanites; Black replied that such tactics were fitting for a war against "hostile barbarians"—"if the death of your whole population be their purpose, you may defeat it by exterminating theirs." Ingersoll had said that the Old Testament approved of slavery; Black answered: "Subordination of inferiors to superiors is the groundwork of human society.... There can be no question that, when a Jew took a neighboring savage for his

Quaker Carpetbagger

bond-servant, incorporated him into his family, tamed him, taught him to work, and gave him a knowledge of the true God, he conferred upon him a most beneficent boon." To Black, the idea that slavery was wrong was an invention of American abolitionists and Republicans, whom Black considered infidels. A reference to "political preachers"—whom Black compared to Judas—was the closest Black came to alluding even indirectly to Christian opponents of slavery. Thorne wrote his wife that Black's article "is the special pleading of a third rate lawyer. Ingersoll will no doubt make a crushing reply. If he does not, I will do it myself."[25]

Black seems to have been a sincere Christian—he was baptized into the faith by the famous American Protestant evangelist Alexander Campbell, cofounder of the Disciples of Christ. Yet the religious views Black expressed in his article reflected, or were reinforced by, the positions he had taken in his political and legal career. Before the war he had been a Pennsylvania doughface, appeasing slavery as the U.S. Attorney General under fellow doughface James Buchanan. While Abraham Lincoln was criticizing Stephen Douglas for being proslavery, Black criticized Douglas for not being proslavery enough. During the Civil War, Black supported restoration of the Union, but would have allowed the South to keep its slaves. He helped write President Johnson's unsuccessful veto messages against Congress's Reconstruction statutes. As a lawyer, Black won a Supreme Court victory on behalf of the right to jury trial in the *Milligan* case, but he won other victories

Jeremiah Black, whose shaky Christian apologia J. Williams considered rebutting (Brady-Handy Photograph Collection, Library of Congress).

9. Returning Home

in which the Court limited the federal government's power to enforce civil rights. Black denounced abolitionism, and the "Radical" Republican Reconstruction program after the war, as the fruit of New England Puritan fanaticism.[26]

Black's remarks reconciling Christianity with slavery and wars of extermination would have provided useful material for J. Williams's rebuttal—but, as J. Williams had predicted, Ingersoll saved his supporters from the necessity of defending him. In the *North American Review* for November, Ingersoll published a stinging rebuttal to Black, taking full advantage of what he deemed Black's fateful concessions.[27] Apparently, J. Williams now felt no need to add to what Ingersoll said.

"I shall speak on temperance three or four times before the Election," J. Williams announced to Mary. "I spoke at Middleburg lately. It is not a party matter." But John J. Mott, the Republican chairman for North Carolina, was working to make sure it *was* a party matter, and that Republicans would be on the anti-prohibition, "wet" side of the debate. Mott's strategy was to saddle the Democrats with prohibition and ally with the policy's "wet" opponents. Mott happened to be the federal collector of internal revenue in North Carolina, responsible for collecting the federal liquor tax, so he had extra incentive to resist any effort to close the distilleries.[28]

Many North Carolina Republicans, like J. Williams, disagreed with their chairman. So delicate was the issue that Orlando Hubbs, the prohibition-sympathizing white congressman from the Second District, stayed out of North Carolina at the time of the prohibition election, pleading ill-health. Less temporizing was James Walker Hood, the former Chester County resident who had left his Kennett Square home in hopes of finding a religious calling. He had come to North Carolina in the middle of the Civil War to evangelize for the African Methodist Episcopal Zion (AMEZ) church. After some time in North Carolina as a churchman and a black Republican politician, Hood was now the AMEZ bishop for Virginia, North Carolina and South Carolina. Bishop Hood was a prohibitionist and came out against Mott's wet crusade. Despite all this, black voters voted overwhelmingly against prohibition, and helped give a crushing defeat to the policy. According to the final count, prohibition got 48,370 votes and the "wet" anti-prohibition side got 166,325.[29]

Eugene continued to wish to leave "hot old N.C." and return to Pennsylvania, "and as for Papa he does not have the kind of company here he likes and if he don't own [admit] it I am sure he prefers to be in Chester Co. and he always told me he was willing to go back to the old place."

Quaker Carpetbagger

Columbus Foster wanted to come north as well, but Eugene didn't want his help, adding "I am tired of darkies." Eugene did mention a neighbor who thought "this neighborhood can't do without me, but they cannot change my mind." Also, Eugene believed that J. Williams would lose his forthcoming will case: "[H]e is entirely to [sic] hopefull and gives too much credit to what people say." Eugene was correct: Thorne lost the case when a jury ruled in favor of the "Carpet Will" in February 1882.[30]

Eugene was not the only one thinking of leaving the area. Many black people were moving from eastern North Carolina to work in the Mississippi cotton fields and the Georgia turpentine industry, or to try their luck in Indiana and the Midwest. Eugene reported on this with his customary sensitivity: "[W]hen I was in [nearby] Louisburg two wagon loads of negroes started for Georgia or some where—I do not know where—they went off happily with the usual good by Bill; good by Henry & they went off laughing; The negroes seem to know no trouble." Eugene himself was still decided on moving back north, though he said his brother Caleb Pusey would remain in North Carolina.[31]

In an application to the president, J. Williams sought a federal job. President Garfield was no longer in charge—he had been shot by a disgruntled office-seeker, and then died under his doctor's care, despite J. Williams's optimistic declaration that "Garfield is getting well in despite of Doctors and assassins." Garfield's place was now occupied by Chester Alan Arthur of New York. Possibly following up on the patronage promises of Congressman Hubbs, or perhaps making a bid for office as a Pennsylvanian and not a North Carolinian, J. Williams had some Chester County friends and associates write to Arthur and back his candidacy "for some of the vacant foreign missions." Ex-Congressman Washington Townsend, who had recommended J. Williams to Warren County voters, now recommended J. Williams to the President on character and qualification grounds, noting the "considerable attention" Thorne had said he gave "to international law." Townsend described J. Williams as a former Chester County resident "now a resident of North Carolina." William B. Waddell was a Chester County lawyer and politician who had served in local government and in the Pennsylvania legislature. Waddell endorsed what Townsend had said. So did Major Edward B. Moore, who had been the editor of the *West Chester American Republican* from 1866 to 1878. Major Moore had written a complimentary article on the eve of J. Williams's departure for North Carolina in 1869, though he had not always published the numerous articles J. Williams submitted to the *Republican*. Finishing off the recommendations

9. Returning Home

was a note from Joseph and Rebecca Taylor, parents of the late Bayard Taylor, who had "long known" J. Williams. They claimed that if Bayard Taylor were still alive "we have no doubt he would have been pleased to join with us" in recommending J. Williams.[32]

Despite these recommendations, J. Williams's quest for offices did not bear fruit. Developments in North Carolina may have hurt his chances. Opponents of prohibition in North Carolina built on their 1881 triumph by forming, in mid–1882, a Liberal Anti-Prohibition Party. Some former Greenbackers—though probably not J. Williams—joined these Liberals. Under Mott's leadership, the Republicans endorsed the new party's candidates, so as to make a united challenge to the Democrats. The administration in Washington came to the support of this strange amalgam of wets, soft-money men and Republicans. President Arthur—though sometimes credited with a Damascus-road conversion to civil-service reform—was willing to use federal patronage in the South to promote Republican fortunes. While Arthur at first made some gestures toward blacks and carpetbaggers, he soon switched to a new effort to pry native Southern whites loose from the Democrats. This new strategy involved siding with many of the South's anti–Democratic insurgent movements, such as the Liberal Anti-Prohibitionists in North Carolina. (In North Carolina, this strategy would bear fruit in a one-time, not permanent, increase of Republican vote totals.) For J. Williams, this meant that his record as a carpetbagging prohibitionist could not have helped him, which may be why he went through Pennsylvania channels in his failed self-promotion efforts.[33]

His known anti–Christian views could not have helped J. Williams, either. Robert J. Ingersoll, more famous than Thorne, had put many Republican presidents and other politicians under obligation by campaigning for them. Still, no Republican president had rewarded Ingersoll with a federal job. Rumors that Ingersoll might get the Berlin mission had provoked opposition that proved decisive. Thorne's notoriety as an "infidel," though not as great as Ingersoll's, may have been another factor in his being passed over for patronage jobs. J. Williams was probably aware of this, which makes his willingness to write a second anti–Christian polemic in response to Jeremiah Black all the more remarkable.[34]

Eugene continued to plan his move back to Pennsylvania. He proclaimed in February that he had begun packing. "I stuck it out" in North Carolina "only to be a Sader [sic] and a wiser man." Bantering with Peter Hershey, Eugene sarcastically sang the praises of the "corn cakes and ash cake and fat meat," of cotton and hogs and defending Southern honor at the point of a gun. He joked in coarse language about selling some black people to Peter. Eugene's animadversions targeted high freight rates and a local politician who was supposedly the son of the commander at the Andersonville prisoner of war camp who "Starved our soldiers to death."[35]

After all this, Eugene's plans to move back to Pennsylvania did not come off. He visited his mother in Fountain Hill—apparently Mary was renting the old place from Peter Hershey. But the plan for a permanent move did not work, and Eugene went back to North Carolina to join J. Williams, who was already there. Mary wrote J. Williams in September that this situation "has made me very unhappy all summer, but I hope it will teach [Eugene] not to make such a move again. It has cost him untold trouble and expense." As for Peter Hershey, he "has to be in Lancaster nearly all the time." Mary wished "much love to all our kind friends in the South and to good kind Aunt Margaret."[36]

Down in Henderson in April 1883, J. Williams wrote to Mary in Lancaster to congratulate Annie on the birth of another son, Ralph. "I suppose you might have preferred a daughter," J. Williams wrote his wife, "but until women can vote perhaps it is well as it is." Eugene and Caleb Pusey were with J. Williams, Eugene's plans for returning north not being heard of again. Probably responding to a concern of Mary's, J. Williams wrote, "I do not need any more clothing." The fruit crop—apples and strawberries—was doing well. J. Williams wrote his wife at the end of April: "All the trees are in full leaf. The weather could not be more beautiful. I have never been more busy in my life than I have been this spring ... all well."[37]

Meeting in June 1883, the Progressive Friends Meeting authorized a one-hour free-for-all discussion of religion. J. Williams had come up from North Carolina and he made his contribution. The minutes tried to summarize him:

> J. Williams Thorne thought the word Religion ambiguous, as now understood; an obstruction to the progress of human beings. He could not distinguish between the real and the ideal. If evolution doesn't go fast enough, let us have revolution. Some persons worship God and sell whiskey. Let us worship man, work for him, and not for an indefinite God. If we do that which injures our fellow-men, we injure the divinity within ourselves....
>
> J.W. Thorne thought Webster's meaning of the word religion the best. He said religious means "deferential." The Puritans thought they were religious, but they were not deferential, and did wickedly, while professedly worshipping God. All that is worthy of worship should be religion.[38]

9. Returning Home

Then in the fall of 1883, disaster struck. Peter Hershey had been making some bad investments, or worse. Faced with creditors or possibly criminal prosecution, he cheated a local bank out of some money and fled out west, abandoning his wife Annie and his children. Peter took with him J. Williams's niece Anulette Humphrey, who had been staying with Peter, supposedly innocently, to do housekeeping duties when Annie was away in the South. Before fleeing Pennsylvania, Peter met with Annie and arranged for all of their property to be assigned to one John S. Rohrer, who would be responsible for using the property to pay off creditors. The property thus assigned included the old Thorne estate at Fountain Hill, which would have to be sold like the other property in order to satisfy the debts Peter owed. (The census of 1920 lists Peter Hershey working as a janitor in Illinois, with a wife named "Anna."[39])

At the Progressive Friends meeting in 1884, still listed as hailing from North Carolina, J. Williams contributed some remarks which might be seen as having a personal application, as far as the summary in the minutes can disclose. He "said that motherhood should take precedence of a desire for greatness or fame. Give women an opportunity to vote. Republicanism is not true of this country while they are held in bondage. All sorts of oppression should end." When a testimony was proposed on education, Thorne joined in the debate—possibly to emphasize the need for including temperance instruction in the schools, but the minutes revert to vagueness on the specifics of what J. Williams said. The final testimony did indeed discuss the need for temperance education, and added: "[W]e would urge upon all to consider the petition now in circulation in the State, asking that Temperance text books be introduced into the schools, and give it their support." The following year, the Pennsylvania legislature passed a law requiring the public schools to give instruction on the harmful effects of alcohol.[40]

The Progressive Friends meeting of 1885 featured another freewheeling discussion of religion, and J. Williams had his contribution to make: "I think that true religion is that religion which teaches man to be wiser, and makes the world better and happier, here and now. That instead of religion teaching that we must flatter God and supplicate him in order to prevent some dreadful things which will happen to us if we do not worship him, it should teach man those things needful to the moral and intellectual advancement of civilization." On another subject, he "had noticed a great change in the country within the last forty years with regard to temperance. There was not anything like so much drunkenness in proportion to the population as formerly. The time had gone by when liquor was consumed by three-fourths of the people of our land, and the reason was that public feeling against it had been raised to fever heat. He believed that the time is coming when the traffic will be entirely killed."[41]

Facing the failure of their North Carolina adventure, and wishing to be back with their abandoned daughter, J. Williams and Mary came back to southeastern Pennsylvania for good. Until Fountain Hill was sold off, J. Williams and Mary lived in a log cabin where they had lived during the building of Fountain Hill back in the 1840s. At first J. Williams thought he would be able to buy the Fountain Hill property, but ultimately he could not afford it. He acquired an estate just across the county line in Lancaster county. After Mary and J. Williams had moved into their new home in 1886, Mary wrote Eugene: "We like our new house very much, with its stone walls and slate roof and plenty of nice windows with two panes, and so firm and substantial and warm, you must come and see us.... The land is good for fruit and vegetables, and papa will bring it out with Annie and Edgars help. It looks wild now but can be made a beautiful place, it is in a grove of Chestnuts, I want them to call it 'Chestnut Hill.'" Eugene and his wife Unity had just had a baby, and Mary suggested the name Percy: "[I]t is a good old English name and the name of an english poet 'Percy Byschey Shelly' [sic] and sounds a little like Pusey." Eugene did not follow his mother's advice about naming his child after the famous atheist poet Percy Bysshe Shelley.[42]

At the time Thorne moved back to Pennsylvania, North Carolina's prior enthusiasm for obtaining immigrants from out of state or from beyond the seas had diminished. After the war, both Republicans and Democrats had worked to recruit migrants to North Carolina, but by 1886 the state's own immigration agent warned against "promiscuous immigration"—only the most select candidates should be encouraged. In 1887, the State Agriculture Department said the people of the state were against "foreign and promiscuous immigration" from "Swedes, Hungarians, Chinese and other foreigners." Welcoming out-of-state capital was deemed a good thing, but out-of-staters personally coming to the Tar Heel State no longer seemed so desirable. The feeling seems to have been mutual, as immigration and migration rates were low. A *Handbook* for potential immigrants to America, published in 1880, warned against settling in North Carolina and several other Southern states, which were "ruled too much by the pistol, the rifle, and the shot-gun, to make life agreeable there."[43]

Contacting a Raleigh lawyer in 1886, J. Williams made an unsuccessful

9. Returning Home

effort to get his full salary for his term as a legislator in 1875. After all, he figured, the House had expunged his expulsion, so there was no longer any reason to withhold the pay he should have collected for attending on the legislature during its entire term. The lawyer J. Williams consulted poured cold water on this idea, saying it wouldn't work, and returned the affidavit J. Williams had prepared to back up his claim.[44]

By the time of his 70th birthday on Christmas 1886, J. Williams had lost his wife Mary, who had died earlier in the month, on the 6th. The two had been married forty years. The Chestnut Hill household now comprised J. Williams, Annie, and his grandchildren Edgar and Ralph.[45]

Anyone who listened to J. Williams at the Progressive Friends gathering at Longwood in June 1887 would not have noticed any loss of his fighting spirit—quite the contrary. "Intemperance is the very basis of murder, and if you have the right to punish murder by hanging, you have the still stronger right of abating that which really causes the murder. Murders increase exactly in proportion as the temperance cause is lessened in strength. It is then sufficient, nay, it is obligatory that we shall apply the law if we can.... We have only begun the agitation of this subject. Every State in the Union will yet have Prohibition; furthermore it will be the greatest reform that has ever been effected in any community."[46]

J. Williams Thorne was back at home.

10

Speaking His Mind

In an article for the *West Chester Village Record* in early 1888, J. Williams denounced the mainstream educational system as aristocratic and "anti republican." Youth imbibed aristocratic notions from learning about the lives of warriors and conquerors, which Thorne saw as "infinitely more demoralizing than the dime novel" because the lives of great figures were taught as "good books" endorsed by schools. "The dramas of Shakespeare are generally sensational and immoral. There is scarcely anything in them in harmony with well ordered family life in Chester County." With future rulers imbibing such aristocratic principles, it is no wonder that when they got into government they would rule on behalf of "the wealthy capitalist." Bad education could be blamed for various examples of aristocratic oppression, such as the U.S. Supreme Court, which had struck down the Civil Rights law in 1883 (leaving private parties free to practice racial discrimination unless hindered by state law). In a digression, J. Williams proposed to make the Supreme Court "elective for short terms," and to divide the country into judicial districts of 2,000 population which would elect juries to decide cases without judges. Returning more specifically to his ostensible topic, J. Williams objected to Chester County teachers' being regularly "crammed with new notions about education and the science of teaching." J. Williams concluded on a constructive note, praising local teachers' conventions and noting the improvement in teaching in the past forty years. The article was fairly rambling and discursive, taking in many topics besides the ostensible one of teacher training.[1]

In an update to this article, a letter to the *Village Record* dated March 9, J. Williams replied to some criticism of his earlier article by the newspapers' editors. The editors said that American colleges produced "leading Senators and men prominent in every business and profession." J. Williams, though, called college education "a great fashionable sham." The aristocrats of England "are all college bred, yet, as all her history proves, with a very low minimum result of sense and justice." The House of Lords

10. Speaking His Mind

and the colleges of Oxford were a "dead weight" resisting progressive reforms, which had to come from the people. The U.S. Senate, made of "the same sort of stuff" as American colleges, was likewise an aristocratic dead weight, foisted on the country by "the college-bred aristocratic leaders of the federal party." From that, J. Williams segued into Congressional attempts to restrict the immigration of "[t]he hard-working Chinese or Irish immigrant." If Jesus and the disciples were to come to the U.S., they would at best meet a "chilly" reception "at the hands of such refined college-bred people as [George] Edmunds [R–VT] and [John] Ingalls [R–KS]."

This led to a discussion of the persecution of the Mormons, since Sen. Edmunds had sponsored a bill to crack down on their polygamous practices. While polygamy was "not in accord with the highest ideal of marriage relationship," neither was the celibacy the Roman Catholic Church imposed on priests and monks, yet it was as wrong to prosecute Mormon marriage practices as it would be to prosecute Catholic non-marriage practices. Going back again to his ostensible topic of education, J. Williams linked "the Greek and Latin classics" with the Dark Ages and said they had nothing helpful to guide citizens of the American republic. "Most of the great men of modern times do not owe their greatness to college training.... Of this Washington, Franklin and Lincoln are illustrating examples."[2]

To local newspaper readers, J. Williams expounded on a "Lunar Cycle Rule" for predicting the weather. Articles like "The Coming Winter as Indicated by the Lunar Cycle Rule" and "'The Lunar Cycle Rule' and What of it as an Indication of Weather Futures" gave J. Williams's views on this theory.[3]

In 1887, the Pennsylvania state legislature had proposed a prohibition amendment to the state Constitution. The dominant state Republican Party, reportedly as part of a political deal with the Chester County delegation to the party convention, had approved this measure. The legislature would have to vote on the amendment again in 1889, and if they approved again, the people would vote on the proposal. Meanwhile, the legislature of 1887 passed a so-called "high license" law, tightening the requirements, and raising the fees, for applying for a liquor license. For applicants who surmounted the legal hurdles, the decision whether to let them sell booze was pretty much up to the discretion of the Quarter Sessions judges in each county. Some drys supported the high-license law as a first step toward prohibition, while influential wets approved the law as a way to make the liquor business more respectable, and more defensible in the face of prohibitionist attacks.[4]

Quaker Carpetbagger

In the Progressive Friends Meeting of 1888, J. Williams showed his opposition to government licensing of saloons, even under the new law's stricter standards:

> When we abolish the use of liquor in our county our jails and poor houses will be emptied at once. I know you would not permit a man to keep a dangerous dog, and yet it would be better for us were hundreds of mad dogs turned loose in Chester county every year than that any saloons should be licensed, because we would not put up with the mad dogs for one minute while we do put up with the saloon.... The very men who license the liquor seller are far worse than the sellers themselves. See what the intelligent citizens of Chester county are doing. See what the political parties are doing. See what the ministers of the Gospel and those who attempt to teach you religion are doing. These are the things we shall have to look after.[5]

The Temperance testimony issued by the Meeting declared: "To legalize this wicked traffic is to legalize crime. We therefore oppose all License, high or low, and demand the unconditional abolition by Constitutional law both State and National of the importation, manufacture and sale of all alcoholic beverages." Despite J. Williams's animadversions against Christian ministers, the meeting even praised the Women's Christian Temperance Union and other Christian Prohibitionists, though "we beg them to avoid all ecclesiasticism" and not to undermine religious liberty in the Constitution.[6]

It is quite possible that J. Williams was not present for the 1889 meeting of the Progressive Friends, or that he had some illness preventing him from speaking, because there is no record of his taking part in the debates—even though the Meeting set aside a day of discussion of prohibition. This was quite timely, since the legislature had approved the Prohibition amendment a second time, submitting the matter to a popular vote on June 18. In this election, while prohibition won the vote of the majority of the *counties*, most *voters* rejected the measure. The no votes were concentrated in the large urbanized counties and—a fact that was apparently noticed by many Progressive Friends—large numbers of no voters were foreign-born laborers. With statewide prohibition defeated, the Progressive Friends would have to start from scratch, since they did not propose to rely on the license law.[7]

J. Williams took no recorded part in the Progressive Friends meeting of 1890.[8]

Opposite: **Statue of Frances Willard in the U.S. Capitol. Willard was the head of the Women's Christian Temperance Union, praised by the Progressive Friends in spite of theological differences (Wikimedia Commons).**

10. Speaking His Mind

Quaker Carpetbagger

The recollection of a visit to Mount Vernon, General Washington's former home, around 1879, prompted an article by J. Williams in 1891. This was among the more "conventional" articles J. Williams wrote, in that he did not agitate his favorite political or reform causes. He told what he remembered of his Mount Vernon trip, and added remarks about Washington's lack of selfishness and greed. "In these latter days we are in great need of a few Washingtons, but where shall we find them?"[9]

In the 1891 Progressive Friends gathering, J. Williams was indubitably present again. A retrospective paper on the Meeting's history prompted some of J. Williams's reflections: "The most of those who aided in the organization are lying in the cemetery yonder. They have consecrated this place to free thought and speech. I know of no place where all sects can have as free expression as here. Let no one think that because slavery is abolished there are no weighty questions needing our consideration.... Do not suppose we have attained to perfection. We come here to teach and be taught, not to dogmatize."[10]

In other remarks, J. Williams touched on religion, and in addition to his animadversions on the Bible, he spoke of the unknowability of spiritual matters and his doubts as to the immortality of the soul. "Some people lose their minds. If the mind is immortal, it cannot be lost. Where is it then?"[11]

In more worldly subjects, a controversy was emerging in the Meeting over their positions on immigration and suffrage. The Meeting had long testified in favor of a letting women vote on the same terms as men. While agreeing on the need to remove sex discrimination from the voting laws, a dispute arose over whether some of the male population—especially illiterate and foreign-born voters—should be deprived of the franchise. These doubts were accentuated by the tendency of the less educated voters to oppose women's suffrage—and probably the recent Prohibition referendum was in Friends' minds as well. Discussion began over possible literacy and English proficiency tests for voters, or even a requirement that naturalized citizens wait twenty years before they could vote. The minutes laconically record a "very lively discussion" in which J. Williams participated—though we may readily suppose that J. Williams, on this as on other occasions, was against suffrage restrictions. The Meeting agreed to postpone these delicate matters until the following year.[12]

The 1892 meeting of the Progressive Friends adopted a string of resolutions on various subjects—opposing private race discrimination, opposing the Chinese Exclusion laws ("a gross violation of the principle of

10. Speaking His Mind

hospitality to which our government is committed, and an unjustifiable indignity towards a humble, and in the main industrious and not unworthy, class of immigrants"), and urging the Columbian exposition not to sell alcohol, and to be open on Sunday. Another proposed resolution that prompted debate would call on certain immigrants to be excluded from the country: those who were "illiterate and vicious, the criminal and pauper, the self-ungoverned and ungovernable classes." This resolution was voted down after the Meeting heard pleas for the immigrants.[13]

On June 4—the Saturday after the Meeting had officially adjourned, but apparently while some Friends were still in the vicinity—J. Williams may have read a poem of his own composition to at least some members of the Meeting. As a poet, J. Williams was no Milton—truth be told, he was not even a Bayard Taylor—but the poem put into rhyme many of his reform ideas. The composition was dated December 21, 1891, and includes end notes. Perhaps J. Williams wanted his poem to be on the official program, but had to settle for reading it to an interested audience after the Meeting's sessions had formally adjourned.[14]

The poem expressed fear that J. Williams's beloved country, which ought to be a place "Where man's progressive nature shall be free/ To strive for higher good immortally," contained abuses that contradicted these noble purposes and threatened the American dream. Despite "proud boasts" that "the Slave-curse has vanished from the land," the country faced a new slave power: "the robber 'Bulls and Bears,' ... the "gambling Millionaires/ Monopolists of money and of land." The laws excluding Chinese immigrants contradicted American Christians' boasts about their faith—now, J. Williams sarcastically declared, the Chinese "may learn how Christian faith is fraught/ With more of good than that Confucius taught." While the Chinese were unjustly kept out of the country, booze was unjustly let in—the poem rhetorically asked America, "Shall pauper making wines and brandies be/ Brought from all lands, unhindered, unto thee?/ While all thy ports are closed 'gainst poor humanity." Restrictive immigration laws "would have kept away/ Jesus and his disciples, in their day"—such laws would "disgrace/ A Russian despot." Perhaps alluding to the immigration debate in the Meeting, J. Williams asked if "freedom's Goddess" (perhaps meaning the recently completed Statue of Liberty) would, "when is reached thy vaunted open door/ Welcome the pauper rich, send back the pauper poor." In a prose endnote, J. Williams continued his diatribe: "The opponents of free immigration, if assembled in convention, would, no doubt adopt, as expressing their sense of Christian justice, the following resolutions. *Resolved*, first, that the earth is the Lord's. *Resolved*, second, that he has given it to his saints. *Resolved*, third, that we are his saints."[15]

According to the poem, women's suffrage would herald an era of Prohibition: "The true republic that is yet to be,/ Will rest on suffrage to both sexes free./ Then the saloon with all its ills shall die." Implicitly rebuking some of his fellow Progressive Friends who would enfranchise educated women while denying the ballot to the uneducated of both sexes, J. Williams declared: "'Tis unrestricted suffrage only can/ Securely hold the liberties of man."[16]

Mormons were persecuted for their polygamy, even though the Mormon's "life is as the Bible taught.... And wilt thou [America] in virtue's guise arrayed,/ When reason fails, ask persecution's aid?" In an endnote, J. Williams explained (in prose) that he did not advocate polygamy, which is "far below the highest idea of true marriage." However, at least "the social evil" (a euphemism for prostitution) was absent in Utah, and the abolition of polygamy would lead to its replacement by prostitution. Eliminating polygamy and prostitution would require "a change in our present social system." Persecution was not the answer.[17]

Naturally, J. Williams took a swipe at organized religion:

> —The Bible as a Fetich [fetish] we adore
> And send by thousands to each heathen shore,
> Yet all its highest teachings we ignore.
> For now with mightiest war-ships is the plan,
> To herald "peace on earth, good will to man." ...
> No Christian Church or nation lives to-day;
> All but the shadowy name has passed away.

In an endnote, J. Williams proclaimed: "The author challenges the world to refute this statement in a public discussion, either through the Press or on the platform."[18]

A weighty Friend named Henry S. Kent proposed a testimony on suffrage in the 1893 Progressive Friends meeting. This proposal rejected any distinctions in voting rights based on "the accident of sex, color, or nationality," and said that "virtue and intelligence" should be the only criteria on which the vote should be granted. To make sure that the virtuous and intelligent—of all sexes and colors—were the only ones with the vote, the resolution called for "the exclusion of crime and ignorance from the exercise of the franchise" and proposed that "every citizen be required to give evidence that he or she understands at least the rudiments of free govern-

10. Speaking His Mind

ment before the responsibility of the franchise can be safely entrusted to him."[19]

J. Williams made his opposition clear: "I have long advocated that people have the use of the elective franchise whether or not they are ignorant." Massachusetts had adopted a literary test for voters, and look what followed: "Mississippi had a bitter hatred against the former slaves, and thinking to deprive them of their rights followed the example of Massachusetts and enacted a similar law. They escaped the censure it would otherwise have brought upon them, by pointing to Massachusetts and saying 'why we are only following the example of Massachusetts.'" To J. Williams, "Russia is no more a despotism than is the United States so long as we disfranchise one individual unjustly. The principle is the same whether it be one or many." And where was the link between virtue and education? "Let us consider now who is responsible for the liquor traffic in the United States. Is it the low, degraded classes? Not at all. It is the judges of our courts—the educated judges who bring all this misery upon us." Indeed, Pennsylvania's high-license law, empowering judges to decide who would operate saloons, was by dry standards a failure. The judges gave liquor licenses to applicants who (as a later study found) were often backed by court and police officials, and other respectable people, even church officials. (There were also plenty of illegal liquor establishments that stayed open in exchange for well-placed bribes, though to prohibitionists, this simply meant there needed to be more laws and stricter enforcement.) To J. Williams, it wouldn't be necessary to disenfranchise anyone to get Prohibition, so long as women's suffrage was adopted: "If the women vote for the next hundred years, whether or not the men do, the world will be far better than it is to-day. The saloons and gambling hells will certainly be abolished if no other good is accomplished."[20]

Many in the Progressive Friends meeting, like J. Williams, were uncomfortable at the disenfranchisement provisions of the suffrage resolution, but were worried that rejection of the resolution would include rejection of women's suffrage, which the resolution also supported. So the Meeting agreed to vote on two new resolutions—the first one endorsed universal adult suffrage without literacy tests or other restrictions, while the second resolution simply ignored literacy tests and confined itself to condemning voting discrimination if based on "sex, color or nationality." This latter resolution passed, while the first one—for universal adult suffrage—failed, though J. Williams presumably voted for it. "This," proclaimed the minutes with seeming relief, "ended the discussion on this subject."[21]

Quaker Carpetbagger

Next up for debate was a subject which, for the Progressive Friends, was less controversial—the Prohibition question. A proposed resolution on the subject supported "making use of our ballots in such a way as shall strike the most effective blow for the total Prohibition of the liquor traffic in all its branches."[22]

J. Williams's contribution to the discussion was recorded in the minutes as follows:

> The first temperance tract was written in this country in 1818. Until that time it had always been advised to use liquor temperately as a medicine. If I could believe that it is useful for a medicine I should certainly believe that it is not harmful to use temperately. The time will come when total Prohibition must exist all over the country. In many counties of North Carolina where I am acquainted they have abolished licenses and having no other use for the jails and poor houses use them as granaries. The South and West will I think obtain total prohibition before Pennsylvania or New York. We are making immense progress, how ever.[23]

The temperance testimony was adopted unanimously.[24]

A resolution supporting practical and ethical education for the youth of the country gained J. Williams's support. J. Williams deplored the lack of practicality in much modern education. "We must learn to excel in little things. If we could all be Miltons or Newtons we would be of as little use as any nation on the face of the globe."[25]

Another resolution which would be to J. Williams's taste was on the financial question. The proposed testimony would read in part: "[F]or many years past the Financial Policy of our National Government by the contraction and manipulation of our circulating medium, has played into the hands of the monied few, and built up in this country a powerful money monopoly wholly at the expense of the industrial and producing classes which threatens, if not speedily changed, the peace and liberty of our whole people." The debate included some sallies by supporters of Henry George's Single Tax ideas; J. Williams affirmed his belief in the labor theory of value in evaluating land as well as anything else. The testimony on the financial question was postponed until the following year.[26]

In 1894, the financial resolution was again postponed for a year. The meeting did get to hear a speech from the celebrity reformer Henry George himself, with his "Single Tax" proposal for a tax on land. J. Williams, replying to George, got in an opportunity to speak about the financial issue after all: "I thank the gentleman for his excellent address, and it has much sound sense in it, but I think we may reach the same conclusion by another route. My idea is that Congress should pass a law giving us

10. Speaking His Mind

money at 2per cent, and using this to run the government. This would at once kill the 'bulls and bears.' No man or corporation of men could then monopolize money, because they could not possibly compete with the government, it being a stronger corporation than any monopoly can possibly be."[27] This was his program back from when he ran unsuccessfully for Congress from North Carolina in 1878.

Another prohibition resolution, which said the issue was "one of the most important and should be made the dominant issue of the hour," sparked discussion of the importance of prohibition compared to other reforms. An amendment, adopted 30–10, reclassified Prohibition as *a* dominant issue of the hour. J. Williams agreed that it was not *the* dominant issue, because of the importance of the issue of women's suffrage, which would in any case "naturally" lead to prohibition. "Woman suffrage is much stronger than the other issue, because if we were forming a new government the first question would be 'who shall have a voice in the government?'" As for the prohibition issue itself:

> There are eight counties in Pennsylvania where they have absolute Prohibition, and they have no use for their jails except as storehouses. In the South I have been where they have prohibition and it does prohibit. In Wyoming and Utah too they are ahead of us on this problem. We owe it to the most enlightened people of Chester county, that there is a saloon open in the county. Is it the poor foreigners who grant licenses? No, it is the honorable judges the very representatives of the intelligence of the county, who are asked for, and who grant the licenses. It is one of the most outrageous things imaginable, and the fugitive slave law was an inanity in comparison.

Here the minutes record J. Williams's remarks being met with applause. Later J. Williams elaborated on the importance of prohibition: "If we abolish the saloons we will be 1000 years nearer the millennium than we are with them. There is no question, unless it be that of woman suffrage which can begin to equal this one in importance." The amended prohibition resolution passed unanimously.[28]

In August 1894, J. Williams went blind. He still wanted to write articles for the local papers, so when he had something to write, he dictated it to Annie.[29]

In 1895, the Progressive Friends resolved to their satisfaction the much-postponed financial question, adopting a resolution saying that "no corporation should be allowed to issue money or control its volume and that all money should be issued by the national government and in sufficient volume to do the business of the country for cash." Noticeable by its absence from the records of the debate was the name of J. Williams

Thorne, which would mean that he wasn't there or that he could not speak—otherwise he would have contributed his bit to the debate on a subject near to his heart.[30]

As 1895 ended and J. Williams approached his 79th birthday, his health took a turn for the worse, and J. Williams's grandson Edgar sent Eugene a letter and a telegram asking Eugene to come to his father's bedside. Eugene, despite his earlier protestations, was still in North Carolina, working as a storekeeper in Henderson. Even now Eugene didn't want to leave North Carolina, writing Edgar that he was too busy to come north: "I know iff [sic] papa should drop off how hard it will be for Annie all alone." Eugene briefly gave some of the local news in North Carolina, adding, "Please excuse me for not coming up—give my love to Papa iff alive also Annie & Mary."[31]

Later that month—December 1895—Eugene wrote again, this time to Annie. Eugene had adopted a somewhat more empathetic tone—also, medical concerns seemed to have shifted from J. Williams to Edgar. Edgar had shown signs of mental illness—he had sent a letter that made Eugene worry about his condition. Now Edgar was apparently in Henderson. Eugene said Annie should "watch Edgar close he might harm his self ... iff Ed does not get better you had best take him to an asylum where he can have Special treatment for his trouble." Eugene might be able to come up north in February.[32]

One possible source of good cheer that Christmas was an apparent cash gift to Thorne from some of his friends. E. Clayton Walton, a Philadelphia businessman who sent the money, was almost apologetic, saying that he had simply planned to send his own gift and the other friends chipped in on their own initiative. Though "we may neither one feel the full significance attached to the day in a religious sense, yet I know we can take up the spirit of 'Peace on Earth' etc. & feel kindly toward all, which is the most important thing. Since spending that Sabbath day with thee, I have told several of thy friends of the very pleasant time I had & they wished to forward their good wishes & also contributed small amounts which I enclose in one piece."[33]

In a January 1896 article, J. Williams urged, as he had since at least 1878, that the federal government loan out money at 2 percent interest. "This money should be based on the relative commodity value of gold, silver, copper, iron, lead and the two principal varieties of coal.... This money, resting on the credit of the National Government for their face commodity value, would command it in any part of the civilized world,

10. Speaking His Mind

and take the place of bills of exchange, as being far more convenient ... the principal mines should be under control of the Government. Such control might or might not be necessary, but could be determined by a little experience." It was also necessary "to limit land holding to such a degree as shall render an injurious monopoly of it impossible." This would leave land "open to the free and equitable use of all." J. Williams humbly averred that his proposed system would be "the first truly honest financial system" which the world "has ever yet known," and an inspiration to other countries. J. Williams described how he had previously put forward his ideas in the *Lancaster Inquirer*, together with a challenge to "Hon. Marriott Brosius"—his congressional representative—"or any other competent person to meet me in the discussion of this question, either in the inquirer [sic] or on the platform. This challenge has thus far remained unanswered, which," J. Williams breezily declared, "I take to mean that no one has any objection to the new financial system as I have presented it."[34]

Edgar's mental issues were sufficiently worrisome that his family sent him to a mental hospital. By March, the doctors released him, believing that he had recovered sufficiently.[35]

Though he could not attend the Progressive Friends meeting for 1896, J. Williams began work on an address which could be read to the Meeting on his behalf. He did not finish the address, given his other business, his bad health, and his blindness.[36]

Annie wrote to J. Williams's sister Caroline Lippincott (formerly married to Washington Hanway), asking Caroline to come. Caroline wrote back sorrowfully from West Chester that she and her family were themselves too sick to come, but that in case "anything should take place," Joseph W. Passmore might be able to help bring everyone together. She added, "[D]ear Annie my sympathies are with you all, but nothing any one can do or say—is of any avail in this last sad hour that sooner or later comes to us all."[37]

Edgar left the family home, apparently without telling his mother and grandfather where he was going. In early March 1897 he wrote from Florida giving a vague account of working in various Southern locations and getting into some unspecified "trouble" in Mississippi. He wrote to ask his mother for the return of some money—apparently money he had earned, but which Annie was holding for him. When the letter reached the Thorne place in Lancaster county, Annie was away doing unspecified "nursing duties"—and perhaps looking for Edgar—so J. Williams forwarded Edgar's missive to Annie. Writing to Annie—or, rather, probably dictating to the teenage Ralph—J. Williams thought Annie should come back to the Thorne place and send the money from there. "Ralph has rede to me as well as he could still I feel a little in the dark in regard to what the great world is doing." This may have been J. Williams's last letter—he died on May 18.[38]

The next month, on "a beautiful, bright June day," the Longwood Progressive Friends Meeting met for its annual deliberations. In the afternoon, someone read a memorial resolution for J. Williams Thorne:

> He was a man sui generis. He furnished a factor in the constitution of the Longwood movement without which it could never be quite complete.... The sweetness of his temper, even under rebuke and rebuff was phenomenal. He could not be angered. Envy and strife and ill-will seemed to find no lodgment in his spirit.... From youth to ripe age his efforts of tongue and pen have been freely given to the cause of human progress ... during the nearly half century of the existence of this association he has faithfully done his part to promote its beneficent ends and keep it loyal to its original conception and first love, the struggle for freedom from every form of bondage, physical, social or ecclesiastical.... Of the accumulation of rubbish which the world calls wealth, he died poor; but in character, which is permanent riches, he has left to us, his survivors, a large estate.[39]

There was more. A member, F.A. Hinckley, read J. Williams's unfinished address, which was to have been read at the prior year's Meeting. J. Williams began with the "selfevident" remark that "the world does not belong to a few aristocratic individuals, but to all the people in it." From this he deduced several conclusions, starting from the idea that "the present constitution of society is on a false basis, and that this false social basis is the cause of almost all the crime and unhappiness which afflict human nature." Other conclusions followed, from free immigration to free trade in non-harmful goods. There should be a ban on "alcoholic liquors, or any commodity injurious to the health of the people." The states would soon have "something approaching universal suffrage." The "signs of the times" pointed to it. Misguided "educational aristocrats" would impose a literacy test for voting—yet all but three of the barons at Runnymede had been illiterate. It was "the educated classes" who were responsible for "all the despotisms inflicted on the world," while "uneducated British criminals" had made Australia and New Zealand "the most free and prosperous portions of the British Empire." On the international scene, settlement of disputes by arbitration and not war could soon become "an inviolable rule all over the world." Arbitration would also be a useful reform for the settlement of individual disputes, in place of the existing justice system: "Those who have had most experience in our so-called courts of justice, have found

10. Speaking His Mind

that in almost all cases their efforts to obtain justice, have been similar to those of sick persons taking poisons as remedial agents, the remedy in nearly all cases proving worse than the disease."[40]

And there Thorne's paper stopped. F.A. Hinckley said: "When all the people of the world are as earnestly devoted to the principles of honesty, temperance and peace as was J. Williams Thorne, we will have an infinitely better condition of things than exists to-day."

Epilogue

An obituary notice printed in several American papers (in whole or in part) briefly mentioned J. Williams's abolitionist and Underground Railroad activities, then added that he went to North Carolina on account of his "land interests" and ended up in the legislature. "During his membership in" the legislature, the obit continued, "he was most persistently and vigorously attacked by the southern members."[1] The reason for the persistent attacks was not mentioned, but the reader could infer that it had to do with J. Williams's racial egalitarianism, especially since it was the "southern members" of the legislature who attacked him. What the obituary meant by "southern members," in describing a legislature where J. Williams was the only "carpetbag" member, was not specified, though the writer may have been using "southerner" as shorthand for white southern Democrats.

D.T. Smithwick, a dentist and an official in the Sons of the American Revolution, married into J. Williams's family and wrote a letter, now at the Warren County Library, about J. Williams's experience in North Carolina. After coming to Warren County for the purpose of "upbuilding the South" ("they did try to teach negros in all the better ways of life"), J. Williams, in Smithwick's account, experienced misfortunes—loss of most of his property, his children mostly going "bad," their "farm implements & tools not suited to Southern farming." It was "a sad ending of a splendid people who came to us in love."[2]

H.G. Jones, curator of the North Carolina Collection at the University of North Carolina at Chapel Hill, published an article about J. Williams in 1977, and apparently did a version of the article for the Associated Press seven years later. Jones's articles gave a brief description of the expulsion proceedings in the House, as well as an explanation: "The case relating to Thorne was prejudiced against him from the beginning. After all, he was a 'carpetbagger,' a Republican, a vegetarian, a teetotaler, a poet, and a critic of evangelical religion."[3]

Epilogue

Eric Anderson's 1981 study of North Carolina's "Black Second" Congressional district during the late 19th century had some brief comments on J. Williams, most notably this one: "Born in Pennsylvania, Thorne was one of the few Republicans who lived up the Democratic caricatures of the reforming Yankee. He apparently actually practiced 'social equality' with Negroes, and as a member of the constitutional convention of 1875 was one of the three delegates to oppose a measure requiring separate schools for blacks and whites. He was a vegetarian, a believer in women's rights, and unorthodox in religion."[4]

Ward M. McAfee's 1998 study *Religion, Race, and Reconstruction* describes J. Williams's legislative expulsion as a manifestation of Southern evangelical Protestant intolerance, with ramifications for religious controversies then roiling the country. McAfee claims that J. Williams was without defenders, rejected by "traditional Quakers" as well as others. (In fact, Republicans generally came to J. Williams's defense, including the prominent North Carolina Quaker legislator Nereus Mendenhall.) Apropos of the Thorne case, McAfee suggests that that Republicans wanted "a movement with elements of a conservative (Protestant) evangelical religious crusade" that could reclaim some Southern votes from the Democrats—who were vulnerable because of the controversial support they gave to their large Catholic constituency. McAfee sees it as significant that a black legislator (Hanson Hughes) opposed J. Williams, calling Hughes one of Thorne's "leading accusers." (Hughes actually managed to avoid most of the debating and voting on J. Williams's expulsion, citing alleged family illness.[5])

At least J. Williams has not been without honor in his own native area. Mark E. Dixon, in a 2011 book profiling various "hidden" figures in Chester County history, devotes a five-page section to J. Williams. Local historians include J. Williams among the Underground Railroad conductors. A project celebrated by J. Williams, the People's Hall in Ercildoun, is still standing and maintained as a meeting place, but is in need of repairs.[6]

A table prepared in 2012 by the Research Division of the North Carolina General Assembly listed disciplinary actions that had historically been taken against members. J. Williams's 1875 expulsion was briefly described, but not the expungement of the proceedings against him in 1880.[7]

Historians give a brief nod to J. Williams's rescue of the free black man John Brown from kidnapping and slavery. Lucy Maddox's 2016 book on the Parker sisters' kidnapping mentions the Brown case and the burning of J. Williams's barn, though J. Williams is not referred to by name,

Epilogue

but simply as "John Brown's employer." The John Brown case is put in the context of the activities of the infamous Gap Gang of criminals.[8]

R.J.M. Blackett's *The Captive's Quest for Freedom*, a study focusing on fugitive slaves, includes a brief reference to the John Brown case as part of a discussion of the kidnapping of Pennsylvania's free blacks. J. Williams and his barn aren't mentioned.[9]

By the time of J. Williams's death, North Carolina Republicans had finally achieved their dream of overthrowing the Democrats in coalition with dissatisfied ex–Democrats. A "fusion" movement of Republicans and agrarian radicals took over the state and ran it for about half a decade. Democrats turned to racial appeals and violence to rally white support and drive blacks out of politics. Finally, Democrats secured power as they disenfranchised most black voters and brought most white voters back into Democratic ranks. The methods of disenfranchisement included a literacy test—which J. Williams had deplored in both Massachusetts and Mississippi—and from which illiterate whites were exempt through a "grandfather clause." J. Williams's call for universal suffrage, even for the poor and uneducated, had collapsed in his former adopted state.[10]

The Democratic resurgence in North Carolina actually helped promote one of J. Williams's other favorite reforms—prohibition. Fearful that prohibitionists would threaten Democratic dominance with yet another third-party movement, Democratic leaders began supporting statewide dry initiatives. In 1903 the Democratic legislature made most of the state's rural areas into legally dry enclaves. Meanwhile, with legislative authorization, many local communities awarded government-run stores a monopoly on the sale of liquor, which was not strictly in keeping with prohibition, but which did reduce the political influence of saloons and other private liquor sellers. In 1908, Democratic lawmakers ordered another referendum on statewide prohibition—and unlike the 1881 referendum, this one passed, largely because black voters, traditionally skeptical about prohibition, were no longer so numerous as before. The legislative package had some leaky exceptions, but North Carolina was now officially in the Dry column.[11]

Tar Heel drys, as members of the Democratic coalition, turned their attention to closing loopholes, increasing enforcement, and ratifying national Prohibition. The collapse of national Prohibition also signaled the collapse of state prohibition, as local communities were again empowered to set up government-run liquor stores, and did so.[12]

J. Williams's dream of a dry millennium had even more difficulty in

Epilogue

Pennsylvania, which one wet periodical called "the Gibraltar of the liquor traffic." The drys—now under the leadership of the Anti-Saloon League, a heavily Protestant organization—made no attempt at statewide prohibition, and attempted instead to gain a formal restoration of the local option system, which had been abolished in 1875 by a wet legislature. Formal local option was never approved, but in some rural counties a *de facto* local option was instituted by electing dry judges and successfully petitioning them to deny all liquor-license applications, under the law of 1878. By the First World War, Pennsylvania jumped on the bandwagon for national Prohibition, and passed its own enforcement laws. A national magazine wasn't impressed, referring to Pennsylvania during Prohibition as a "bootlegger's Elysium." With the end of federal Prohibition, this Gibraltar/Elysium state was officially wet again. North Carolina's and Pennsylvania's experiences, in various forms and permutations, were repeated throughout the country, and J. Williams's vision of liquor chased out of society by law was dashed.[13]

J. Williams would have been interested, though not amused, to see his beloved temperance crusade saddled with a label he would have hated—"conservative." For instance, historian Stephen Prothero includes a chapter on prohibition in his book *Why Liberals Win the Culture Wars*. Prothero portrays the prohibition movement as a conservative crusade, one of many such crusades defeated by "liberals."[14]

In fact, to J. Williams, the prohibition crusade was linked to another favorite cause—votes for women. Many woman suffrage supporters (like J. Williams) hoped, and many wets feared, that women voting meant dry victories. The adoption of the Nineteenth Amendment guaranteeing women's suffrage, the year after the Eighteenth Amendment enacting Prohibition, would have been seen by J. Williams as an equal cause of rejoicing. He would have been disappointed at how the repeal of national Prohibition was helped when influential women turned against it.[15]

The disenfranchised black citizens of Warren County suffered from their loss of political power. In Norlina, near Warrenton, a dispute between a black customer and a white storeowner led to the lynching of two black men, including the one who had argued with the clerk. A confrontation later ensued between white and black mobs, in which the white clerk was shot and wounded. Matthew Bullock, the brother of the clerk's lynched adversary, was charged with attempted murder of the clerk. When Matthew Bullock fled to Canada and was arrested there, the NAACP got involved, and a sympathetic Canadian magistrate, to the applause of the

Epilogue

Canadian press, released Bullock. The governor of North Carolina said he would not send witnesses to testify in Canada: "[H]e did not propose to send reputable white men to a foreign country to bandy words with 'nigger societies.'" Bullock seems to have kept a low profile thereafter.[16] It took time for blacks' constitutional right to vote to be restored in North Carolina and the rest of the South.

The causes of integrated public schools and the right to interracial marriage had been so controversial in 1875 that J. Williams had been joined by only one or two other state Constitutional Convention delegates in championing those causes. Even most Republican and black delegates refused to back him up. The right to integrated education and interracial marriage were recognized by the U.S. Supreme Court in 1954 and 1967, respectively.[17]

Nowadays, someone in Thorne's position, expelled from a state legislature for an allegedly blasphemous pamphlet, would probably be reinstated fairly quickly by the courts. Three decisions of the U.S. Supreme Court point strongly in that direction. A decision in 1952 prevented the states from censoring allegedly blasphemous material. A Maryland case decided in 1961 declared the right of atheists and other religious dissidents to hold public office. And a ruling in 1966 affirmed that a state legislature could not exclude a member for exercising his First Amendment rights (the protagonist of the latter case was Julian Bond, son of Lincoln University President Horace Mann Bond, whom we shall see shortly).[18]

One of J. Williams's stances was that the 1851 violence in Christiana, in which a slaveholder was killed trying to recover his "property" with federal assistance, was an example of heroic resistance by slaves to their oppressors. It took some time for the official mainstream to come around to the views of abolitionists like J. Williams concerning the Christiana events of 1851. When officialdom and the Lancaster Historical Society commemorated the 60th anniversary in 1911, a moral-equivalence view was in vogue. On a rainy September 9, various dignitaries, including the governor of Pennsylvania, spoke at the base of a proposed obelisk commemorating the "riots." The obelisk, through a snafu, had not been delivered, but when it was installed on the actual anniversary (September 11), it had a list of the defendants on one side, as well as declarations on adjoining sides that Edward Gorsuch had "died for law" while Castner Hanway "suffered for freedom." A descendant of Gorsuch, and a surviving black "rioter," each received special medallions produced by the Philadelphia Mint.[19]

Complicating the ceremonies was a crime that had stained Chester

Epilogue

County in the previous month. In August 1911, Edgar Rice, a white steel-company policeman who formerly worked for the county, encountered Zachariah Walker, a black steelworker from the South who had used his day off to go barhopping and was reportedly drunk and disorderly (the encounter took place on the public roads, but apparently with the importance of the new and influential steel mills, Rice felt at liberty to walk his old beat despite his private status). When the encounter, in the vicinity of Coatesville, was over, Walker had shot Rice to death and the authorities took Walker, who had been injured, to the hospital. An angry mob removed Walker from the hospital, dragged him to a farm in East Fallowfield, and burned him alive. This lynching, in J. Williams's old stomping grounds, was recalled by the speakers at the Christiana commemoration. Governor John K. Tener and the local Congressman used their speeches to condemn the lynching and promise punishment for the perpetrators. In fact, prosecutions of several alleged lynch-mob members resulted in a string of not-guilty verdicts, with nobody being convicted.[20]

The centennial celebrations of Christiana in 1951 at first seemed to have a similar moral-equivalence focus between the slavehunters defending "law" and the resisters defending "freedom." However, the final speech at the event, by Lincoln University President Horace Mann Bond, turned the focus onto William Parker, the leader of the resistance, and emphasized his heroic role, with implied parallels to the reemerging civil rights movement of the time.[21]

By the 2001 commemoration, the focus was unambiguously on J. Williams's theme of heroic resistance, with the Christiana clash, in the course of elaborate sesquicentennial ceremonies, placed in the context of the black struggle for equality and justice.[22]

A few more of J. Williams's causes may be mentioned in connection with their modern fate. Banks, and the "bulls and bears" of the stock market, continue to exist. Arbitration has not caught on as a substitute for war. Vegetarians are numerous enough to form an influential market. Tobacco is socially less and less acceptable. Christians and non–Christians—when so inclined—continue to clash.

It is virtually inevitable that any discussion of J. Williams will include the term "gadfly." Is there any word which sums him up better? For most of his life, though staying in southeastern Pennsylvania to farm, he "thought globally and acted locally"—discussing the issues of the day with his neighbors and with those who came from remote parts of the country to take part in the Progressive Friends meetings in J. Williams's own

Epilogue

locality. He helped the fugitive slaves who came to his neighborhood, and fought against the "reverse underground railroad" that kidnapped local free blacks into slavery. After moving to North Carolina, he tried to be active both there and in Pennsylvania, promoting quite a variety of causes popular with postwar "Liberals" or radicals. For a few years he was popular enough with Warren County's black population to be elected by them to several positions, though the established black politicians did not seem to like the interloper, and his political star eventually fell. Without good connections, and with too much of a tendency to be voluble in controversial causes, he couldn't get a federal patronage job, which he seemed to yearn to do as financial security eluded him despite his hard work as a farmer. Family misfortunes brought him back to Pennsylvania for good, where he apparently became accepted as a local "character." Those who knew him best commented on his constant cheerfulness and optimism, even in situations that did not make for much optimism.

When history didn't come to him, he came to it. The history to which he came, or which came to him, was sufficiently dramatic that J. Williams Thorne's life is worth reading about.

Appendix I
Memorial Resolution on J. Williams Thorne Adopted by the Progressive Friends Meeting, Longwood, 1897

All who have been accustomed to attend the "Longwood Yearly Meeting of Progressive Friends" will now notice a vacant place on the front seat in the body of this house. The venerable form of J. Williams Thorne on whose head nature had placed her white coronal, is not here.

In thinking and speaking of him we cannot move in the memorial rut.

He was a man sui generis. He furnished a factor in the constitution of the Longwood movement without which it could never be quite complete.

But withal his was a character made up of a throng of glorious qualities.

The sweetness of his temper, even under rebuke and rebuff was phenomenal. He could not be angered. Envy and strife and ill-will seemed to find no lodgment in his spirit. "He loved his fellow men, his blows fell only on their crimes." His well stored mind covering a wide range of subjects, and his retentive memory made him available and valuable in the pursuit of truth.

From youth to ripe age his efforts of tongue and pen have been freely given to the cause of human progress.

He stood in the strength of his years in the forefront of the fierce moral crusade against chattel slavery. The creeds of the churches were all too narrow for him, but on the broad platform of the Progressive Friends he found room to stand; and during the nearly half century of the existence of this association he has faithfully done his part to promote its beneficent ends and keep it loyal to its original conception and first love, the struggle for freedom from every form of bondage, physical, social or ecclesiastical.

Appendix I

He had no part with dogmatic theology, but he had unbounded faith in the upward tendencies and the divine destiny of man.

Of the accumulation of rubbish which the world calls wealth, he died poor; but in character, which is permanent riches, he has left to us, his survivors, a large estate.

Appendix II
J. Williams Resorts to Satire to Defend What He Considers the Principles of a True Republic, 1877

Undated leaflet from the Thorne family papers. This describes state Senator J. Williams Thorne's unsuccessful efforts to defend his vision of universal suffrage and justice for the poor in North Carolina. This was presumably in early 1877.

RESOLUTIONS INTRODUCED BY
J. WILLIAMS THORNE, SENATOR FROM WARREN.
Resolutions.

Some time ago I introduced into the Senate a series of resolutions based on the true republican principle that "all just powers of government are derived from the consent of the governed." These resolutions the Senate refused to pass, and indefinitely postponed them. I then introduced another series of resolutions of a directly opposite character. These were, if anything, still more distasteful than the former, and the Senate refused to accept them. The first series has already been published. I now publish both series in juxtaposition. The public will then be able to see how very difficult it is, to adapt resolutions to the fastidious taste of legislators.

J. WILLIAMS THORNE.

DECLARATORY OF THE EQUALITY BEFORE THE LAW OF THE WHITE AND COLORED RACES.

WHEREAS, It is self evident that social law is above all other law,[1] and never was nor ever can be, the creature of legislation; and,

WHEREAS, Social equality and equality before the law have no necessary dependence on each other; and,

Appendix II

WHEREAS, In a truly republican government, in the language of our State Constitution, "All political power is vested in, and derived from the people; all government of right originates from the people, is founded upon their will only, is instituted solely for the good of the whole." And,

WHEREAS, The same Constitution further reminds us, that "a frequent recurrence to fundamental principles is absolutely necessary to preserve the blessings of liberty"; therefore,

The General Assembly of North Carolina do resolve, That dwelling no longer on the past of the State, whether for the weal or the woe of its people, but looking hopefully forward to such vitally important legislative reforms, as must mould for us a grand future of harmonious freedom, greatness and stability of government, we accept and reaffirm as the only just basis of legislation, the great axiomatic declaration of Thomas Jefferson, that "all just powers of government are derived from the consent of the governed."

2. That in full accord with this unimpeachable declaration, and bound by our oaths of office to represent justly the whole people, and to guard and protect with unfaltering firmness their equal rights before the law, we hereby declare and affirm our determined resolution, never to give encouragement or consent to any form of legislation that has for its object the abridgement of the right of suffrage or the annulment of the voice of any class of our people as a governing power.

3. That, recognizing and accepting as we do, the wise words of a wise law giver of old, "that the best form of government is that in which an injury done to the least and weakest member of it, is felt to be an injury to all,"[2] we will, in all our acts of legislation, guard and protect with jealous watchfulness, the laboring poor, of whatever race or color not only in the exercise of their political rights, but against the monopolizing grasp of avaricious power; thus adopting and reaffirming the noble and just declaration of John C. Calhoun, that "they, who dig the wealth from the soil, have a right to it against the universe."

4. Not recognizing a necessity for the subversion or destruction of the political rights of any one class of citizens, that another may have relief from real or imaginary oppression; but believing, as we do, that simply justice done to all classes, will be found to be the only full and efficient relief to all, we can never consent to legislate from the poor and weak, either directly or indirectly, those fundamental principles of a true republic that constitute their representative and suffrage power—the only efficient and

sure protection they can have against encroachment on their rights by the rich and strong.

RESOLUTIONS OF
J. WILLIAMS THORNE.
SENATOR FROM WARREN,
Declaratory of the Inequality before the Law of the various Classes and Races.

WHEREAS, It is self-evident that social law is not above all statute law, but for the purpose of preventing unequal, improper and degrading association of the lower with the higher classes of society, may be, and frequently is the creature of legislation; and,

WHEREAS, When a distinguished Senator so eloquently declared that social law is not coequal with, nor above divine law, he must have meant, that when Jesus taught by precept and example, that the poor and ignorant were, at least, as good and socially as worthy of recognition, as the wealthy and educated, he intended to inculcate the rightfulness of such association, only in a religious sense, and not as an applicable guide for the enlightened modern states men. And,

WHEREAS, The golden rule, "do unto others as you would have others do unto you," was never intended as a rule of life for individuals of different classes, but only for people of the same class. And,

WHEREAS, Association is, usually, the result of artificial enforcement, rather than of natural affinity. And,

WHEREAS, The social and political welfare of the wealthy and educated classes, will be greatly endangered, if they are to have no more civil and political rights than the poor and ignorant. And,

Whereas, The experience of all mankind in all ages, has abundantly shown, that there can be no safety for the wealthy and educated classes, where the poor and ignorant are their coequals in political power. And,

WHEREAS, the best form of government is not as the old Greek law-giver declared, "that, in which an injury done to the least and weakest member of it, is felt to be an injury to all"; but that in which the wealthy and educated classes are best protected in the tenure of their property and governing power, and in which the ignorant laboring poor are best subordinated and controlled. And,

WHEREAS, Justinian and Blackstone have declared as an axiomatic principle that all law not founded in justice, is null and void. And,

Appendix II

WHEREAS, The practical administration of such a principle in government can only be beneficial to the poor and laboring classes; while it must endanger the prosperity of the wealthy. And,

WHEREAS, In the eloquent language of one of South Carolina's most distinguished sons, the declaration of Thomas Jefferson, that "all men are created equal," is a mere "rhetorical flourish," having no foundation in truth.[3] And,

WHEREAS, The first section of the first article of our State Constitution, is but an amplified embodiment of the same senseless declaration, of impossible application in any system of government and having no practical influence on legislation. And,

WHEREAS, Jefferson's other declaration that "all just powers of government are derived from the consent of the governed," puts the governing power into the hands of the poor and ignorant many, who are not sufficiently interested in the welfare and happiness of the wealthy and educated few. And,

WHEREAS, If he could have foreseen the unhappy condition of the wealthy and educated classes in the Eastern Counties of North Carolina, brought about by his unfortunate declaration, he would have blotted it out of existence, and never raised either voice or hand in behalf of what he deemed the oppressed and unrepresented colonies. And,

WHEREAS, A learned and eloquent Senator has justly characterized the high-sounding declaration of that eminent statesman, John C. Calhoun, that "they who dig the wealth from the soil have a right to it against the universe," as "neither true in law nor in fact." And,

WHEREAS, If it were made true, both in law and in fact, there would, at once, be inaugurated such a mighty social revolution that the very foundations of society would be broken up and the very rich, as well as the very poor, so necessary to the welfare and happiness of each other, would vanish and be seen no more in the land. Therefore,

That General Assembly of North Carolina do resolve: That, rejecting the glittering generalities of the Declaration of Independence about the "equal rights of all men," as self-evidently false in theory, and impossible in practice; and believing, as we do, that the only safe and proper governing power of a nation, is in its wealth and intelligence, we hereby declare and affirm our determined resolution, to legislate as far as possible, the governing power of the State, out of the hands of the uneducated, ignorant poor, and into the hands of its wealthy and educated people.

2. That we do this in the highest and best interests of all classes, fully

J. Williams Resorts to Satire

assured, as we are that the rich and strong are the natural protectors and proper guardians of the poor and weak. In the terse and apt language of Goldsmith:

A "just experience tells in every soil,
"That those who think must govern those who toil."

3. That the history of all civilized nations conclusively shows that a true republic—a government founded on the suffrages of all the governed—is about the worst form of government ever devised for people of Wealth, education and culture.

4. That we shall never cease to regret the rash and hasty separation we made in 1776 from our good old mother country, England, where the poor, without complaint, are content to labor for the glory and aggrandizement of the rich.

5. That we rejoice "with exceeding great joy," in the long wished for power, now in our hands, to relieve the State of its present odious elective county government, and to substitute therefor one modeled closely after our favorite aristocratic English system, which has worked so long and so well, and with such entire satisfaction to all the wealthy and educated people of that great and enlightened nation.

Chapter Notes

Chapter 1

1. John W. Moore, *History of North Carolina: From the Earliest Discoveries to the Present Time*, Vol. 2 (Raleigh: Alfred Williams & Co., 1880), 413.
2. J. Williams Thorne, *North Carolina in the 19th Century: The Great Ecclesiastical Trial of J. Williams Thorne, Representative from Warren County, Who Was Expelled for Opinion Sake, by the House of Representatives of North Carolina, on February 24, 1875*, 42; House Journal, 1874–75, 432, 460–61, 465.
3. Edward King, *The Great South* (Hartford: American Publishing Company, 1875), i–ii, 469.
4. *Great South*, 468.
5. *Great South*, 468.
6. *Great South*, 469.
7. "The Ecclesiastical Court," *Raleigh News*, February 24, 1875, 1; "Expelling a Member," *Raleigh Daily Sentinel*, February 24, 1875, 2.

Chapter 2

1. William K. Klingaman and Nicholas P. Klingaman, *The Year Without Summer: 1816 and the Volcano That Darkened the World and Changed History* (New York: St. Martin's Press, 2013), 86, 152, 193, 195, 237.
2. Klingaman and Klingaman, 1–16.
3. Sadsbury Monthly Meeting records, October (Tenth Month) 7, 1814, courtesy of Ancestry.com; *Fallowfield Friends' Meeting House Ercildoun Pennsylvania One Hundredth Anniversary* (Anniversary Committee: 1911), 41; *Rules of Discipline of the Yearly Meeting of Friends, Held In Philadelphia* (Philadelphia: Kimber, Conrad & Co., 1806), 44–45. Joseph Williams Thorne's letter to his mother, January ("1st mo.") 10, 1834, identifies her as "Margaret" on the envelope. Letter courtesy of Nancy Plumley.
4. Genealogical chart, provided to the author by Nancy Plumley.
5. Envelope enclosing letter from Joseph Thorne to his mother, January ("1st mo.") 10, 1834, Thorne, "Westtown School," courtesy of Nancy Plumley. The 1830 and 1840 census records for Joseph Thorne the elder are obtainable at FamilySearch.org. Distances estimated from Google Maps. The Find A Grave Web site indicates that Joseph Jonathan Thorne and Margaretta Thorne are buried in the Fallowfield Meeting cemetery. Matlack says that Joseph J. Thorne was known as "Joseph Thorne of Fallowfield, as a means of distinguishment from two others of the same name, his uncle Joseph living in New Jersey, and his cousin, a doctor of Philadelphia." J. Chalkley Matlack, unpublished manuscript on the Thorne family, courtesy of Nancy Plumley, 17.
6. George Johnston, *The Poets and Poetry of Chester County Pennsylvania* (Phladelphia: J.P. Lippincott, 1890), 258.
7. "Boyhood Memories," *The Children's Friend*, May 1868, in Matlack, 27–29.
8. Matlack, 17.
9. William Jones, "Rekindling the Spark of Liberty: Lafayette's Visit to the United States 1824–25," November 2007, http://www.schillerinstitute.org/educ/hist/lafayette.html; Douglas R. Harper, *West Chester to 1865: That Elegant and Notorious Place* (West Chester, PA: Chester County Historical Society, 1999), 263–65.

171

Chapter Notes—2

10. "The Sheep Washing," *The Children's Friend*, May 1868, in Matlack, 24–27.

11. Stanley Harrold, *Border War: Fighting over Slavery before the Civil War* (Chapel Hill: University of North Carolina Press, 2010), 28; "What Right Had a Fugitive Slave of Self-Defence against His Master?" *The Pennsylvania Magazine of History and Biography* 13, No. 1 (April 1889): 106–109; H. Robert Baker, *Prigg v. Pennsylvania: Slavery, the Supreme Court and the Ambivalent Constitution* (Lawrence: University Press of Kansas, 2012), 74–75.

12. Carol Wilson, *Freedom at Risk: The Kidnapping of Free Blacks in America, 1780–1865* (Lexington: University Press of Kentucky, 1994), 10; Harrold, 2; Julie Winch, "Philadelphia and the Other Underground Railroad," *The Pennsylvania Magazine of History and Biography* 111, No. 1 (January 1987): 3–25. The work of Mason and Dixon is discussed in Edwin Danson, *Drawing the Line: How Mason and Dixon Surveyed the Most Famous Border In America* (New York: John Wiley and Sons, 2001). For Judge Darlington, see Harper, 193–94.

13. Beverly C. Tomek, *Pennsylvania Hall: A "Legal Lynching" in the Shadow of the Liberty Bell* (New York: Oxford University Press, 2014), 6–7; Arthur Zilversmit, *The First Emancipation: The Abolition of Slavery in the North* (Chicago: University of Chicago Press, 1967), 124–37, 162–64.

14. Baker, 48–52; Harrold, 21–22.

15. Baker, 73–79.

16. Dumas Malone, *The Public Life of Thomas Cooper, 1783–1839* (Columbia: University of South Carolina Press, 1961).

17. H. Larry Ingle's *Quakers in Conflict: The Hicksite Reformation* (Knoxville: The University of Tennessee Press, 1986), gives a detailed account of the split between the Hicksites and the Orthodox. "Fallowfield Monthly Meeting was established in 1811 by Western Quarterly Meeting out of London Grove Monthly Meeting. The Orthodox branch of this monthly meeting was discontinued in 1838, and its members were transferred to London Grove Monthly Meeting (Orthodox). Fallowfield Monthly Meeting (Hicksite) was the forerunner of the current Fallowfield Monthly Meeting of Friends." Fallowfield Monthly Meeting finding aid, http://web.tricolib.brynmawr.edu/speccoll/mm/fallomm.xml. The Find A Grave Web site records Joseph W. Thorne's parents as being buried in the Fallowfield Burying Ground belonging to what was the Hicksite Monthly Meeting.

18. J. Williams Thorne, "A Sketch of Old Westtown School. As It was Fifty Years Ago Compared With Its Beauty of To-day. A Wonderful Seat of Learning," *Village Record* (article datelined July 5, 1892; clipping in possession of Nancy Plumley, copy in possession of author); "A List of Students at Westtown School from 1799 to 1872. Males," in Watson W. DeWees, *A Brief History of Westtown Boarding School with a General Catalogue of Officers, Students, etc.* (Philadelphia: Sherman and Company, 1872), 112; Watson W. DeWees and Sarah B. DeWees, *Centennial History of Westtown Boarding School 1799–1899* (Philadelphia: Westtown Alumni Association, 1899), 102–03, 108; "Report of the Westtown Boarding School Committee," April 14, 1837, Friends Historical Collection, Swarthmore (online access); "History," https://www.westtown.edu/page.cfm?p=524 ("Non-Quakers were admitted for the first time in 1933...").

19. Ingle, 195; Bruce Dorsey, "Friends Becoming Enemies: Philadelphia benevolence and the neglected era of American Quaker History," *Journal of the Early Republic* (Fall 1998): 395–428, at 419–20; DeWees and DeWees, *Centennial History*, 101.

20. Thorne, "Westtown School," DeWees and DeWees, 94–95; "Report of the Westtown Boarding School Committee."

21. Thorne, "Westtown School."

22. J.W. Thorne to his mother, January ("1st mo.") 10, 1834; Thorne, "Westtown School."

23. Nancy Plumley, genealogical notes for the Thorne family, in author's possession.

24. Thorne, "Westtown School."

25. Thorne, "Westtown School."

26. North Carolina Constitution of 1776, Art. XXXII, http://avalon.law.yale.edu/18th_century/nc07.asp; Leon Hühner, "The Struggle for Religious Liberty

in North Carolina, with Special Reference to the Jews," *Publications of the American Jewish Historical Society* 16 (1907): 37–71, at 46–52, 68–71; Ira Rosenswaike, "Further Light on Jacob Henry," in Leonard Dinnerstein and Mary Dale Palson, eds., *Jews in the South* (Baton Rouge: Louisiana State University Press, 1973), 47–51; Leonard Rogoff, *Down Home: Jewish Life in North Carolina* (Jewish Heritage Foundation of North Carolina, 2010), 39–44; Edward Eitches, "Maryland's 'Jew Bill,'" *American Jewish Historical Quarterly* (September 1970–June 1971): 258–78; "Speech of H.M. Brackenridge," in H.M. Brackenridge, ed., *Speeches on the Jew Bill* (Philadelphia, 1829), 59–100, at 90–91. A later edition of the book Brackenridge relied on may have been Samuel Clark, ed., *The American Orator. Selected Chiefly from American Authors; for the Use of Schools and Private Families* ("Gardiner. Printed at the Intelligencer Office" (copyright registered in the federal district court of Maine), 1828), 46–49.

27. Christopher Densmore, "Be Ye Therefore Perfect: Anti-Slavery and the Origins of the Yearly Meeting of Progressive Friends in Chester County, Pennsylvania," *Quaker History* 93, No. 2 (Fall 2004): 28–46, at 34; Albert J. Wahl, "Longwood Meeting: Public Forum for the American Democratic Faith," *Pennsylvania History: A Journal of Mid-Atlantic Studies* 42, No. 1 (January 1975): 42–69, at 45; "The Call for a Convention," *National Enquirer*, December 30, 1836, 59; Tomek, 60–61.

28. Tomek, 60–61; *National Enquirer*, February 27, 1837, 78; *National Enquirer*, March 18, 1837, 1–2. The East Fallowfield Antislavery Society resolutions are dated "Third Mo. (March)," in the Quaker style of designating months by number, indicating the overlap between the Fallowfield antislavery group and the local Quakers.

29. *National Enquirer*, April 29, 1837, 25.

30. *Pennsylvania Freeman*, March 15, 1838; Roland H. Woodwell, *John Greenleaf Whittier: A Biography* (Haverhill, MA: Trustees of the John Greenleaf Whittier Homestead, 1985), 103–06.

31. "Communications," *Pennsylvania Freeman*, March 15, 1838.

32. Woodwell, 106–09; "Governor Joseph Ritner," http://www.phmc.state.pa.us/portal/communities/governors/1790-1876/joseph-ritner.html; Edward Price, "The Black Voting Rights Issue in Pennsylvania, 1780–1900," *The Pennsylvania Magazine of History and Biography* 100, No. 3 (July 1976), 356–73, at 356–63. For a detailed account of the burning of Pennsylvania Hall, see Tomek.

33. Jesse Kersey, *A Narrative of the Early Life, Travels and Gospel Labor of Jesse Kersey, late of Chester County, Pennsylvania* (Philadelphia: T. Ellwood Chapman, 1851), 42, 44–45, 83–87, 91, 96, 112, 121, 136, 282–83; "A Paraphrase of a Sermon by Jesse Kersey, an eminent Minister of the Society of Friends," in J. Williams Thorne, *North Carolina in the 19th Century*. As will be seen in a later chapter, Joseph showed this poem as evidence that he was not an atheist. The same poem (with a few minor differences) is published in Johnston, *Poets and Poetry of Chester County*, 258–59, under the title "NATURE PROMPTING TO DEVOTION" and without any mention of Kersey.

34. Kersey, 133.

35. Thomas D. Hamm, "George F. White and Hicksite Opposition to the Abolitionist Movement," in Brycchan Carey and Geoffrey Plank, *Quakers and Abolition* (Urbana: University of Illinois Press, 2014), 43–55, at 46.

36. Hamm, op. cit. For an example of the disownment policy, see *Rules of Discipline of the Yearly Meeting of Friends*, 73–74.

37. 1840 census records for Joseph Thorne the elder available at FamilySearch.com.

38. *Pennsylvania Freeman*, June 30, 1841, cited in Harrold, 106, 237, n27.

Chapter 3

1. E. Fuller Torrey, *The Martyrdom of Abolitionist Charles Torrey* (Baton Rouge: Louisiana State University Press, 2013), 78–79.

2. Baker, 101, 108–10, 112–24.

3. Baker, 140–49.

4. In my analysis of southeastern Pennsylvania's black community, I relied

on Carl Douglas Oblinger, "New Freedoms, Old Miseries: The Emergence and Disruption of Black Communities in Southeastern Pennsylvania, 1780–1960" (Ph.D. diss., Lehigh Universtity, 1988).

5. Reinhard O. Johnson, *The Liberty Party 1840–1848: Antislavery Third-Party Politics in the United States* (Baton Rouge: Louisiana State University Press, 2009), 5; Manisha Sinha, *The Slave's Cause: A History of Abolition* (New Haven: Yale University Press, 2016), 220–27; Carol Faulkner, *Lucretia Mott's Heresy: Abolition and Women's Rights in Nineteenth Century America* (Philadelphia: University of Pennsylvania Press, 2011), 64–66; Woodwell, 67–68.

6. Richard H. Sewell, *Ballots for Freedom: Antislavery Politics in the United States 1837–1860* (New York: W.W. Norton, 1980), 24–29; Faulkner, 69–70, 107–08; Ralph Volney Harlow, *Gerrit Smith: Philanthropist and Reformer* (New York: Henry Holt and Company, 1939), 154–56, 158; Torrey, 1–19, 49–53.

7. Sewell, 43–106; Johnson, 36–47; Torrey, 54–65, Harlow, 146–72.

8. Johnson, 153–54, 298; Faulkner, 108; Densmore, 28–46, at 30–31, 33; *National Anti-Slavery Standard*, November 28, 1844, 3.

9. Dorothy Sterling, *Ahead of Her Time: Abby Kelley and the Politics of Antislavery* (New York: W.W. Norton, 1991), 104–05, 172–73, 179, 186–87, 188–89, 190, 192, 196–202; *National Anti-Slavery Standard*, December 12, 1844, 4; *ibid.*, December 29, 1844, 3.

10. *National Anti-Slavery Standard*, December 29, 1844, 3; *ibid.*, January 2, 1845, 3; Densmore, 33.

11. "Letter from Mr. Pennock," *National Anti-Slavery Standard*, February 6, 1845, 2; Densmore, 34; Clara Marshall, *The Women's Medical College of Pennsylvania. An Historical Outline* (Philadelphia: B. Blackiston, Son & Co., 1897), 10; "Dr. Bartholomew Fussell," https://www.findagrave.com/memorial/75892887/bartholomew-fussell; "Dr. Edwin Fussell," https://www.findagrave.com/memorial/91907565/edwin-fussell.

12. "Letter from Mr. Pennock"; Densmore, 34.

13. Densmore, 34–35.
14. Densmore, 35.
15. Densmore, 35.
16. Densmore, 35; People's Hall Web site, http://www.peoples-hall.org/; John Milton, *Areopagitica*, https://www.dartmouth.edu/~milton/reading_room/areopagitica/text.html; Thorne, *Ecclesiastical Trial*, 37.
17. Thorne, "Ecclesiastical Trial," 37–39.
18. Densmore, 33.
19. Densmore, 35–36.
20. Genealogical table of Pusey family, courtesy of Nancy Plumley; information from Ancestry.com.
21. Chester County Agriculture Society, 1858 Report, in *Report of the Transactions of the State Agricultural Society, for the Years 1861-62-63*, Vol. 6 (Harrisburg, PA: Singerly & Myers, State Printers, 1863), 317.
22. Chester County Agricultural Society report, 317–18.
23. Genealogical Chart, Joseph Williams Thorne, courtesy of Nancy Plumley. For the time of Caleb's birth, see chapter 6.
24. Harper, *West Chester*, 346.
25. R.J. Houston, "Recollections of J. Williams Thorne. A Very Pleasing Account of a Philosopher and General Scholar," *Lancaster Examiner*, letter dated May 22, 1897, clipping in Thorne family papers.
26. Asa Earl Martin, "The Temperance Movement in Pennsylvania Prior to the Civil War," *The Pennsylvania Magazine of History and Biography* 49, No. 3 (1925): 195–230, at 216; Harper, *West Chester*, 616–17; Harry M. Chalfant, *Father Penn and John Barleycorn* (Harrisburg, PA: The Evangelical Press, 1920), 74–75; Joshua L. Baily, "Give Us Something Permanent," in J.N. Stearns, ed., *The Constitutional Prohibitionist, or Prohibition by the People* (New York: National Temperance Society and Publication House, 1887), 11.
27. Thomas D. Morris, *Free Men All: The Personal Liberty Laws of the North, 1780–1861* (Baltimore: Johns Hopkins University Press, 1974), 117–19.
28. Morris, 118–19.
29. Milt Diggins, *Stealing Freedom Along the Mason-Dixon Line: Thomas McCreary, the Notorious Slave-Catcher from Maryland* (Baltimore: Maryland Historical Society, 2015), 7–10.

30. Diggins, 11–12.
31. Diggins, 24–25; Ralph Clayton, *Cash for Blood: The Baltimore to New Orleans Domestic Slave Trade* (Bowie, MD: Heritage Books, 2002), 112–14.
32. Diggins, 26–42.
33. Diggins, 25–26, 33–37.
34. Diggins, 21, 23, 31, 35–38.
35. R.C. Smedley, *History of the Underground Railroad in Chester County and the Neighboring Counties* (Lancaster, PA: Printed by John A. Hiestand, 1883), 131–32; "Fugitive Slave Act of 1850," http://avalon.law.yale.edu/19th_century/fugitive.asp.
36. Smedley, 67–68; Thomas Whitson, Esq. (not the same Thomas Whitson), "The Early Abolitionists of Lancaster County," *Journal of the Lancaster County Historical Society* 15, No. 3 (1911); grave site, https://www.findagrave.com/memorial/156831127/thomas-whitson. Whitson discussed his disunionist, anti-Constitution views in a letter to Samuel May, April 16, 1857, available online at https://www.digitalcommonwealth.org/search/commonwealth:dv144r931.
37. Frederick J. Blue, *The Free Soilers: Third Party Politics 1848–54* (Urbana: University of Illinois Press, 1973), 1–15; Johnson, 75–91; Sewell, 135–69; Randy Barnett, "From Antislavery Lawyer to Chief Justice: The Remarkable but Forgotten Career of Salmon P. Chase," Georgetown Public Law and Legal Theory Research Paper No. 12–122 (2013), http://scholarship.law.georgetown.edu/facpub/1027.
38. Sewell, 163–64; Harlow, 183–92; "1849 Platform of the Liberty Party," http://alexpeak.com/twr/libertyparty/1849/; In Memoriam, William Goodell (Chicago: Guilbert and Winchell, Printers, 1879), 27–30, 33; Gerald Sorin, *The New York Abolitionists: A Case Study of Political Radicalism* (Westport, CT: Greenwood, 1971); William Goodell, *The Democracy of Christianity, or; An Analysis of the Bible and Its Doctrines in Their Relation to the Principles of Democracy*, Vol. 1 (New York: Cady and Burgess, 1849).
39. Smedley, 67, 131–32.

Chapter 4

1. Smedley, 131–32.
2. Pauli Murray, *Proud Shoes: The Story of an American Family* (New York: Harper, 1956), 86, 96–97.
3. J. Williams Thorne (Nancy Plumley, ed.), "J. Williams Thorne's unedited 1875 Account of The Christiana Riot and a brief biography," pamphlet courtesy of Nancy Plumley.
4. Thomas P. Slaughter, *Bloody Dawn: The Christiana Riot and Racial Violence in the Antebellum North* (New York: Oxford University Press, 1991), 46–47.
5. Quoted in Lucy Maddox, *The Parker Sisters: A Border Kidnapping* (Philadelphia: Temple University Press, 2016), 69.
6. "Thorne line," genealogical chart courtesy of Nancy Plumley; "Washington M. Hanaway" (sic), 1850 federal census, Schedule I, Free Inhabitants in West Marlborough Township in the County of Chester.
7. Slaughter, 43–45, 52–75.
8. Slaughter, 76–93.
9. Slaughter, 97–99; John F. Coleman, *The Disruption of the Pennsylvania Democracy, 1848–1860* (Harrisburg: The Pennsylvania Historical and Museum Commission, 1975), 37–38, 42, 44–47, 168; William C. Armor, *Lives of the Governors of Pennsylvania* (Norwich, CT: T.H. Davis and Company, 1874), 411–12; Philip Shriver Klein, *President James Buchanan: A Biography* (University Park: Pennsylvania State University Press, 1962), 217.
10. Slaughter, 112–133.
11. Don Fehrenbacher, *The Dred Scott Case: Its Significance in American Law and Politics* (New York: Oxford University Press, 1978), 242–46, 250–65, 276–80, 285–90, 293–302, 305–12; Diggins, 79; R.J.M. Blackett, *The Captive's Quest for Freedom: Fugitive Slaves, the 1850 Fugitive Slave Law, and the Politics of Slavery* (New York: Cambridge University press, 2018), 280–91.
12. Elijah Lewis, "List of Visitors to Moyamensing Prison during the incarceration of Elijah Lewis, I. Castner Hanway, Joseph Scarlet from 26 9 month to 12 of 12 month, 1851," copy courtesy of Nancy Plumley; Slaughter, 116, 122;

Chapter Notes—5

Hans L. Trefousse, *Thaddeus Stevens: Nineteenth-Century Egalitarian* (Mechanicsburg, PA: Stackpole Books, 2001), 84.
13. Slaughter, 133–38.
14. Diggins, 88–93.
15. Diggins, 93–105.
16. Diggins, 105–11, 135–43.
17. George B. Carr, *John Miller Dickey, His Life and Times* (Philadelphia: The Westminster Press, 1929), 150–160; Horace Mann Bond, *Education for Freedom: A History of Lincoln University, Pennsylvania* (Princeton, NJ: Princeton University Press, 1976), 98–9, 203–4, 212.
18. Morris, *Free Men All,* 155–56; Diggins, 56–59.
19. Receipts for the *Pennsylvania Freeman* for the month of October 1852, *Pennsylvania Freeman*, Thursday, November 25, 1852, Issue 48, 192; Mary Jones Pusey Thorne to her sisters, February 10 and 11, 1852 (additions to letter at later dates), Thorne family papers; "Amelia Bloomer," https://www.biography.com/people/amelia-bloomer-9216245.
20. Carl J. Guarneri, *The Utopian Alternative: Fourierism in Nineteenth-Century America* (Ithaca: Cornell University Press, 1991), 356–59.
21. Elizabeth Cady Stanton, Susan B. Anthony, and Matilda Joslyn Gage, *History of Woman Suffrage*, Vol. 1 (Rochester: Charles Mann, 1889), 350 ff; *The Proceedings of the Women's Rights Convention, Held at West Chester, PA June 2 and 3, 1852* (Philadelphia: Merrihew and Thompson, Printers, 1852).
22. Densmore, 37–39.
23. Densmore, 39 ff. For Oliver Johnson, see Steven Raffo, "Oliver Johnson, Abolitionist: 1831–1865" (Ph.D. diss., City University of New York, 2000).
24. Courtesy of Nancy Plumley.
25. Maddox, 2–3, 179.
26. Sandy Dwayne Martin, *For God and Race: The Religious and Political Leadership of AMEZ Bishop James Walker Hood* (Columbia: University of South Carolina Press, 1999), 23–26.
27. Wahl, 45; Densmore, 41; Murray, 85; "Call for a General Religious Conference, with a view to the establishment of a Yearly Meeting in Pennsylvania," in Progressive Yearly Meeting, *Proceedings*, Fifth Month, 1853, 3–4.

28. "Call"; Sadsbury (Lancaster County) Monthly Meeting minutes, June 9, 1852; Memorial resolution for Castner Hanway, Progressive Yearly Meeting Proceedings, 1893, 34–36.
29. "Call."
30. Diggins, 145–67.
31. Diggins, 169–73.
32. Courtesy of Nancy Plumley.
33. Courtesy of Nancy Plumley.
34. "Annual Meeting of the Pennsylvania A.S. Society," *The Liberator*, November 12, 1852, 821; "Visit to Pennsylvania," *The Liberator*, December 31, 1852, 210.
35. Emma Worrell, "Memories of Longwood Meeting," *Friends' Intelligencer* 75, No. 35 (August 31, 1918): 547–48; Wahl, 48–49.
36. "Proceedings," 7; Wahl, 49–50.
37. Worrell.
38. "Proceedings," 31–33.
39. "Proceedings," 27–31.
40. "Proceedings," 33–37.
41. "Proceedings," 37–39.
42. "Proceedings," 39.
43. "Proceedings," 10.
44. "Proceedings," 12–26.
45. Maddox, 72–73; Blackett, 293; Smedley, 107–08.

Chapter 5

1. Timothy Larsen, *Crisis of Doubt: Honest Faith in Nineteenth-Century England* (New York: Oxford University Press, 2006), 136–54; Betty Fladeland, *Abolitionists and Working-Class Problems in the Age of Industrialization* (Baton Rouge: Louisiana State University Press, 1984), 132–53.
2. Wahl, 19; Progressive Friends Proceedings, 1854, 7.
3. More information about Dickey and the founding of the Ashmun Institute (later Lincoln University) is in Carr, *John Miller Dickey*; Murray, *Proud Shoes*, 103–07; and Bond, *Education for Freedom*, 81–118.
4. *First Annual Report of the Transactions of the Pennsylvania State Agricultural Society* (Harrisburg: Printed by A. Boyd Hamilton, state printer, 1854).
5. Coleman, 73–75; Martin, "Temperance Movement in Pennsylvania," 218–19.

Chapter Notes—5

6. Coleman, 76–77; Martin, 219–21.
7. Wahl, 20; Progressive Friends, 1855 proceedings, 7.
8. Proceedings, 7–8, 17–18.
9. Raffo, 168–69.
10. Coleman, 78, 84. For the Williamson case, see Nat Brandt and Yanna Kroyt Brandt, *In the Shadow of the Civil War: Passmore Williamson and the Rescue of Jane Johnson* (Columbia: University of South Carolina Press, 2007).
11. Proceedings, 1856, 11, 29–42.
12. Coleman, 90–99, 172.
13. J. Smith Futhey and Gilbert Cope, *History of Chester County, Pennsylvania, with Genealogical and Biographical Sketches* (Philadelphia: Louis H. Everts, 1881), 307.
14. Excerpt from Thorne family history compiled by T. Chalkley Matlack, 18, Thorne family papers. "First Debate: Ottawa, Illinois," https://www.nps.gov/liho/learn/historyculture/debate1.htm. The Matlack narrative, which is not always accurate, refers to "Ottawo," but Google Maps confirms that Ottawa is in the same location Matlack gives for "Ottawo" ("about 83 miles west, southwest of Chicago").
15. Larsen, 153–54.
16. *Report of the Transactions of the Pennsylvania State Agricultural Society*, 317–19, 322. This volume contains state and local agricultural society reports going back to 1858. See *Report*, 19.
17. *Report*, 296–97, 306, 299, 125, 126; *Lancaster Examiner and Herald*, October 20, 1858, 1.
18. Morris, *Free Men All*, 168–71, 193–94; Harper, *West Chester to 1865*, 683–84; "John Brown's Harper's Ferry Raid," https://www.battlefields.org/learn/collections/john-browns-harpers-ferry-raid; Annie Thorne Hershey, "Honors to John Brown," letter to the editor, undated newspaper clipping (perhaps the West Chester *Daily Local News*) in Thorne family papers.
19. "Kidnapping case," *Lancaster Examiner and Herald*, March 3, 1860, 1; "Kidnapping Case," *Lancaster Examiner and Herald*, November 28, 1860, 2; "Taking Revenge," *National Antislavery Standard*, November 10, 1860, 1.
20. "Kidnapping case," *Lancaster Examiner and Herald*, March 3, 1860, 1; "Kidnapping Case," *Lancaster Examiner and Herald*, November 28, 1860, 2.
21. *Examiner and Herald*, "Kidnapping case" articles of March 3 and November 28. For the Maryland law enslaving free blacks who came in by the northern border, see Melba Joyce Boyd, *Discarded Legacy: Politics and Poetics in the Life of Frances E.W. Harper, 1825–1911* (Detroit: Wayne State University Press, 1994), 40.
22. "Kidnapping case," November 28, 1860.
23. *Ibid.*; American Anti-Slavery Society, *The Fugitive Slave Law And Its Victims* (New York: The Society, 1861), 132–33.
24. *Fugitive Slave Law and Its Victims*, 133; Pamela Scott, "Emancipation in the President's Neighborhood, 1850: The Story of African American Coachman William Williams," https://www.whitehousehistory.org/emancipation-in-the-presidents-neighborhood-1850.
25. Proceedings, 10, 16.
26. Mark E. Dixon, *The Hidden History of Chester County: Lost Tales from the Delaware and Brandywine Valleys* (Charleston, SC: The History Press, 2011), 80.
27. Proceedings, 9; "Abraham Lincoln, The Slave-Hound of Illinois," by "W.P.," *The Liberator*, June 22, 1860, 3. See also Lincoln's remark in the seventh debate in Alton, Illinois: "Why then do I yield support to a Fugitive Slave law? Because I do not understand that the Constitution, which guaranties that right, can be supported without it." https://www.nps.gov/liho/learn/historyculture/debate7.htm.
28. Proceedings, 9, 13.
29. Dixon, 82.
30. "Taking Revenge."
31. "Taking Revenge"; Warrant for Francis Wilson, October 21, 1860, Chester County Archives; "Christianity as Part of the Law of Pennsylvania," *Dickinson Law Review* 15, No. 1 (October 1910): 1–24, at 18 ("The Jew, the Mohammedan, the adherent of any theistic creed who attributes to his Deity the power and disposition to punish falsehood, and the Christian are impartially received as witnesses"). The Pennsylvania legislature adopted a statute in 1909 enacting that nobody's religious

Chapter Notes—5

opinions would affect his capacity to testify, Act. No. 90, adopted April 23, 1909, Laws of Pennsylvania, 1909 session, 140. And see *Com. v. Tresca*, 45 Pennsylvania Superior Court Reports, 619 (applying the new statute and declaring that it supersedes previous rules).

32. "Taking Revenge."
33. "Taking Revenge"; Kenneth Silverman, *Lightning Man: The Accursed Life of Samuel F.B. Morse* (Cambridge, MA: Da Capo Press, 2003), 70 (describing the founding of the *Observer* by Samuel Morse's brothers); Peter J. Wallace, "'The Bond of Union': The Old School Presbyterian Church and the American Nation, 1837–1861" (Ph.D. diss., University of Notre Dame, 2004), http://www.peterwallace.org/bond-union/ ("the *New York Observer* was formally a nondenominational paper, but after 1840 its editor was in the Old School, and it engaged more with Old School issues than any other denomination").
34. Raffo, 173.
35. "Kidnapping Case," November 28, 1860.
36. Morris, 216–18; Coleman, 177.
37. Wahl, 30; "Com. v. Edward Mackay," *Lancaster Examiner and Herald*, August 28, 1861, 3.
38. Abraham Lincoln to Eliza P. Gurney, September 4, 1864, cited in William C. Kashatus, *Abraham Lincoln, the Quakers, and the Civil War* (Santa Barbara: Praeger, 2014), 3–4; "A Case of Proscription," *Christian Union*, March 10, 1875; "Chester County Militia Fines and Exonerations," https://bit.ly/2W26P6v; Mary Pusey Thorne to Libbie Paxson, n.d., Thorne family papers, and accompanying notes by Nancy Plumley.
39. Mary Pusey Thorne, *ibid*.
40. *Ibid*. Other evidence of J. Williams's non-pacifist tendencies can be found in a letter by his daughter Annie to her husband Peter Hershey while J. Williams was in North Carolina. "Papa is getting his gun in order to shoot thieves or at them any how." Annie to Peter, 1879 (no date given but probably in September), Thorne family papers. This is particularly significant since J. Williams had denounced the alleged inconsistency of a witness in the "carpet will" case, who had been a conscientious objector in the Civil War but was willing to bear arms against potato thieves; see Chapter 8.

41. Mary to Anna, September 17, 1861, Thorne family papers; genealogical charts by Nancy Plumley.
42. J. Williams Thorne to William Darlington, Esq., May 19, 1862, Chester County Historical Society.
43. Edward B. Moore, "J. Williams Thorne and His Place," *West Chester Republican*, reprinted in *Lancaster Evening Express*, August 11, 1869, typescript in Thorne family papers.
44. Andrew Rolle, *John Charles Fremont: Character as Destiny* (Norman: University of Oklahoma Press, 1991), 182–93, 197–201, 205–09; "David Hunter," https://www.nps.gov/fopu/learn/historyculture/david-hunter.htm.
45. John G. Barrett, *The Civil War in North Carolina* (Chapel Hill: University of North Carolina Press, 1963), 127–28; Norman D. Brown, *Edward Stanly: Whiggery's Tarheel "Conqueror"* (Tuscaloosa: University of Alabama Press, 1974), 202–11; Judkin Browning, *Shifting Loyalties: The Union Occupation of Eastern North Carolina* (Chapel Hill: University of North Carolina Press, 2011), 77, 101; Ruth Levitt, "Vincent Colyer (1824–1888): Controversial American Humanitarian," *Quaker History* 104, No. 2 (Fall 2015): 1–17, at 4–5.
46. Douglas R. Harper, *If Thee Must Fight: A Civil War History of Chester County, Pennsylvania* (West Chester: Chester County Historical Society, 1990); Harper, *West Chester*, 697, 700; Brown, 211; Levitt, 5.
47. Thomas F. Curran, *Soldiers of Peace: Civil War Pacifism and the Postwar Radical Peace Movement* (New York: Fordham University Press, 2003), 42–44, 55, 57; Progressive Friends Meeting, 1862 proceedings, 9, 14.
48. Proceedings, 1862, 6, 10–11.
49. Proceedings, 1862, 13–14.
50. Proceedings, 1862, 10, 15–16.
51. Wahl, 29; Kashatus, 47–49, 54.
52. Harper, *If Thee Must Fight*, 197.
53. Quarter Sessions Dockets; Commonwealth vs. Sylvester Gordon; April Sessions 1863; #477, Lancaster County Archives, Lancaster, PA.

Chapter Notes—6

54. 1863 Proceedings, 7, 17; Wahl, 58n57.
55. 1863 Proceedings, 9–10.
56. Harper, *If Thee Must Fight*, 223.
57. Harper, *If Thee Must Fight*, 223–25; Richmond Croom Beatty, *Bayard Taylor: Laureate of the Gilded Age* (Norman: University of Oklahoma Press, 1936), 168–69, 264–65 (for Thorne's friendship with Taylor's parents, see Joseph and Rebecca Taylor to Chester Arthur, January 12, 1882, Thorne family papers); David G. Smith, "Race and Retaliation: The Capture of African Americans During the Gettysburg Campaign," in Peter Wallenstein and Bertram Wyatt-Brown, eds., *Virginia's Civil War* (Charlottesville: University of Virginia Press, 2005), 137–151.
58. *National Anti-Slavery Standard*, December 19, 1863, 1.
59. *National Anti-Slavery Standard*, December 3, 1864, 3.
60. 1865 Proceedings, 7, 8, 14.
61. Genealogical Tables prepared by Nancy Plumley; Joseph Thorne estate administration papers, Chester County Archives; Matlack, 18.
62. Futhey and Cope, 307.

Chapter 6

1. J. Williams Thorne, Obituary of James Fulton, *National Anti-Slavery Standard*, July 4, 1868, 3.
2. Newspaper reports of the incident include "A Curious Question About the Age of a Voter," *Chicago Republican*, November 2 (Monday), 1868, 5; "Cutting a Vote Down to a Close Point," *New York Herald*, November 3, 1868, 10; *Cincinnati Daily Gazette*, November 11, 1868; "Three Minutes Too Soon," *Macon Weekly Telegraph*, November 20, 1868, 6. These stories referred to the October election, which in 1868 was held on October 13, as mentioned in the testimony in an unrelated Congressional voter-fraud investigation. See Report of the Committee on Elections on the contested-election case of *Myers v. Moffett*, in "Digest of Election Cases," 41st Congress, 2nd Session, Mis. Doc. No. 152, 564 ff.
3. Price, 365–67.
4. D.T. Smithwick, D.D.S., to "Miss Mable," September 29, 1928, Warren County Memorial Library. For an example of the use of the term "colony," see Eugene Thorne to "Mother Sister and Brother," May 15, 1881.
5. Richard Nelson Current, *Those Terrible Carpetbaggers* (New York: Oxford University Press, 1988), 127–28.
6. Moore, "J. Williams Thorne and His Place."
7. William C. Harris, *William Woods Holden: Firebrand of North Carolina Politics* (Baton Rouge: Louisiana State University Press, 1987), 266–68; North Carolina Land Company, *A Statistical and Descriptive Account of the Several Counties of the State of North Carolina, United States of America* (Raleigh: Nichols and Gorman, 1869), 4.
8. *Statistical and Descriptive Account*, 56–57.
9. Francis Charles Anscombe, *I Have Called You Friends: The Story of Quakerism in North Carolina* (Boston: The Christopher Publishing House, 1959), 139–147; Allen Jay, *The Autobiography of Allen Jay* (Philadelphia: John C. Winston Co., 1910), 219–221; B. Russell Branson, "A Period of Change in North Carolina Quakerism," *Bulletin of Friends Historical Association* 39, No. 2 (Autumn 1950): 74–86, at 75–79.
10. Margaret Newbold Thorpe, "A 'Yankee Teacher' in North Carolina," *The North Carolina Historical Review* 30, No. 4 (October 1953): 564–82. The only local Quaker Margaret Thorpe recorded meeting was at the time of her first arrival in September 1869: "Our 'thee' and 'thou' made us a pleasant acquaintance, a kindly faced middle-aged Friend who introduced himself and talked to us for some time, and when he left us cordially invited us to visit his home; but as he and his family live down by 'The Dismal Swamp' a hundred miles from here, we probably will never have the opportunity to accept his invitation." "Yankee Teacher," 569.
11. Anscombe, 104–07; Branson, 84–85.
12. Manly Wade Wellman, *The County of Warren North Carolina 1586–1917* (Chapel Hill: University of North Carolina Press, 1959), 119, 163; Thorpe, 571–72.
13. Wellman, 135, 154; Eric Anderson,

Chapter Notes—6

Race and Politics in North Carolina: The Black Second (Baton Rouge: Louisiana State University Press, 1981), 36.

14. Wellman, 140–48; Lizzie Wilson Montgomery, *Sketches of Old Warrenton, North Carolina* (Raleigh: Edwards and Broughton Printing Company, 1924), 271–73.

15. Wellman, 154, 158; Anderson, 36–37, 86–87.

16. Anderson, 22–28; Thorpe, 569.

17. J. Williams Thorne, "Mrs. Harper," *Philadelphia Press*, December 15, 1868, 2; Boyd, *Discarded Legacy*; James William Clark, Jr., "Frances Ellen Watkins Harper, 1825–1911: A Literary Biography" (master's thesis, Duke University, 1967).

18. *The Pennsylvania School Journal* 19, No. 3 (September 1870): 57, 87; Advertisement, The Misses Mordecais' School for Young Ladies, *The Occident, and American Jewish Advocate* 25, No. 11 (February 1868), back matter following 591; "Rosa Mordecai 1839–1936," https://jwa.org/encyclopedia/article/mordecai-rosa; Guarneri, 356–59; Montgomery, 133–42. An account of the Mordecai family is found in Emily Bingham, *Mordecai: An Early American Family* (New York: Hill and Wang, 2003).

19. Undated poem, Thorne family papers. A note from Annie Thorne Hershey says that this is "Aunt Elizas letter to J. Williams Thorne written about 1870 when Papa went south."

20. Annie Thorne to Peter Hershey, April 5, 1869, Thorne family papers, and accompanying notes by Nancy Plumley.

21. Smithwick to "Miss Mable," September 29, 1928, Warren County Memorial Library; Mary J. Pusey Thorne to Eugene and Annie Thorne, August 8, 1869; J. Williams Thorne to Eugene Thorne, October 3, 1870; Mary J. Pusey Thorne to Annie Hershey, November 22, 1873. These letters are in the Thorne family papers.

22. Annie Thorne to Peter Hershey, January 9, 1870, Thorne family papers; Nancy Plumley genealogical notes.

23. Anne Pusey to Annie Thorne, July 30, 1870, Thorne family papers.

24. Wedding announcement for Peter Hershey and Annie Thorne; Mary J. Pusey Thorne to Annie and Peter, August 21, 1870; J. Williams Thorne to Mary J. Pusey Thorne, Sept. 5th, 1870. All these items are in the Thorne family papers.

25. J. Williams Thorne to Mary J. Pusey Thorne, September 5, 1870; J. Williams Thorne to Mary J. Pusey Thorne, September 24, 1870; J. Williams Thorne to Eugene Thorne, October 5, 1870. All in Thorne family papers.

26. *Lancaster Examiner and Herald*, November 2, 1870, 3.

27. Michael Hill, ed., *The Governors of North Carolina* (Raleigh: Office of Archives and History, 2007), 19–20, 70–72; Max Longley, "North Carolina Maverick: The Remarkable William Woods Holden," HistoryNet, https://www.historynet.com/remarkable-william-woods-holden.htm; Wellman, 158, 161–62; Allen W. Trelease, *White Terror: The Ku Klux Klan Conspiracy and Southern Reconstruction* (New York: Harper and Row, 1971), 189–225; Thorpe, 571. For Octavius Catto and the Philadelphia riot that ended his life, see Daniel R. Biddle and Murray Dubin, *Tasting Freedom: Octavius Catto and the Battle for Equality in Civil War America* (Philadelphia: Temple University Press, 2010).

28. Longley; Gordon B. McKinney, *Zeb Vance: North Carolina's Civil War Governor and Gilded Age Political Leader* (Chapel Hill: University of North Carolina Press, 2004), 288–294.

29. Unmarked, undated news clipping in possession of Nancy Plumley. The 1872 date is established because a speaker denounced Horace Greeley, the Democratic/Liberal Republican candidate who ran against President Grant in that year. Andrew L. Slap, *The Doom of Reconstruction: The Liberal Republicans in the Civil War Era* (New York: Fordham University Press, 2006), 126–98. The presence of William Parker at Lincoln University's commencement in 1872 is confirmed by Susan Goodman, *Republic of Words: The Atlantic Monthly and its Writers* (Lebanon, NH: University Press of New England, 2011), 23–24.

30. J. Williams to M.J. Pusey Thorne, February 22, 1872, Thorne family papers.

31. Sheriff's return on a writ of *fieri facias*, August term 1872, Court of Com-

Chapter Notes—7

mon Pleas of Chester County, Thorne family papers. A writ of *fieri facias* is defined thus: "A writ of execution that directs a marshal or sheriff to seize and sell a defendant's property to satisfy a money judgment." *Black's Law Dictionary*, 8th ed. (St. Paul: Thomson West, 2004), 659.

32. Annie Hershey to Peter Hershey, September 8, September 26, and (n.d.), 1872; Mary J.P. Thorne to Annie Hershey, November 22, 1873. All in Thorne family papers. Notes by Nancy Plumley describe the Lippincott family.

33. Fladeland, 150–163. I put Barker's encounter with Thorne, and Thorne's ensuing pamphlet, in 1873, though the pamphlet is undated. Internal evidence indicates a publication date in 1873, especially since the pamphlet says George Francis Train had "lately" been arrested. See J. Williams Thorne, "Reply to Jos. Barker's Lecture, Comparing Infidels and Christians," n.d., 4, Thorne Family Papers. For more about Train, see below.

34. "A Letter from Rev. Joseph Barker," *Boston Investigator*, September 18, 1872; "Messrs. Bradlaugh and Barker," *Boston Investigator*, October 2, 1872; "A Letter from Joseph Barker," *Boston Investigator*, October 30, 1872; "The Rev. Joseph Barker and Another Noted Methodist Minister," *Boston Investigator*, March 26, 1873.

35. Thorne, "Reply," 1.
36. Thorne, "Reply," 1.
37. Thorne, "Reply," 1–2.
38. Thorne, "Reply," 2, 12.
39. Thorne, "Reply," 2–3.
40. Thorne, "Reply," 3–4."
41. Barbara Goldsmith, *Other Powers: The Age of Suffrage, Spiritualism and the Scandalous Victoria Woodhull* (New York: Alfred A. Knopf, 1998), 337–45, 363–69; Cait Murphy, *Scoundrels in Law: The Trials of Howe & Hummel, Lawyers to the Gangsters, Cops, Starlets, and Rakes Who Made the Gilded Age* (New York: HarperCollins, 2010), 32–40.
42. Thorne, "Reply," 4. Goldsmith gives a detailed account of Woodhull's life—the good, the bad and the ugly. For Train, see Patricia G. Holland, "George Francis Train and the Woman Suffrage Movement, 1867–70," *Books at Iowa* 46 (1987): 8–29, https://doi.org/10.17077/0006-7474.1135; George Francis Train, *The Great Epigram Campaign of Kansas* (Leavenworth: Prescott and Hume, 1867).

43. Thorne, "Reply," 4.
44. Thorne, "Reply," 5.
45. Thorne, "Reply," 6–8.
46. Thorne, "Reply," 8–9, 11.
47. Thorne, "Reply," 9.
48. Thorne, "Reply," 9–10.
49. Thorne, "Reply," 10–11.
50. Thorne, "Reply," 12.
51. Thorne, "Reply," 12.
52. Mark Wahlgren Summers, *The Ordeal of the Reunion* (Chapel Hill: University of North Carolina Press, 2014), 335–46; Wellman, 170.
53. Mary J. Pusey Thorne to Annie Hershey, November 22, 1873; Thorne family papers.
54. Smithwick to "Miss Mable," September 29, 1928, Warren Memorial Library; Thorpe, 570, 572, 574–76, 578.
55. Mary J. Pusey Thorne to Annie Hershey, January 22 1874.
56. Progressive Friends Records, 9.
57. Anderson, 41; J. Williams Thorne flyer, "Citizens of Warren County, Read and Judge for Yourselves," May 12, 1874, with covering note of May 27, 1874; Thorne family papers. This flyer is also reproduced in Thorne's *Ecclesiastical Trial*, 28–33.
58. Thorne, "Read and Judge"; Ward M. McAfee, *Religion, Race and Reconstruction: The Public School in the Politics of the 1870s* (Albany: State University of New York Press, 1998), 126–53; Summers, 346, 351.
59. Thorne, "Read and Judge."
60. Thorne, "Read and Judge."
61. Thorne, "Read and Judge."
62. Thorne, "Read and Judge."
63. Thorne, "Read and Judge."
64. Thorne, "Read and Judge."
65. Wellman, 169.
66. Wellman, 170.

Chapter 7

1. J. Williams Thorne affidavit, February 16, 1886, Thorne family papers; McAfee, 151–73; Paul Yandle, "Different Colored Currents of the Sea: Reconstruction North Carolina, Mutuality, and the Political Roots of Jim Crow, 1872–1875,"

Chapter Notes—7

in Paul D. Escott, ed., *North Carolinians in the Era of the Civil War and Reconstruction* (Chapel Hill: University of North Carolina Press, 2008), 221–68, at 234–46; Paul D. Escott, *Many Excellent People: Power and Privilege in North Carolina, 1850–1900* (Chapel Hill: University of North Carolina Press, 1985), 166; "Resolution in Relation to Civil Rights Bill," General Assembly Acts and Resolutions 1874–75, 367–68, December 1874 (no date specified).

2. North Carolina House Journal 1874–75, 238; J.G. de Roulhac Hamilton, *Reconstruction in North Carolina* (New York: Columbia University, 1914), 604, 607.

3. Jacob C. Davis to J.W. Thorne, February 22, 1875 and accompanying genealogical note by Nancy Plumley; Thorne family tree drawn up by Nancy Plumley.

4. Davis to Thorne, February 22, 1875.

5. Daniel J. Whitener, *Prohibition in North Carolina* (Chapel Hill: University of North Carolina Press, 1946), 59–60.

6. North Carolina House Journal 1874–75, 261; R.D.W. Connor, *A Manual of North Carolina* (Raleigh: E.M. Uzzell, 1913), 525, 528. The clause pertaining to belief in God is still in the North Carolina Constitution, though the 1961 decision of the U.S. Supreme Court in *Torcaso v. Watkins* makes this clause unenforceable today. See John Orth, *The North Carolina State Constitution: A Reference Guide* (Westport, CT: Greenwood Press, 1993), 137.

7. Thorne, *Ecclesiastical Trial*, 28.

8. House Journal, 366; *Ecclesiastical Trial*, 39.

9. *Ecclesiastical Trial*, 40.

10. *Ecclesiastical Trial*, 40. Connor, 778, 782; W. McKee Evans, *To Die Game: The Story of the Lowry Band, Indian Guerillas of Reconstruction* (Baton Rouge: Louisiana State University Press, 1971), 213–14; "Richard Montgomery Norment," http://ploughboys.org/richard-montgomery-norment/; Congressional Statutes at Large, Chapter 194, March 4, 1915, 1569 (Mexican War pension for Norment's widow).

11. *Ecclesiastical Trial*, 40.

12. *Ecclesiastical Trial*, 40–41; Max Longley, "Oaths," North Carolina History Project, https://northcarolinahistory.org/encyclopedia/oaths/.

13. House Journal, 355, 446–47, 462–63; Chapter 79, North Carolina Session Laws 1874–75, 92; *(Raleigh) Weekly Era*, March 4, 1875, 2; Anderson, 93, 199 (confirming that Carter was black); Monroe N. Work, Thomas S. Staples, H.A. Wallace, Kelly Miller, Whitefield McKinlay, Samuel E. Lacy, R.L. Smith and H.R. McIlwaine, "Some Negro Members of Reconstruction Conventions and Legislatures and of Congress," *The Journal of Negro History* 5, No. 1 (January 1920): 63–119 (confirming that the other dissenters, apart from Thorne, were black).

14. *Ecclesiastical Trial*, 42; House Journal, 432, 460–61, 465; "The Ecclesiastical Court," *Raleigh News*, February 24, 1875; Connor, 553, 689; "Gudger, Hezekiah Alexander," NCPedia, https://www.ncpedia.org/biography/gudger-hezekiah-alexander. Moring later became speaker, see Connor, 477.

15. North Carolina House Journal 1874–75, 4; Robert C. Kenzer, *Enterprising Southerners: Black Economic Success in North Carolina, 1865–1915* (Charlottesville: University Press of Virginia, 1997), 90; *State v. Hughes*, 72 NC 25 (1875). Warren and Granville Counties no longer border each other, because in 1881 the legislature carved out a new county—Vance—from parts of Warren, Franklin and Granville Counties. Vance now stands between Warren and Granville. See David Leroy Corbitt, *The Formation of the North Carolina Counties 1663–1943* (Raleigh: Division of Archives and History, 1987), 102, 211–12. For a map of Warren County prior to the creation of Vance, see R.D. Paschall, "Map of Warren County N.C.," 1874.

16. House Journal, 465–66; Connor, 246–47.

17. *Ecclesiastical Trial*; "Second Night's Session," *Raleigh Daily News*, February 25, 1875, Thorne family papers (both motions as summarized by Mr. Finger; see below); "Nathaniel Macon," NCPedia, https://www.ncpedia.org/biography/macon-nathaniel-0; Max Longley, *For the Union and the Catholic Church: Four Converts in the Civil War* (Jefferson, NC: McFarland, 2015), 52; J. Herman Schauinger, *William Gaston: Carolinian* (Milwaukee: Bruce, 1949).

18. *Ecclesiastical Trial.*
19. House Journal, 489.
20. Connor, 635; House Journal, 490; Roland H. Bainton, *Here I Stand: A Life of Martin Luther* (Nashville: Abingdon Press, reprint edition, 2013), 342; "Ecclesiastical Court"; *Ecclesiastical Trial.*
21. "Expelling a member," *Raleigh Daily Sentinel*, February 24, 1875, 2; "Obliged to Publish," *Raleigh Daily Sentinel*, February 24, 1875, 2.
22. "Expelling a member"; "Nereus Mendenhall," NCPedia, https://www.ncpedia.org/biography/mendenhall-nereus; Abbie Rogers, "Confederates and Quakers: The Shared Wartime Experience," *Quaker History* 99, No. 2 (Fall 2010): 1–19, at 6–7.
23. "Expelling a member."
24. "Expelling a member."
25. House Journal, 490; Connor, 855, 644.
26. House Journal, 500–1.
27. House Journal, 501; "Second Night's Session"; F.A. Sondley, *Asheville and Buncombe County* (Asheville: The Citizen Company, 1922), 88. This volume combines an article by Sondley and an article by Theodore F. Davidson titled "Genesis of Buncombe County," so publication information and pagination are the same.
28. "Report: To Accompany bill H. R. 1628," June 16, 1874, Report No. 660, House of Representatives, 43d Congress, 1st Session; U.S. Senate Journal, 1874–75 session, 158, 335, 426; Chapter 230, An Act for the Relief of Montraville Patton of Buncombe County, North Carolina, March 3, 1875, U.S. *Statutes at Large*, Volume 18, Part 3, 666.
29. "Second Night's Session"; "Sidney Michael Finger," https://www.ncpedia.org/biography/finger-sidney-michael.
30. House Journal, 502–04; Work, et. al., "Some Negro Members," 77; "Albert Bigelow, 1848–1922," North Carolina History Project, https://northcarolinahistory.org/encyclopedia/albert-Rbigelow-1848-1922/; H.G. Jones, "Legislator Expelled for Views" (AP article), *Durham Sun*, May 4, 1977, North Carolina Collection Clipping File, 1976–1989, UNC Library, Chapel Hill.
31. House Journal, 502; John Preston Arthur, *Western North Carolina: A History (From 1730 to 1913)* (Raleigh: Edward Buncombe Chapter, Daughters of the American Revolution, 1914), 202. I classify Spears and Gash as Democrats based on their vote in the speakership contest at the beginning of the House session; see House Journal 5–6. Spears and Gash voted for the successful Democratic candidate Robinson.
32. House Journal, 502.
33. House Journal, 503, 518. Concerning the right of recording a protest, see Orth, 85–86.
34. J. Williams Thorne, affidavit, February 16, 1886, Thorne family papers; "Resolution in Favor of Witnesses in the Matter of J. Williams Thorne," March 16, 1875, Laws and Resolutions of the NC General Assembly, 1874–75, 398.
35. "In Demand," *Raleigh Daily Times*, February 25, 1875, 1; Thorne family papers. This editorial is quoted in *Ecclesiastical Trial*, 48–49.
36. Philip Hamburger, *Separation of Church and State* (Cambridge: Harvard University Press, 2002); Steven K. Green, *The Second Disestablishment: Church and State in Nineteenth-Century America* (New York: Oxford University Press, 2010), 275–91; 201–78.
37. "God in Politics," *Chicago Daily Tribune*, February 28, 1875.
38. Reprinted in the *New York Times*, March 6, 1875; *Chicago Daily Tribune*, March 12, 1875 (*Republican* editorial from February 25).
39. "A Religious Test Applied," *The Napa Register*, April 10, 1875, 2.
40. "A Case of Proscription," *Christian Union*, March 10, 1875, 206; Goldsmith, 219, 389–418.
41. Roderick Bradford, *D.M. Bennett: The Truth Seeker* (Amherst, NY: Prometheus Books, 2006), 17–19, 25–106.
42. *The Truth Seeker*, March 1, 1875, 1.
43. Hamburger, 288–93; Sydney E. Ahlstrom and Robert Bruce Mullin, *The Scientific Theist: A Life of Francis Ellingwood Abbot* (Macon, GA: Mercer University Press, 1987), vi–ix, 76, 81–95.
44. Ahlstrom and Mullin, 95, 101–104; Hamburger, 294–96.
45. "Freedom Trampled Under Foot"

(article dated March 1), *The Index*, March 11, 1875, 117; *The Index*, March 25, 1875, 133.

46. Reprinted in the *Wheeling Daily Intelligencer*, March 18, 1875, 2.

47. Quoted in "Thorne's Defense," by "J.G.J.," *The Spiritualist at Work*, May 22, 1875, 1.

48. *Ibid.* For the connections among Spiritualism, reformism and secularism, see Goldsmith, 33–7, 48–9, 139; Ahlstrom and Mullin, 103.

49. *The Index*, April 1, 1875, 149.

50. *Ecclesiastical Trial*; Current, 297–88.

51. Warren Allen Smith, *Who's Who in Hell* (New York: Barricade Books, 2000), 764; Samuel P. Putnam, *400 Years of Freethought* (New York: The Truth Seeker Company, 1894), 710 ("Mr. Moore is well known in the Liberal ranks to-day, and has been a persistent worker for Freethought").

52. *Ecclesiastical Trial*, 2–3.

53. *Ecclesiastical Trial*, 4–6.

54. Article reprinted from *Philadelphia Times*, April 21, in *The Index*, May 20, 1875, 233.

55. *Christian Union*, April 21, 1875, 334.

56. Progressive Friends Proceedings, 1875, 4.

57. Progressive Friends Proceedings, 1875, 16.

58. Progressive Friends Proceedings, 1875, 14–16.

59. Progressive Friends Proceedings, 10, 15–16; Irwin Unger, *The Greenback Era: A Social and Political History of American Finance, 1865–1879* (Princeton: Princeton University Press, 1964), 195 ff.

60. Progressive Friends Proceedings, 10–11, 17; Chalfant, 83–88.

Chapter 8

1. S.H. Preston, "An Appeal" (article dated July 20), *The Truth Seeker*, August 1, 1875, 5.

2. Hamilton, 605–06; Escott, 165–67.

3. *Ibid.*; Genealogical chart from Nancy Plumley.

4. J. Williams to Annie, August 18, 1875 (written on the back of a letter of that date from Eugene to Annie), Thorne family papers.

5. Hamilton, 634–38; Moore, 410, 415–16; Eric Anderson, "James O'Hara of North Carolina: Black Leadership and Local Government," in Howard N. Rabinowitz, ed., *Southern Black Leaders of the Reconstruction Era* (Urbana: University of Illinois Press, 1982), 107, 123n12; William Alexander Graham, https://www.ncpedia.org/biography/graham-william-alexander.

6. Convention Journal, September 18, 1875, 89.

7. Yandle; Elizabeth Balanoff, "Negro Legislators in the North Carolina General Assembly, July, 1868–February, 1872," *The North Carolina Historical Review* 49, No. 1 (January 1972): 22–55, at 35.

8. Convention Journal, September 25, 1875, 130; William J. Simmons, *Men of Mark: Eminent, Progressive and Rising* (Cleveland: George M. Rewell & Co., 1887), 422–26.

9. Convention Journal, September 27, 5, 137–38.

10. John Hope Franklin, *The Free Negro in North Carolina, 1790–1860* (Chapel Hill: University of North Carolina Press, 1995 edition), 35–37.

11. Convention Journal, 261–65; Simmons, 871–76; Anderson, *Race and Politics*, 62–63. For Tourgée, see Mark Elliott, *Color-Blind Justice: Albion Tourgée and the Quest for Racial Equality from the Civil War to Plessy v. Ferguson* (New York: Oxford University Press, 2006).

12. Constitutional Convention Journal, 40; J. Williams Thorne, letter to the editor, *Daily Constitution*, undated clipping in Thorne family papers.

13. McAfee, 177–180; Unger, 120–26, 269–85; Roy Morris, Jr., *Fraud of the Century: Rutherford B. Hayes, Samuel Tilden, and the Stolen Election of 1876* (New York: Simon and Schuster, 2003), 66.

14. Hamburger, 397–328; McAfee, 189–98.

15. Ahlstrom and Mullin, 103–05; National Liberal League, *Equal Rights in Religion. Report of the Centennial Congress of Liberals, and Organization of the National Liberal League at Philadelphia, on the Fourth of July, 1876. With an Introduction and Appendix* (Boston: National

Chapter Notes—8

Liberal League, 1876), 6. Until its issue of April 12, 1877, *The Index* repeated the mistake, and then it gave the correct name, J. Williams Thorne. See p. 170 of the April 12 issue. J. Williams was listed as being from Warren, North Carolina, while other executive committee members were listed by hometown.

16. Anderson, *Race and Politics*, 48, 54; Mary J. Pusey Thorne to Annie, November 5, 1876, Thorne family papers. For Ingersoll, see Susan Jacoby, *The Great Agnostic: Robert Ingersoll and American Freethought* (New Haven: Yale University Press, 2013). The most famous speech Ingersoll gave in 1876 was his unsuccessful nomination speech for James G. Blaine at the Republican convention (see Morris, 75–76); Annie Hershey to Peter Hershey, October 14, 1877 ("Mother is eating lunch with Aunty and Papa. Eugene and Unity have gone to church…"). October 14 was a Sunday.

17. *Ibid.*, November 9 addendum; Morris, *Fraud of the Century*, 164 ff; Escott, 169; Hamilton, 654; Moore, 429–31. The gubernatorial race is described in Sandra Porter Babb, "The Battle of the Giants: The Gubernatorial Election of 1876 in North Carolina" (master's thesis, University of North Carolina at Chapel Hill, 1970).

18. Unger, 286–321, 347–49; Polly Guerin, *The Cooper-Hewitt Dynasty of New York* (Charleston, SC: The History Press, 2012), 37–47.

19. Mary J. Pusey Thorne to Anne Pusey, November 30, 1976, Thorne family papers.

20. North Carolina Senate Journal, 1876–77, 2, 32, 33.

21. Senate Journal, 94, 106, 134.

22. Senate Journal, 162; "Robinson, James Lowrie," https://www.ncpedia.org/biography/robinson-james-lowrie.

23. Whitener, 60; Senate Journal, 73, 83, 89, 90, 91, 97, 140, 185; House Journal, 150, 174, 186–87; Chapter 35, "An Act to Prevent the Sale of Spirituous Liquors Within Three Miles of Shocco Chapel and of the People's Hall, in Warren County," *Laws and Resolutions of the State of North Carolina, 1876–77* (Raleigh: Raleigh News, 1877), 80–81; John Hill Wheeler, *Reminiscences and Memoirs of North Carolina and Eminent North Carolinians* (Columbus, OH: Columbus Printing Works, 1884), 153–54.

24. Senate Journal, 138, 241–42, 154; Chapter 38, "An Act to prevent the sale of malt or spirituous liquor on Sunday," North Carolina Session Laws 1876–77, 83–84.

25. Escott, 170; Anderson, *Race and Politics*, 56–58.

26. "Remarks of J. Williams Thorne, Senator from Warren, on the bill establishing county government," no date, Thorne family papers; "The Wolf and Shepherds: A Fable," in *The Works of the English Poets*, Vol. 18 (London: 1810), 539, 557–58.

27. "Resolutions Introduced by J. Williams Thorne, Senator from Warren," no date, Thorne family papers; Holley Ulbrich, "John C. Calhoun," March 6, 2003, *Dictionary of Unitarian and Universalist Biography*, http://uudb.org/articles/johnccalhoun.html. I have been unable to find a source for the alleged Calhoun quote.

28. "Resolutions."

29. Morris, *Fraud of the Century*, 232–34, 246–49; Mary J. Pusey Thorne to J. Williams Thorne, March 4, 1877, Thorne family papers; Senate Journal, 652.

30. Connor, 625, 862; Senate Journal, 770–71.

31. Senate Journal, 703, 781; Report of Committee on S.B. 878, Thorne family papers; email interview, Dr. Kevin Luskus, MD, February 14, 2019.

32. Senate Journal, 855–65; http://ncgovdocs.org/guides/sessionlawslist.htm.

33. Mary Thorne to Annie, May 6 and May 5, 1877, Thorne family papers.

34. Progressive Friends Proceedings, 11; Annie Hershey to Mary J. Pusey Thorne, July 5, 1877; Annie Hershey to Peter Hershey, September 5, 1877; Annie Hershey to Peter Hershey, September 23, 1877; Annie to Peter, September 28, 1877, Thorne family papers.

35. Annie Hershey to Peter Hershey, October 16, 1877, October 21, 1877, October 25, 1877, October 29, 1877; Peter Hershey to Annie Hershey, October 30, 1877.

36. Mary J. Pusey Thorne to Annie and J. Williams, November 11, 1877 (incomplete letter), Thorne family papers.

37. "Ann Pusey v. Caleb P. Wickersham,"

Chapter Notes—8

West Chester Local News, December 6, 1877, Thorne family papers; Susanna Taylor probate records, Chester County archives.

38. J. Williams Thorne, "The Carpet Will Case of Kennett Square," *West Chester American Republican*, January 19, 1878, and January 22, 1878, Thorne family papers.

39. "J. Williams Thorne, Why he was Arrested in Pennsylvania," March 25, 1878, 1; "Embracery," in *Black's Law Dictionary*, 561; Papers in *Commonwealth v. Thorne*, Quarter Sessions Docket S, October 1873–1879, Chester County Archives; Wilmer W. MacElree, *Side Lights on the Bench and Bar of Chester County* (West Chester: Self-published, 1918), 366. "Wilmer W. MacElree, born in 1859, was a lawyer, district attorney, and historian in Chester County, Pennsylvania, practicing law until the age of 93. He wrote books concerning nature and the area around the Brandywine, such as *Down the Eastern and Up the Black Brandywine*, *Along the Western Brandywine*, and *Around the Boundaries of Chester County*. He died on January 16, 1960." https://legacy.lib.utexas.edu/taro/utcah/01387/cah-01387.html.

40. Mary J. Pusey Thorne to Annie, March 3, 1878 (incomplete letter); Peter Hershey to Caleb Pusey Thorne, September 30, 1877, Thorne family papers.

41. "Why he was Arrested in Pennsylvania."

42. Bond for Thorne, April 23, 1878, Hayes to Bull, May 25, 1878, papers in *Commonwealth v. Thorne*.

43. Stewart Rapalje, *A Treatise on Contempt* (New York: L.K. Strouse and Company, 1884), 14, 70–72; Richard C. Donnelly, "Contempt by Publication in the United States" (1961), *Faculty Scholarship Series*, Paper 4757, http://digitalcommons.law.yale.edu/fss_papers/4757, 240; "Contempt By Publication," *Indiana Law Journal* 23, No. 2, Article 9 (1948): 195–96; John L. Thomas, *The Law of Constructive Contempt: The Shepherd Case Reviewed* (St. Louis: The F.H. Thomas Law Book Co., 1904), 115–22 (Appendix B); Walter Nelles and Carol Weiss King, "Contempt by Publication in the United States. To the Federal Contempt Statute," *Columbia Law Review* 28, No. 4 (April 1928): 401–431.

44. Papers in *Commonwealth v. Thorne*.

45. Ahlstrom and Mullin, 114–24; Bradford, 162; Amy Werbel, *Lust on Trial: Censorship and the Rise of American Obscenity in the Age of Anthony Comstock* (New York: Columbia University Press, 2018), 127–28.

46. See *The Index*, November 21, 1878, 554 (Thorne on the Executive Committee of the National Liberal League of America); *The Truth Seeker*, November 16, 1878, 725 (Thorne on the Executive Committee of the National Liberal League); E.C. Walker, "Show Your Colors," *The Truth Seeker*, March 13, 1880, 167 ("The members of the Executive Committee for Delaware, Florida, Georgia, Maine, Maryland, Minnesota, Nevada, North Carolina, Texas, and Virginia are the same in the organizations. 'Under which king,' comrades, fellow-members of the Executive Committee?").

47. Mary J. Pusey Thorne to Annie Hershey, September 29, 1878, Thorne family papers.

48. Anderson, *Race and Politics*, 53–56, 65–66, 70; Hill, 12.

49. Unger, 347–49, 353–65, 370–78; Matthew Hild, *Greenbackers, Knights of Labor, and Populists: Farmer-Labor Insurgency in the Late-Nineteenth-Century South* (Athens: University of Georgia Press, 2007), 20–24; Ralph R. Ricker, *The Greenback-Labor Movement in Pennsylvania* (Bellephonte, PA: Pennsylvania Heritage, 1966), 20–62; Anderson, *Race and Politics*, 67.

50. Unger, 53–58; "A New National Monetary System. A Letter to a Northern Newspaper, by J. Williams Thorne, of Ridgeway, N.C.," Thorne family papers.

51. "National Monetary System."
52. "National Monetary System."
53. "National Monetary System."

54. "Radical Pow-wow," *Wilson Advance*, November 1, 1878, 3, Thorne family papers.

55. Anderson, *Race and Politics*, 70.

56. Anderson, *Race and Politics*, 71–74. Kitchin briefly affiliated with the Populists in the 1890s because of their support for free silver; see https://www.ncpedia.org/biography/kitchin-william-hodge.

57. Hild, 37–38; Jeffrey J. Crow and Robert F. Durden, *Maverick Republican in*

Chapter Notes—9

the Old North State: A Political Biography of Daniel L. Russell (Baton Rouge: Louisiana State University Press, 1977), 34–38.

Chapter 9

1. Mary J. Pusey Thorne to Annie Hershey, letters of December 1, 15, and 26, 1878, Thorne family papers.
2. Mary J. Pusey Thorne to Annie Hershey, December 26, 1878, Thorne family papers; Vincent P. DeSantis, *Republicans Face the Southern Question—The New Departure Years, 1877–1897* (New York: Greenwood Press, 1969), 66–103.
3. Beatty, 229–34, 263, 267–68, 321–23, 351–61; Mary J. Pusey Thorne to Annie Hershey, December 26, 1878, Thorne papers.
4. B.F. Fries to J. Williams Thorne, April 1, 1879, Chester County Historical Society; *Geo. P. Rowell & Cos American Newspaper Directory* (New York: George P. Rowell and Company, 1879), 261, 296; B.F. Fries, "Another D.L. Society," *Direct Legislation Record*, January 1896, 6–7; W. Fitzhugh Brundage, *A Socialist Utopia in the New South: The Ruskin Colonies in Tennessee and Georgia, 1894–1901* (Urbana: University of Illinois Press, 1996), 238n26.
5. Annie to Mary, June 1, 1879; Mary to Annie, June 8, 1879, and June 22, 1879; Mary to Annie, July 20, 1879, Thorne family papers.
6. Progressive Friends Meeting proceedings 1879, 5–6, 12, 16, 29.
7. Progressive Friends Meeting Proceedings 1879, 15–16, 28–29.
8. Progressive Friends Meeting Proceedings 1879, 17, 25; Hugh T. Lefler, *History of North Carolina* (New York: Lewes Historical Publishing Company, 1956), 597–601, 611, 614–19; Escott, 178; "Assigned estate of Peter Hershey and Wife. Inventory and appraisement," filed October 4, 1883, Chester County archives.
9. Progressive Friends Meeting Proceedings, 1879, 21–22, 11.
10. Mary J. Pusey Thorne to Annie Hershey, July 20, 1879; Mary to Annie, August 17, 1879; Thorne family papers. For Edgar's delicate health, see also Annie to Mary (August) 24, 1879; Mary to Annie, December 18, 1879, Thorne family papers.
11. Annie Hershey to Peter Hershey, September 14, 1879, Thorne family papers. For Mary Bayard Clarke, see Terry Armistead Crow and Mary Moulton Barden, eds., *Live Your Own Life: The Family Papers of Mary Bayard Clarke, 1854–1886* (Columbia: University of South Carolina Press, 2003).
12. Three letters from Annie to Peter, c. September 1879; undated letter from Annie to Peter, written from Chester County; Peter to Annie, September 18, 1879; Peter to Annie, September 19, 1879; Annie to Peter, September 19, 1879; Mary to Annie, October 28, 1879; Mary to Annie, December 18, 1879; Mary to Annie, January 4, 1880; Mary to Annie, January 20, 1880, Thorne family papers.
13. Mary to Annie, January 20, 1880, Thorne family papers; Ron Chernow, *Grant* (New York, Penguin Press, 2017), 883–903.
14. J. Williams Thorne to Joshua and Mary Brinton, February 18, 1880, Thorne family papers.
15. Lefler, 623–28; Hamilton, 199, 204–05; North Carolina Senate and House Journals, Special Session 1880, 4–6.
16. Whitener, 61–62; North Carolina Senate and House Journals, Special Session 1880, 67, 134; *Charlotte Democrat*, April 2, 1880, 3; "Sec. 444 Motion to Expunge," in *Mason's Manual of Legislative Procedure* (St. Paul: West Publishing Company, 1989), 289.
17. "J.W. Thorn," letter to the editor (dated April 23, 1880), *The Truth Seeker*, May 1, 1880, 285; Bradford, 177–183, 233; Chernow, 899–902.
18. Mary to Annie, August 27, 1880; Mary to Annie, partial letter dated September 20, 1880, Thorne family papers; Anderson, *Race and Politics*, 68, 83, 84–93; "1880 Presidential election," https://www.270towin.com/1880_Election/. For the Greenbackers, their 1880 campaign, and their attempt to crack the South, see Mark A. Lause, *The Civil War's Last Campaign: James B. Weaver, the Greenback-Labor Party & the Politics of Race and Section* (Lanham, MD: University Press of America, 2001).
19. Foster to "Miss Thorne" (Mary Thorne), December 14, 1880; biographical note on Columbus Foster by Nancy Plumley; Eugene to Mary, December 19, 1880.

20. Whitener, 63–68. The election was ordered to be held on the first Thursday in August, which in 1881 meant August 4.

21. Columbus Foster to Mary, March 14, 1881; Eugene to Mary, February (?) 1881; Eugene to Mary, November 27, 1881, Thorne family papers.

22. Eugene to Mary, May 15, 1881, Thorne family papers.

23. Eugene to Mary, May 15, 1881, J. Williams to Mary, July 23, 1881, Thorne family papers; Corbitt, 211–12, 214–15; Eugene to Mary, November 27, 1881 (Eugene says he is summoned to jury duty in Vance County court).

24. *The Truth Seeker*, May 22, 1880, 331; *The Truth Seeker*, June 5, 1880, 362; *The Index*, June 10, 1880, 278; Ahlstrom and Mullin, 123–24; Bradford, 215–27.

25. William Norwood Brigance, *Jeremiah Sullivan Black: Defender of the Constitution and the Ten Commandments* (Philadelphia: University of Pennsylvania Press, 1934), 249–51; Robert G. Ingersoll and Jeremiah S. Black, "The Christian Religion," *The North American Review* 133, No. 297 (August 1881): 109–152, at 129, 137, 139, 148; J. Williams to Mary Thorne, July 23, 1881. The August issue of the *North American Review* had presumably come out before the cover date, which often happens with magazines.

26. Brigance, 20–22, 62–65, 76–77, 128–29, 145–57, 161–79, 198–203; "Alexander Campbell," https://www.christianitytoday.com/history/people/denominationalfounders/alexander-campbell.html. James Garfield, a friend of Black's despite their political differences, was also a member of the Disciples of Christ. Brigance, 77, 147. Garfield would probably have defended Christianity in different terms from those of his fellow Disciple. During the war, Garfield declared: "Before God I here record my conviction that the spirit of slavery is the soul of the rebellion and the incarnate devil which must be cast out before we can trust in any peace as lasting and secure." Allan Peskin, *Garfield: A Biography* (Kent, OH: Kent State University Press, 1999), 140.

27. Robert G. Ingersoll, "The Christian Religion. Part II," *The North American Review* 133, No. 300 (November 1881): 477–522.

28. J. Williams Thorne to Mary Thorne, July 23, 1881; Whitener, 68–71; Anderson, *Race and Politics*, 97; "John James Mott," https://www.ncpedia.org/biography/mott-john-james.

29. Whitener, 71–73; Anderson, *Race and Politics*, 96–7; Martin, *For God and Race*, 47–96.

30. Eugene to Mary, November 27, 1881, Thorne family papers. *Thorne v. Wickersham*, Appearance Docket 50, #385, Chester County Archives.

31. Anderson, *Race and Politics*, 29–30, 80; Nell Irvin Painter, *Exodusters: Black Migration to Kansas after Reconstruction* (Lawrence: University Press of Kansas, 1986), 251–52; McKinney, 353–54; Eugene to Mary, January 8, 1882, Thorne family papers.

32. J. Williams Thorne to Mary Thorne, July 23, 1881, Thorne family papers. For Garfield's shooting, defective medical care and death, see Candice Millard, *Destiny of the Republic: A Tale of Madness, Medicine and the Murder of a President* (Anchor Books, 2012); Townsend, Waddell, Moore and Joseph and Rebecca Taylor to Chester A. Arthur, January 12, 1882, Thorne family papers; Futhey and Cope, 327, 383, 384, 386, 387, 388, 391.

33. Whitener, 75 ff; DeSantis, 151–62.

34. Jacoby, 178–79.

35. Eugene to Mary (and Peter), February 3, 1882, Thorne family papers.

36. Mary to J. Williams, "Sun Sept (?) 1882," Thorne family papers.

37. J. Williams to Mary, April 7, 1883; April 16, 1883; April 30, 1883, Thorne family papers.

38. Progressive Friends Proceedings, 1883, 4–6.

39. "Assigned estate of Peter Hershey and Wife. Inventory and appraisement," filed October 4, 1883, Chester County archives; Peter Hershey to "Father Thorn," September 17, 1883; undated note by Annie Hershey; partial letter from Peter Hershey, probably from 1884; J. Williams to Mary, April 28, 1884; J.R. Buckwalter to Annie Hershey, July 30, 1884; Lydia Ann Thorne Mews (sister of J.W. Thorne) to Mary, June 25, 1884, Thorne family papers; Census record on Peter Hershey,

Chapter Notes—10

Year: *1920*; Census Place: *Stonington, Christian, Illinois*; Roll: *T625_299*; Page: *7A*; Enumeration District: *28*; Image: *972*, provided via Ancestry.com; information from Nancy Plumley.
40. Progressive Friends Proceedings 1884, 10, 12, 15–16; Chalfant, 98–101.
41. Progressive Friends Proceedings, 1885, 35, 73.
42. J. Williams to Mary, March 10, 1884, Thorne family papers; note by Nancy Plumley; Mary to Eugene, April 4, 1886, Thorne family papers.
43. Lefler, 590–92; *Handbook of the United States of America and Guide to Emigration* (Old House, 2014, originally published 1880), 105.
44. J. Williams Thorne, affidavit, February 16, 1886, and associated legal correspondence, Thorne family papers.
45. Genealogical information about Mary J. Pusey Thorne, courtesy of Ancestry.com; Genealogical charts by Nancy Plumley.
46. Progressive Friends proceedings, 1887, 3, 27.

Chapter 10

1. J. Williams Thorne, "What Constitutes an Education," undated newspaper clipping, Thorne family papers.
2. J. Williams Thorne, "What Constitutes a True Education," *Village Record*, letter dated March 9, 1888, but clipping itself undated, Thorne family papers; "George Franklin Edmunds," http://bioguide.congress.gov/scripts/biodisplay.pl?index=E000056; "On this day," http://movies2.nytimes.com/learning/general/onthisday/harp/0506.html; "John James Ingalls," http://bioguide.congress.gov/scripts/biodisplay.pl?index=I000012.
3. Both articles are in the Thorne family papers, one undated, the other dated May 17, 1888.
4. Chalfant, 102–03; Earl Clifford Kaylor, Jr., "The Prohibition Movement in Pennsylvania, 1865–1920," vols. 1 and 2 (Ph.D. diss., Pennsylvania State University, 1963), 259–63, 284–92.
5. Progressive Friends proceedings, 1888, 86.
6. Progressive Friends proceedings, 1888, 102.
7. Progressive Friends proceedings, 1889; Kaylor, 263–78.
8. Progressive Friends proceedings, 1890.
9. J. Williams Thorne, "Mount Vernon: Washington's Home," newspaper clipping in Thorne family papers, letter dated February 11, 1891.
10. Progressive Friends proceedings 1891, 14.
11. Progressive Friends proceedings 1891, 41.
12. Progressive Friends proceedings 1891, 50–53.
13. Progressive Friends proceedings 1892, 49–50. For the laws against Chinese immigrants, see Lucy E. Salyer, *Laws Harsh as Tigers: Chinese Immigrants and the Shaping of Modern Immigration law* (Chapel Hill: University of North Carolina Press, 1995).
14. "The True Republic. Read before the Longwood Yearly Meeting, of Progressive Friends, June 4, 1892," Thorne family papers; https://www.timeanddate.com/calendar/?year=1892&country=1.
15. "The True Republic"; "Liberty Island Chronology," https://www.nps.gov/stli/learn/historyculture/liberty-island-a-chronology.htm.
16. "The True Republic."
17. "The True Republic."
18. "The True Republic."
19. Progressive Friends proceedings, 1893, 7.
20. Progressive Friends proceedings, 1893, 12–14; Kaylor, 294–303.
21. Progressive Friends proceedings, 1893, 14.
22. Progressive Friends proceedings, 1893, 14–15.
23. Progressive Friends proceedings, 1893, 26.
24. Progressive Friends proceedings, 1893, 26.
25. Progressive Friends proceedings, 1893, 26–27, 31–32.
26. Progressive Friends proceedings, 1893, 27, 44.
27. Progressive Friends proceedings, 1894, 91–96.
28. Progressive Friends proceedings 1894, 59, 64–65, 69.
29. Note by Nancy Plumley (attached

to letter from Walton to Thorne); "Death's Work. J. Williams Thorne," *Local News*, May 18, 1897, clipping in Thorne family papers.
30. Progressive Friends proceedings, 1895, 86–87.
31. Eugene to Edgar, December 12, 1895, Thorne family papers.
32. Eugene to Annie, December 19, 1895, Thorne family papers.
33. E. Clayton Walton to J. Williams, Christmas 1895, Thorne family papers.
34. J. Williams Thorne, "The Financial Situation," clipping from unnamed newspaper, letter dated January 28, 1896, Thorne family papers; Marriott Brosius, http://bioguide.congress.gov/scripts/biodisplay.pl?index=b000892.
35. Frank Hartman to Annie Hershey, March 3, 1896, Thorne family papers.
36. Progressive Friends proceedings, 1897, 116.
37. Caroline Lippincott to Annie Hershey, May 18, 1896, Thorne family papers.
38. Edgar Hershey to Annie (?), March 4, 1897; J. Williams to Annie, March 13, 1877, Thorne family papers; note by Nancy Plumley attached to this letter.
39. Progressive Friends proceedings, 1897, 90, 100–01.
40. Progressive Friends proceedings, 1897, 116–118.

Epilogue

1. *Evening Star* (Washington, D.C.), May 19, 1897, 2; *Baltimore Sun*, May 20, 1897, 2; *San Diego Evening Tribune*, May 20, 1897, 1; *New York Tribune*, May 20, 1897, 7; *Portland Morning Oregonian*, May 20, 1897, 2; *San Diego Union*, May 20, 1897, 1.
2. Smithwick letter, Warren County library.
3. Jones, "Legislator Expelled for Views," *Durham Sun*, May 4, 1977; Jones, "In Light of History," *Statesville Record & Landmark*, August 9, 1984, 7-H.
4. Anderson, *Race and Politics*, 48.
5. McAffee, 182.
6. Dixon, 80–84; "People's Hall," http://www.peoples-hall.org/About%20People's%20Hall.html.
7. "Disciplinary Action by the General Assembly Against Members of the House or Senate," https://www.ncleg.net/library/Documents/DisciplinaryActionsAgainstMembers.pdf.
8. Lucy Maddox, *The Parker Sisters: A Border Kidnapping* (Philadelphia: Temple University Press, 2016), 73–74.
9. Blackett.
10. There are many historical descriptions of these events, including Escott, 241–62; Crow and Durden; Helen G. Edmonds, *The Negro and Fusion Politics in North Carolina* (Chapel Hill: University of North Carolina Press, 1951).
11. Whitener, 116–71.
12. Whitener, 171–226.
13. Kaylor, 325–86; Annie Anderson, "Prohibition," *The Encyclopedia of Greater Philadelphia*, https://philadelphiaencyclopedia.org/archive/prohibition/. For the history of national Prohibition in general, see John Kobler, *Ardent Spirits: The Rise and Fall of Prohibition* (Greenwich, CT: Fawcett Books, 1973).
14. Stephen Prothero, *Why Liberals Win the Culture Wars (Even When They Lose Elections): The Battles That Define America from Jefferson's Heresies to Gay Marriage* (New York: HarperOne, 2016), 139 ff.
15. Alexander Keyssar, *The Right to Vote: The Contested History of Democracy in the United States* (New York: Basic Books, 2000), 186–87, 194; Kobler, 340–42.
16. John C. Weaver, "Black Man, White Justice: The Extradition of Matthew Bullock, an African-American Residing in Ontario, 1922," 34 Osgoode Hall L.J. 627 (1996).
17. The battle over segregated public schools is described in J. Harvie Wilkinson III, *From Brown to Bakke: The Supreme Court and School Integration: 1954–1978* (New York: Oxford University Press, 1979). The battle over interracial marriage is described in Sheryll Cashin, *Loving: Interracial Intimacy in America and the Threat to White Supremacy* (Boston: Beacon Press, 2017).
18. *Joseph Burstyn, Inc. v. Wilson*, 343 U.S. 495 (1952); *Torcaso v. Watkins*, 367 U.S. 488 (1961); *Bond v. Floyd*, 385 U.S.

116 (1966); Anthony Rice, *A Legacy Transformed: The Christiana Riot in Historical Memory* (Dissertation, Lehigh University, 2012), 307–08. For developments in the law of blasphemy, see Leonard Levy, *Blasphemy: Verbal Offenses Against the Sacred, from Moses to Salman Rushdie* (New York: Knopf, 1993).

19. Rice, 207–35.
20. Rice, 245. The lynching and its aftermath is described in Dennis B. Downey and Raymond M. Hyser, *Coatesville and the Lynching of Zachariah Walker: Death in a Pennsylvania Steel Town* (Charleston, SC: History Press, 2011).
21. Rice, 257–89, 302–13.
22. Rice, 357–80.

Appendix II

1. By the phrase "other law" is not meant a law of nature or of the universe, but simply law statutory (J. Williams's note).
2. (Editor's note:) J. Williams may have been adapting a remark attributed to the Greek lawmaker Solon, which Thomas Paine gives as follows in Volume II of his *Age of Reason*: "The answer of Solon on the question, 'Which is the most perfect popular government,' has never been exceeded by any man since his time, as containing a maxim of political morality. 'That,' says he, 'where the least Injury done to the meanest [i.e., lowest or humblest] individual, is considered as an insult on the whole constitution.'" *The Theological Works of Thomas Paine* (Boston: J.P. Mendum, Investigator Office, 1859), 152fn.
3. This is probably a reference to John C. Calhoun, who deplored the influence of the preamble to the Declaration of Independence. See, for example, John C. Calhoun, "Speech on the Oregon Bill, Delivered in the Senate, June 27, 1848," in *The Works of John C. Calhoun*, Vol. 4 (New York: Appleton and Company, 1854), at 507–512. I could only find the specific term "rhetorical flourish," in connection with the Declaration of Independence, in a purported quote from the *Southern Christian Herald* of Columbia, South Carolina, in L. Maria Child, ed., *The Patriarchal Institution, as Described by Members of Its Own Family* (New York: American Anti-Slavery Society, 1860), 4 ("The substance of the wild and extravagant notions which many seem to entertain respecting liberty is contained in that *rhetorical flourish* of Mr. Jefferson...").

Bibliography

Archives

Chester County Archives, Chester County, Pennsylvania.
Chester County Historical Society papers, Chester County, Pennsylvania.
Friends Historical Collection, Swarthmore College, Swarthmore, Pennsylvania.
Lancaster County Archives, Lancaster County, Pennsylvania.
Thorne family papers, in possession of Nancy Plumley, Pennsylvania.
Warren County Memorial Library, Warren County, North Carolina.

Government and Quasi-Governmental Publications

"Digest of Election Cases," 41st Congress, 2nd Session, Mis. Doc. No. 152.
North Carolina Constitutional Convention Journal, 1875.
North Carolina House of Representatives Journal.
North Carolina Land Company, *A Statistical and Descriptive Account of the Several Counties of the State of North Carolina, United States of America* (Raleigh: Nichols and Gorman, 1869).
North Carolina Senate Journal.
Report of the Transactions of the State Agricultural Society, for the years 61–62–63, Vol. 6 (Harrisburg, PA: Singerly & Myers, State Printers, 1863).

Newspapers and Periodicals

American Republican, West Chester, PA.
Boston Investigator, Boston, MA.
Chicago Republican, Chicago, IL.
Christian Union, New York, NY.
Cincinnati Daily Gazette, Cincinnati, OH.
Daily Sentinel, Raleigh, NC.
Direct Legislation Record.
Evening Express, Lancaster, PA.
The Index.
Lancaster Examiner and Herald, Lancaster, PA.
Macon Weekly Telegraph, Macon, GA.
National Anti-Slavery Standard, New York, NY.
New York Herald, New York, NY.
The Occident and American Jewish Advocate.
Pennsylvania Freeman (earlier published as the *National Enquirer*), Philadelphia, PA.

Bibliography

The Pennsylvania School Journal.
Philadelphia Press, Philadelphia, PA.
The Raleigh News, Raleigh, NC.
The Spiritualist at Work, Chicago, IL.
Times and Chronicle, Cincinnati, OH.
The Truth Seeker, New York, NY.
Village Record, West Chester, PA.
The Weekly Era, Raleigh, NC.
West Chester Local News (later the *Daily Local News*), West Chester, PA.
Wheeling Daily Intelligencer, Wheeling, WV.

Primary Sources

American Anti-Slavery Society. *The Fugitive Slave Law and Its Victims*. New York: The Society, 1861.

Brackenridge, H.M. "Speech of H.M. Brackenridge." In *Speeches on the Jew Bill*, edited by H.M. Brackenridge. Philadelphia, 1829, 59–100.

Clark, Samuel, ed. *The American Orator. Selected Chiefly from American Authors; For the Use of Schools and Private Families.* "Gardiner. Printed at the Intelligencer Office," 1828.

Geo. P. Rowell & Cos American Newspaper Director. New York: George P. Rowell and Company, 1879.

Goodell, William. *The Democracy of Christianity, or; An Analysis of the Bible and Its Doctrines in Their Relation to the Principles of Democracy*, Vol. 1. New York: Cady and Burgess, 1849.

Handbook of the United States of America and Guide to Emigration. Old House, 2014; originally published 1880.

In Memoriam, William Goodell. Chicago: Guilbert and Winchell, Printers, 1879.

Ingersoll, Robert G. "The Christian Religion. Part II." *The North American Review* 133, No. 300 (November 1881): 477–522.

Ingersoll, Robert G., and Jeremiah S. Black. "The Christian Religion." *The North American Review* 133, No. 297 (August 1881).

Jay, Allen. *The Autobiography of Allen Jay*. Philadelphia: John C. Winston Co., 1910.

Kersey, Jesse. *A Narrative of the Early Life, Travels and Gospel Labor of Jesse Kersey, Late of Chester County, Pennsylvania*. Philadelphia: T. Ellwood Chapman, 1851.

King, Edward. *The Great South*. Hartford: American Publishing Company, 1875.

National Liberal League. *Equal Rights in Religion. Report of the Centennial Congress of Liberals, and Organization of the National Liberal League at Philadelphia, on the Fourth of July, 1876. With an Introduction and Appendix*. Boston: National Liberal League, 1876.

Proceedings. Progressive Yearly Meeting, Longwood, PA.

The Proceedings of the Women's Rights Convention, Held at West Chester, PA June 2 and 3, 1852. Philadelphia: Merrihew and Thompson, Printers, 1852.

Thorne, J. Williams. *North Carolina in the 19th Century: The Great Ecclesiastical Trial of J. Williams Thorne, Representative from Warren County, Who Was Expelled for Opinion Sake, by the House of Representatives of North Carolina, on February 24, 1875*. Published in 1875.

Train, George Francis. *The Great Epigram Campaign of Kansas*. Leavenworth: Prescott and Hume, 1867.

Bibliography

Secondary Sources

Ahlstrom, Sydney E., and Robert Bruce Mullin. *The Scientific Theist: A Life of Francis Ellingwood Abbot*. Macon, GA: Mercer University Press, 1987.

Anderson, Eric. "James O'Hara of North Carolina: Black Leadership and Local Government." In *Southern Black Leaders of the Reconstruction Era*, edited by Howard N. Rabinowitz. Urbana: University of Illinois Press, 1982.

_____. *Race and Politics in North Carolina: The Black Second*. Baton Rouge: Louisiana State University Press, 1981.

Anscombe, Francis Charles. *I Have Called You Friends: The Story of Quakerism in North Carolina*. Boston: The Christopher Publishing House, 1959.

Armor, William C. *Lives of the Governors of Pennsylvania*. Norwich, CT: T.H. Davis and Company, 1874.

Arthur, John Preston. *Western North Carolina: A History (From 1730 to 1913)*. Raleigh: Edward Buncombe Chapter, Daughters of the American Revolution, 1914.

Babb, Sandra Porter. "The Battle of the Giants: The Gubernatorial Election of 1876 in North Carolina." Master's thesis, University of North Carolina at Chapel Hill, 1970.

Baily, Joshua L. "Give us Something Permanent." In *The Constitutional Prohibitionist, or Prohibition by the People*, edited by J.N. Stearns. New York: National Temperance Society and Publication House, 1887.

Bainton, Roland H. *Here I Stand: A Life of Martin Luther*. Nashville: Abingdon Press, reprint edition, 2013.

Baker, H. Robert. *Prigg v. Pennsylvania: Slavery, the Supreme Court and the Ambivalent Constitution*. Lawrence: University Press of Kansas, 2012.

Balanoff, Elizabeth. "Negro Legislators in the North Carolina General Assembly, July, 1868–February, 1872." *The North Carolina Historical Review* 49, No. 1 (January 1972).

Barnett, Randy. "From Antislavery Lawyer to Chief Justice: The Remarkable but Forgotten Career of Salmon P. Chase." Georgetown Public Law and Legal Theory Research Paper No. 12–122 (2013), http://scholarship.law.georgetown.edu/facpub/1027.

Barrett, John G. *The Civil War in North Carolina*. Chapel Hill: University of North Carolina Press, 1963.

Beatty, Richmond Croom. *Bayard Taylor: Laureate of the Gilded Age*. Norman: University of Oklahoma Press, 1936.

Biddle, Daniel R., and Murray Dubin. *Tasting Freedom: Octavius Catto and the Battle for Equality in Civil War America*. Philadelphia: Temple University Press, 2010.

Bingham, Emily. *Mordecai: An Early American Family*. New York: Hill and Wang, 2003.

Black's Law Dictionary, 8th ed. St. Paul: Thomson West, 2004.

Blackett, R.J.M. *The Captive's Quest for Freedom: Fugitive Slaves, the 1850 Fugitive Slave Law, and the Politics of Slavery*. New York: Cambridge University Press, 2018.

Blue, Frederick J. *The Free Soilers: Third Party Politics 1848–54*. Urbana: University of Illinois Press, 1973.

Bond, Horace Mann. *Education for Freedom: A History of Lincoln University, Pennsylvania*. Princeton, NJ: Princeton University Press, 1976.

Boyd, Melba Joyce. *Discarded Legacy: Politics and Poetics in the Life of Frances E.W. Harper, 1825–1911*. Detroit: Wayne State University Press, 1994.

Bibliography

Bradford, Roderick. *D.M. Bennett: The Truth Seeker.* Amherst, NY: Prometheus Books, 2006.
Brandt, Nat, and Yanna Kroyt Brandt. *In the Shadow of the Civil War: Passmore Williamson and the Rescue of Jane Johnson.* Columbia: University of South Carolina Press, 2007.
Branson, B. Russell. "A Period of Change in North Carolina Quakerism." *Bulletin of Friends Historical Association* 39, No. 2 (Autumn 1950): 74–86.
Brigance, William Norwood. *Jeremiah Sullivan Black: Defender of the Constitution and the Ten Commandments.* Philadelphia: University of Pennsylvania Press, 1934.
Brown, Norman D. *Edward Stanly: Whiggery's Tarheel "Conqueror."* Tuscaloosa: University of Alabama Press, 1974.
Browning, Judkin. *Shifting Loyalties: The Union Occupation of Eastern North Carolina.* Chapel Hill: University of North Carolina Press, 2011.
Brundage, W. Fitzhugh. *A Socialist Utopia in the New South: The Ruskin Colonies in Tennessee and Georgia, 1894–1901.* Urbana: University of Illinois Press, 1996.
Carr, George B. *John Miller Dickey, His Life and Times.* Philadelphia: Westminster Press, 1929.
Cashin, Sheryll. *Loving: Interracial Intimacy in America and the Threat to White Supremacy.* Boston: Beacon Press, 2017.
Chalfant, Harry M. *Father Penn and John Barleycorn.* Harrisburg, PA: Evangelical Press, 1920.
Chernow, Ron. *Grant.* New York: Penguin Press, 2017.
"Christianity as Part of the Law of Pennsylvania." *Dickinson Law Review* 15, No. 1 (October 1910): 1–24.
Clark, Jr., James William. "Frances Ellen Watkins Harper, 1825–1911: A Literary Biography." Master's thesis, Duke University, 1967.
Clayton, Ralph. *Cash for Blood: The Baltimore to New Orleans Domestic Slave Trade.* Bowie, MD: Heritage Books, 2002.
Coleman, John F. *The Disruption of the Pennsylvania Democracy, 1848–1860.* Harrisburg: The Pennsylvania Historical and Museum Commission, 1975.
Connor, R.D.W. *A Manual of North Carolina.* Raleigh: E.M. Uzzell, 1913.
"Contempt by Publication." *Indiana Law Journal* 23, No. 2, Article 9 (1948).
Corbitt, David Leroy. *The Formation of the North Carolina Counties 1663–1943.* Raleigh: Division of Archives and History, 1987.
Crow, Jeffrey J., and Robert F. Durden. *Maverick Republican in the Old North State: A Political Biography of Daniel L. Russell.* Baton Rouge: Louisiana State University Press, 1977.
Crow, Terry Armistead, and Mary Moulton Barden, eds. *Live Your Own Life: The Family Papers of Mary Bayard Clarke, 1854–1886.* Columbia: University of South Carolina Press, 2003.
Curran, Thomas F. *Soldiers of Peace: Civil War Pacifism and the Postwar Radical Peace Movement.* New York: Fordham University Press, 2003.
Current, Richard Nelson. *Those Terrible Carpetbaggers.* New York: Oxford University Press, 1988.
Danson, Edwin. *Drawing the Line: How Mason and Dixon Surveyed the Most Famous Border in America.* New York: John Wiley and Sons, 2001.
Davidson, Theodore F. *Genesis of Buncombe County.* Asheville: The Citizen Company, 1922.
Densmore, Christopher. "Be Ye Therefore Perfect: Anti-Slavery and the Origins of the

Bibliography

Yearly Meeting of Progressive Friends in Chester County, Pennsylvania." *Quaker History* 93, No. 2 (Fall 2004): 28–46.
DeSantis, Vincent P. *Republicans Face the Southern Question—The New Departure Years, 1877–1897.* New York: Greenwood Press, 1969.
DeWees, Watson W. *A Brief History of Westtown Boarding School with a General Catalogue of Officers, Students, etc.* Philadelphia: Sherman and Company, 1872.
DeWees, Watson W., and Sarah B. DeWees. *Centennial History of Westtown Boarding School 1799–1899.* Philadelphia: Westtown Alumni Association, 1899.
Diggins, Milt. *Stealing Freedom Along the Mason-Dixon Line: Thomas McCreary, the Notorious Slave-Catcher from Maryland.* Baltimore: Maryland Historical Society, 2015.
Dinnerstein, Leonard, and Mary Dale Palson, eds. *Jews in the South.* Baton Rouge: Louisiana State University Press, 1973.
Dixon, Mark E. *The Hidden History of Chester County: Lost Tales from the Delaware and Brandywine Valleys.* Charleston, SC: History Press, 2011.
Donnelly, Richard C. "Contempt by Publication in the United States," 1961. *Faculty Scholarship Series.* Paper 4757, http://digitalcommons.law.yale.edu/fss_papers/4757.
Dorsey, Bruce. "Friends Becoming Enemies: Philadelphia Benevolence and the Neglected Era of American Quaker History." *Journal of the Early Republic* (Fall 1998): 395–428.
Downey, Dennis B., and Raymond M. Hyser. *Coatesville and the Lynching of Zachariah Walker: Death in a Pennsylvania Steel Town.* Charleston, SC: History Press, 2011.
Edmonds, Helen G. *The Negro and Fusion Politics in North Carolina.* Chapel Hill: University of North Carolina Press, 1951.
Eitches, Edward. "Maryland's 'Jew Bill.'" *American Jewish Historical Quarterly* (September 1970–June 1971): 258–78.
Elliott, Mark. *Color-Blind Justice: Albion Tourgée and the Quest for Racial Equality from the Civil War to Plessy v. Ferguson.* New York: Oxford University Press, 2006.
Escott, Paul D. *Many Excellent People: Power and Privilege in North Carolina, 1850–1900.* Chapel Hill: University of North Carolina Press, 1985.
Evans, W. McKee. *To Die Game: The Story of the Lowry Band, Indian Guerillas of Reconstruction.* Baton Rouge: Louisiana State University Press, 1971.
Faulkner, Carol. *Lucretia Mott's Heresy: Abolition and Women's Rights in Nineteenth Century America.* Philadelphia: University of Pennsylvania Press, 2011.
Fehrenbacher, Don. *The Dred Scott Case: Its Significance in American Law and Politics.* New York: Oxford University Press, 1978.
Fladeland, Betty. *Abolitionists and Working-Class Problems in the Age of Industrialization.* Baton Rouge: Louisiana State University Press, 1984.
Franklin, John Hope. *The Free Negro in North Carolina, 1790–1860.* Chapel Hill: University of North Carolina Press, 1995 edition.
Futhey, J. Smith, and Gilbert Cope. *History of Chester County, Pennsylvania, with Genealogical and Biographical Sketches.* Philadelphia: Louis H. Everts, 1881.
Goldsmith, Barbara. *Other Powers: The Age of Suffrage, Spiritualism and the Scandalous Victoria Woodhull.* New York: Alfred A. Knopf, 1998.
Goodman, Susan. *Republic of Words: The Atlantic Monthly and Its Writers.* Lebanon, NH: University Press of New England, 2011.
Green, Steven K. *The Second Disestablishment: Church and State in Nineteenth-Century America.* New York: Oxford University Press, 2010.

Bibliography

Guarneri, Carl J. *The Utopian Alternative: Fourierism in Nineteenth-Century America*. Ithaca: Cornell University Press, 1991.
Guerin, Polly. *The Cooper-Hewitt Dynasty of New York*. Charleston, SC: History Press, 2012.
Hamburger, Philip. *Separation of Church and State*. Cambridge, MA: Harvard University Press, 2002.
Hamilton, J.G. de Roulhac. *Reconstruction in North Carolina*. New York: Columbia University, 1914.
Hamm, Thomas D. "George F. White and Hicksite Opposition to the Abolitionist Movement." In *Quakers and Abolition*, edited by Brycchan Carey and Geoffrey Plank. Urbana: University of Illinois Press, 2014.
Harlow, Ralph Volney. *Gerrit Smith: Philanthropist and Reformer*. New York: Henry Holt, 1939.
Harper, Douglas R. *If Thee Must Fight: A Civil War History of Chester County, Pennsylvania*. West Chester: Chester County Historical Society, 1990.
_____. *West Chester to 1865: That Elegant and Notorious Place*. West Chester, PA: Chester County Historical Society, 1999.
Harris, William C. *William Woods Holden: Firebrand of North Carolina Politics*. Baton Rouge: Louisiana State University Press, 1987.
Harrold, Stanley. *Border War: Fighting Over Slavery Before the Civil War*. Chapel Hill: University of North Carolina Press, 2010.
Hild, Matthew. *Greenbackers, Knights of Labor, and Populists: Farmer-Labor Insurgency in the Late-Nineteenth-Century South*. Athens: University of Georgia Press, 2007.
Hill, Michael, ed. *The Governors of North Carolina*. Raleigh: Office of Archives and History, 2007.
Hühner, Leon. "The Struggle for Religious Liberty in North Carolina, with Special Reference to the Jews." *Publications of the American Jewish Historical Society* 16 (1907): 37–71.
Ingle, H. Larry. *Quakers in Conflict: The Hicksite Reformation*. Knoxville: University of Tennessee Press, 1986.
Jacoby, Susan. *The Great Agnostic: Robert Ingersoll and American Freethought*. New Haven: Yale University Press, 2013.
Johnson, Reinhard O. *The Liberty Party 1840–1848: Antislavery Third-Party Politics in the United States*. Baton Rouge: Louisiana State University Press, 2009.
Johnston, George. *The Poets and Poetry of Chester County, Pennsylvania*. Philadelphia: J.P. Lippincott, 1890.
Kashatus, William C. *Abraham Lincoln, the Quakers, and the Civil War*. Santa Barbara: Praeger, 2014.
Kaylor, Jr., Earl Clifford. "The Prohibition Movement in Pennsylvania, 1865–1920," Vols. 1 and 2. Ph.D. diss., Pennsylvania State University, 1963.
Kenzer, Robert C. *Enterprising Southerners: Black Economic Success in North Carolina, 1865–1915*. Charlottesville: University Press of Virginia, 1997.
Keyssar, Alexander. *The Right to Vote: The Contested History of Democracy in the United States*. New York: Basic Books, 2000.
Klein, Philip Shriver. *President James Buchanan: A Biography*. University Park: Pennsylvania State University Press, 1962.
Kobler, John. *Ardent Spirits: The Rise and Fall of Prohibition*. Greenwich, CT: Fawcett Books, 1973.
Larsen, Timothy. *Crisis of Doubt: Honest Faith in Nineteenth-Century England*. New York: Oxford University Press, 2006.

Bibliography

Lause, Mark A. *The Civil War's Last Campaign: James B. Weaver, the Greenback-Labor Party & the Politics of Race and Section*. Lanham, MD: University Press of America, 2001.
Lefler, Hugh T. *History of North Carolina*. New York: Lewes Historical Publishing Company, 1956.
Levitt, Ruth. "Vincent Colyer (1824–1888): Controversial American Humanitarian." *Quaker History* 104, No. 2 (Fall 2015): 1–17.
Levy, Leonard. *Blasphemy: Verbal Offense Against the Sacred, from Moses to Salman Rushdie*. New York: Knopf, 1993.
Longley, Max. *For the Union and the Catholic Church: Four Converts in the Civil War*. Jefferson, NC: McFarland, 2015.
MacElree, Wilmer W. *Side Lights on the Bench and Bar of Chester County*. West Chester: Self-published, 1918.
McAfee, Ward M. *Religion, Race and Reconstruction: The Public School in the Politics of the 1870s*. Albany: State University of New York Press, 1998.
McKinney, Gordon B. *Zeb Vance: North Carolina's Civil War Governor and Gilded Age Political Leader*. Chapel Hill: University of North Carolina Press, 2004.
Maddox, Lucy. *The Parker Sisters: A Border Kidnapping*. Philadelphia: Temple University Press, 2016.
Malone, Dumas. *The Public Life of Thomas Cooper, 1783–1839*. Columbia: University of South Carolina Press, 1961.
Marshall, Clara. *The Women's Medical College of Pennsylvania: An Historical Outline*. Philadelphia: B. Blackiston, Son & Co., 1897.
Martin, Asa Earl. "The Temperance Movement in Pennsylvania Prior to the Civil War." *The Pennsylvania Magazine of History and Biography* 49, No. 3 (1925): 195–230.
Martin, Sandy Dwayne. *For God and Race: The Religious and Political Leadership of AMEZ Bishop James Walker Hood*. Columbia: University of South Carolina Press, 1999.
Mason's Manual of Legislative Procedure. St. Paul: West Publishing Company, 1989.
Millard, Candice. *Destiny of the Republic: A Tale of Madness, Medicine and the Murder of a President*. New York: Anchor Books, 2012.
Montgomery, Lizzie Wilson. *Sketches of Old Warrenton, North Carolina*. Raleigh: Edwards and Broughton Printing Company, 1924.
Moore, John W. *History of North Carolina: From the Earliest Discoveries to the Present Time*, Vol. 2. Raleigh: Alfred Williams & Co., 1880.
Morris, Jr., Roy. *Fraud of the Century: Rutherford B. Hayes, Samuel Tilden, and the Stolen Election of 1876*. New York: Simon & Schuster, 2003.
Morris, Thomas D. *Free Men All: The Personal Liberty Laws of the North, 1780–1861*. Baltimore: Johns Hopkins University Press, 1974.
Murphy, Cait. *Scoundrels in Law: The Trials of Howe & Hummel, Lawyers to the Gangsters, Cops, Starlets, and Rakes Who Made the Gilded Age*. New York: HarperCollins, 2010.
Murray, Pauli. *Proud Shoes: The Story of an American Family*. New York: Harper, 1956.
Nelles, Walter, and Carol Weiss King. "Contempt by Publication in the United States. To the Federal Contempt Statute." *Columbia Law Review* 28, No. 4 (April 1928): 401–431.
Oblinger, Carl Douglas. "New Freedoms, Old Miseries: The Emergence and Disruption of Black Communities in Southeastern Pennsylvania, 1780–1960." Ph.D. diss., Lehigh University, 1988.

Bibliography

Orth, John. *The North Carolina State Constitution: A Reference Guide*. Westport, CT: Greenwood Press, 1993.

Painter, Nell Irvin. *Exodusters: Black Migration to Kansas After Reconstruction*. Lawrence: University Press of Kansas, 1986.

Peskin, Allan. *Garfield: A Biography*. Kent, OH: Kent State University Press, 1999.

Price, Edward. "The Black Voting Rights Issue in Pennsylvania, 1780–1900." *The Pennsylvania Magazine of History and Biography* 100, No. 3 (July 1976): 356–73.

Prothero, Stephen. *Why Liberals Win the Culture Wars (Even When They Lose Elections): The Battles That Define America from Jefferson's Heresies to Gay Marriage*. New York: HarperOne, 2016.

Putnam, Samuel P. *400 Years of Freethought*. New York: The Truth Seeker Company, 1894.

Raffo, Steven. "Oliver Johnson, Abolitionist: 1831–1865." Ph.D. diss., City University of New York, 2000.

Rapalje, Stewart. *A Treatise on Contempt*. New York: L.K. Strouse and Company, 1884.

Rice, Anthony. "A Legacy Transformed: The Christiana Riot in Historical Memory." Ph.D. diss., Lehigh University, 2012.

Ricker, Ralph R. *The Greenback-Labor Movement in Pennsylvania*. Bellephonte: Pennsylvania Heritage, 1966.

Rogers, Abbie. "Confederates and Quakers: The Shared Wartime Experience." *Quaker History* 99, Number 2 (Fall 2010): 1–19.

Rogoff, Leonard. *Down Home: Jewish Life in North Carolina*. Jewish Heritage Foundation of North Carolina. Chapel Hill: University of North Carolina Press, 2010.

Rolle, Andrew. *John Charles Fremont: Character as Destiny*. Norman: University of Oklahoma Press, 1991.

Salyer, Lucy E. *Laws Harsh as Tigers: Chinese Immigrants and the Shaping of Modern Immigration Law*. Chapel Hill: University of North Carolina Press, 1995.

Schauinger, J. Herman. *William Gaston: Carolinian*. Milwaukee: Bruce, 1949.

Sewell, Richard H. *Ballots for Freedom: Antislavery Politics in the United States 1837–1860*. New York: W.W. Norton, 1980.

Silverman, Kenneth. *Lightning Man: The Accursed Life of Samuel F.B. Morse*. Cambridge, MA: Da Capo Press, 2003.

Simmons, William J. *Men of Mark: Eminent, Progressive and Rising*. Cleveland: George M. Rewell & Co, 1887.

Sinha, Manisha. *The Slave's Cause: A History of Abolition*. New Haven: Yale University Press, 2016.

Slap, Andrew L. *The Doom of Reconstruction: The Liberal Republicans in the Civil War Era*. New York: Fordham University Press, 2006.

Slaughter, Thomas P. *Bloody Dawn: The Christiana Riot and Racial Violence in the Antebellum North*. New York: Oxford University Press, 1991.

Smedley, R.C. *History of the Underground Railroad in Chester County and the Neighboring Counties*. Lancaster, PA: Printed by John A. Hiestand, 1883.

Smith, Warren Allen. *Who's Who in Hell*. New York: Barricade Books, 2000.

Sondley, F.A. *Asheville and Buncombe County*. Asheville: The Citizen Company, 1922.

Sorin, Gerald. *The New York Abolitionists: A Case Study of Political Radicalism*. Westport, CT: Greenwood, 1971.

Stanton, Elizabeth Cady, Susan B. Anthony, and Matilda Joslyn Gage. *History of Woman Suffrage*, Vol. 1. Rochester, New York: Charles Mann, 1889.

Sterling, Dorothy. *Ahead of Her Time: Abby Kelley and the Politics of Antislavery*. New York: W.W. Norton, 1991.

Bibliography

Summers, Mark Wahlgren. *The Ordeal of the Reunion.* Chapel Hill: University of North Carolina Press, 2014.
Thomas, John L. *The Law of Constructive Contempt: The Shepherd Case Reviewed.* St. Louis: The F.H. Thomas Law Book Co., 1904.
Thorpe, Margaret Newbold. "A 'Yankee Teacher' in North Carolina." *The North Carolina Historical Review* 30, No. 4 (October 1953): 564–82.
Tomek, Beverly C. *Pennsylvania Hall: A "Legal Lynching" in the Shadow of the Liberty Bell.* New York: Oxford University Press, 2014.
Torrey, E. Fuller. *The Martyrdom of Abolitionist Charles Torrey.* Baton Rouge: Louisiana State University Press, 2013.
Trefousse, Hans L. *Thaddeus Stevens: Nineteenth-Century Egalitarian.* Mechanicsburg, PA: Stackpole Books, 2001.
Trelease, Allen W. *White Terror: The Ku Klux Klan Conspiracy and Southern Reconstruction.* New York: Harper and Row, 1971.
Unger, Irwin. *The Greenback Era: A Social and Political History of American Finance, 1865–1879.* Princeton, NJ: Princeton University Press, 1964.
Wahl, Albert J. "Longwood Meeting: Public Forum for the American Democratic Faith." *Pennsylvania History: A Journal of Mid-Atlantic Studies* 42, No. 1 (January 1975): 42–69.
Wallace, Peter J. "'The Bond of Union': The Old School Presbyterian Church and the American Nation, 1837–1861." Ph.D. diss., University of Notre Dame, 2004, http://www.peterwallace.org/bond-union/.
Wallenstein, Peter, and Bertram Wyatt-Brown, eds. *Virginia's Civil War.* Charlottesville: University of Virginia Press, 2005.
Weaver, John C. "Black Man, White Justice: The Extradition of Matthew Bullock, and African-American Residing in Ontario, 1922," 34 Osgoode Hall L.J. 627, 1996.
Wellman, Manly Wade. *The County of Warren, North Carolina, 1586–1917.* Chapel Hill: The University of North Carolina Press, 1959.
Werbel, Amy. *Lust on Trial: Censorship and the Rise of American Obscenity in the Age of Anthony Comstock.* New York: Columbia University Press, 2018.
"What Right Had a Fugitive Slave of Self-Defence against His Master?" *The Pennsylvania Magazine of History and Biography* 13, No. 1 (April 1889): 106–109.
Wheeler, John Hill. *Reminiscences and Memoirs of North Carolina and Eminent North Carolinians.* Columbus, OH: Columbus Printing Works, 1884.
Whitener, Daniel J. *Prohibition in North Carolina.* Chapel Hill: University of North Carolina Press, 1946.
Whitson, Thomas, Esq. "The Early Abolitionists of Lancaster County." *Journal of the Lancaster County Historical Society* 15, No. 3 (1911).
Wilkinson, J. Harvie, III. *From Brown to Bakke: The Supreme Court and School Integration: 1954–1978.* New York: Oxford University Press, 1979.
Wilson, Carol. *Freedom at Risk: The Kidnapping of Free Blacks in America, 1780–1865.* Lexington: University Press of Kentucky, 1994.
Winch, Julie. "Philadelphia and the Other Underground Railroad." *The Pennsylvania Magazine of History and Biography* 111, No. 1 (January 1987): 3–25.
Woodwell, Roland H. *John Greenleaf Whittier: A Biography.* Haverhill, MA: Trustees of the John Greenleaf Whittier Homestead, 1985.
Work, Monroe N., Thomas S. Staples, H.A. Wallace, Kelly Miller, Whitefield McKinlay, Samuel E. Lacy, R.L. Smith and H.R. McIlwaine. "Some Negro Members of Reconstruction Conventions and Legislatures and of Congress." *The Journal of Negro History* 5, No. 1 (January 1920).

Bibliography

The Works of the English Poets, Vol. 18. London: 1810.

Worrell, Emma. "Memories of Longwood Meeting." *Friends' Intelligencer* 75, No. 35 (August 31, 1918): 547–48.

Yandle, Paul. "Different Colored Currents of the Sea: Reconstruction North Carolina, Mutuality, and the Political Roots of Jim Crow, 1872–1875." In *North Carolinians in the Era of the Civil War and Reconstruction*, edited by Paul D. Escott. Chapel Hill: University of North Carolina Press, 2008.

Zilversmit, Arthur. *The First Emancipation: The Abolition of Slavery in the North.* Chicago: University of Chicago Press, 1967.

Index

Numbers in ***bold italics*** indicate pages with illustrations

Abbot, Francis Ellingwood 99–100, 122
abolitionism *see* slavery and antislavery
African Americans 3, 4, 8, 9, 10, 17, 19, 20–22, 30, 32, 35–38, 44, 48, 50, 54, 56, 57, 60, 61, 62–63, 66, 69, 70, 73, 74–75, 76, 80, 84, 85, 87, 90–91, 102–3, 106, 107–9, 110, 114, 117, 125, 126, 129, 132, 135, 136, 137, 157, 158, 159, 161
African Methodist Episcopal Church 21
African Methodist Episcopal Zion church (AMEZ) 135
Alberti, George F. 40
Alma 58
American and Foreign Antislavery Society (New Organization) 22, 23
American Anti-Slavery Society (AASS) (Old Organization) 15, 22, 23, 50, 63
American Colonization Society (ACS) 22, 50
American Liberal Union 122, 133, 186*n*46
American Orator 14
American Republican (West Chester, PA) 67, 98, 101, 119, 121, 123, 136
amusements 51, 52
Anderson, Eric 157
Andersonville (Confederate POW camp) 138
Anglicanism 78–79, 83, 92
Annapolis, MD 20
apprenticeship bill 90–91
arbitration: of international disputes 47, 154, 161; in lieu of litigation 154–55
Arch Street Monthly Meeting, Philadelphia, PA 9
Areopagitica 26
Arthur, Chester A. 136–37
Ashmun Institute *see* Lincoln University
atheism 1, 4, 43, 76, 89, 90, 92, 95, 96, 99, 100, 101, 102, 103, 110, 133, 140, 160, 173*n*33, 182*n*6
"Aunt Margaret" 138

Baily, E.W. 85
Baltimore, MD 8, 30, 31, 39–40, 54–55

Baltimore Association 68, 69
Barclay, Robert 14
Barker, Joseph 49, 51, 53, 76–78, 81, 88
Bart, PA 32
Beattie, James 115
Beecher, Henry Ward 58, 79, 81, 99
Bell, F.W. 108
Bennett, D.M. 99, 121–22, ***123***, 130, 133
Berlin (Germany) 137
Bertie County, NC 108
Bible 1, 11, 12, 13–14, 25, 34, 49, 69, 77–82, 89–97, 98, 100, 102, 103, 128, 146, 148; NC bill for Bible reading in public schools 91
Bigler, William 37–38, 40, 44
Birney, James G. 22–23
Black, Jeremiah S. 133–35, ***134***
Blackett, R.J.M. 158
Blackstone, William 116, 121, 167
Blaine, James G. 111, 185*n*16
Bloomer, Amelia 40–41
Bonaparte, Napoleon 13
Bond, Horace Mann 160, 161
Bond, Julian 160
Bond, William 55
Bostock, Franklin 54, 57
Boston Investigator 77
Brackenridge, H.M. 14
Bragg, Braxton 70
Bragg, Thomas 70
Brinton, Joshua 35, 129
Brinton, Mary 129
Brogden, Curtis 4, 90, 122
Brosius, Marriott 153
Brown, Henry Lee 31–32
Brown, John (free black laborer) 54–55, 56–57, 59, 61–62, 157
Brown, John (white abolitionist) 53–54
Buchanan, James 44, 52, 134
Bull, James H. 119–21
Bullock, Matthew 159–60
Buren, Martin van 33

Index

Butler, Judge William 120
Byron, Lord 13

Cabarrus County 89
Caldwell, Tod 75
Calhoun, John C. 115, 166, 168, 185*n*27, 191*n*3
California 59
Campbell, Bernard Moore 31, 39, 40
Campbell, James 44
Campbell, Lewis 31
Canaanites 80, 133
Canada 30, 37, 159–60
capital punishment 47
The Captive's Quest for Freedom 158
"carpetbaggers" 4, 66–67, 68, 87–88, 94, 101, 137, 156
Carter, Hawkins W. 90
Carteret County, NC 14
Catholic Church 48, 92, 98, 111, 143, 157
Catto, Octavius 75
Cecil County, MD 31
Cecil Whig 31, 32
Centennial Ode 126
Charleston, SC 110
Charlotte Democrat 130
Chase, Salmon P. 33
Chester County, PA 4, 5, 7–9, 14, 15–16, 18, 19, 20, 21, 23, 24, 25, 27, 28, 29, 30, 31, 32, 33, 35, 36, 38, 39, 40, 41, 43, 44, 45, 48, 49, 50, 51, 53, 58, 60, 62–63, 66, 68, 71, 73, 74, 75, 76–77, 78, 79, 80, 82, 84, 85, 94, 101, 113, 119, 120, 121, 126–27, 129, 135, 136, 142, 143, 144, 151, 157, 160–61
Chester County Agricultural Society 28, 50, 53
Chester County Antislavery Society 16, 23
Chestnut Hill farm (Lancaster County, PA) 140, 141
Chicago Tribune 98
The Children's Friend 6
Choccoe Creek *see* Shocco Creek
Christian Commission 60
Christian Statesman 100–1
Christian Union 58, 99, 104
Christiana, PA 32, 36–39, *37*, 71
Christiana Resistance (Christiana Riot) 36–39, 160–61
Christianity 1, 3, 10–11, 14, 16, 18, 34, 47, 48, 49, 57, 61, 65, 69, 71, 76–82, 83, 89, 92, 94, 98–100, 101, 102–3, 105, 106, 108, 109, 112, 122, 128, 133–35, 137, 144, 147–48, 161, 177*n*31, 188*n*26
Christmas, Alfred 84–85
Church of England *see* Anglicanism
Cincinnati Times and Chronicle 100
Citizen's Suffrage Association 104
Civil Rights Act of 1875 (including earlier bills which developed into the Act) 87, 102
Claflin Tennessee Celeste (sister of Victoria Woodhull) 79
Clarke, Mary Bayard 129
Clarkson Antislavery Society 16
Clay, Henry 23
Clearfield, PA 111
Coates, Lindley 35
Coatesville, PA 71, 77–78, 120, 161; Market Hall 78
Coley's Springs (school) 117
colonization movement 21, 46, 50
Colyer, Vincent 59–60
Compassville, PA 71
Comstock, Anthony 79, 121–22
Confederate States of America 77, 94, 108
Congregational Friends *see* Progressive Friends
Conservative Party *see* Democratic Party of North Carolina
Cooper, Peter 112
Cooper, Thomas 10–11
Craven County, NC 107, 131
Crews, W.H. 96, 97
Crosby, John Oliver 107–8, 109
Cumberland County, NC 113

Daily Commercial (Wilmington, DE) 66
Daily Constitution (Raleigh, NC) 109–10
Daily Local News (West Chester, PA) *see* *West Chester Local News*
Daily News (Raleigh, NC) 110
Darlington, Chandler 127
Darlington, Isaac 8
Darlington, William 59
David (Biblical king) 80–81
Davis, Elizabeth *see* Elizabeth Davis Thorne
Davis, Jacob C. 88–89
Declaration of Independence 60, 102, 115, 116, 166, 168, 191*n*3
Declaration of Rights (North Carolina) 14
deism 11, 49, 53, 84, 85, 99, 100, 106
Democratic Party 23, 100, 101, 102, 114, 123, 126, 131, 137, 156, 157, 180*n*29
Democratic Party of North Carolina 4, 70, 74–75, 87, 91, 94, 95, 98, 106–10, 112, 114, 122, 123, 125, 135, 137, 140, 157, 158, 183*n*31
Democratic Party of Pennsylvania 43, 65–66
Dickey, John Miller 40, 49–50, 80
Dixon, Mark E. 157
Donovan, Joseph 54–55
Douglas, Stephen 52, 55, 134
Downington Township, PA 30–31

East Fallowfield, PA 5, 21
East Fallowfield Antislavery Society 15–16, 21, 173*n*28

204

Index

East Sadsbury Monthly Meeting (Quaker), Chester County, PA 6
Eaton, William 107
economic depression of 1873 82, 105
Edgecombe county, North Carolina 71, 107
Edmunds, George 143
Eighteenth Amendment 159
Emancipation Proclamation 91; Preliminary (September 22, 1862) 61
England 10, 49, 76–77, 78, 116, 142, 169
Ercildoun, PA 6
Evans, Henry S. 31
ex Parte Milligan 134

Falkener, Richard 86
Fallowfield Monthly Meeting: Chester County, PA 5; Hicksite 11–12, 21, 23, 24–25, 172n17; Orthodox 11–12, 172n17
Fallowfield Preparative Meeting 25
Faust 127
Fayetteville, NC 113
federal liquor tax 132, 135
Fifteenth Amendment (U.S. Constitution) 66
Finger, Sidney M. 96
Florida 59, 153
Foote, J.H. 95
Foster, Columbus 131, 132, 136
"Fot" (obscure reference to a deity) 99
Fountain Hill (J. Williams Thorne's first farm in PA) 27–28, 40, 73, 74, 76, 82, 83, 127, 132, 138, 139, 140
Fourierism 41
Franklin, Benjamin 115, 143
Franklin County, NC 133, 182n15
Free Religious Association 99
Free-Soil Party 33
Fremont, John C. 59, 61
Friends' Association of Philadelphia and Its Vicinity for the Relief of Colored Freed Men 69
Fries, Ben F. 127
Frothingham, O.B. 129
Fugitive Slave Act of 1793 9, 20, 23, 32
Fugitive Slave Act of 1850 32, 36–39, 56
fugitive slaves 8–10, 19, 20, 23, 36, 70; Abraham Lincoln and fugitive-slave law 55, 177n27
Fulton, James 65
Fulton, Joseph 35
Fulton, Mary Dubree Thorne Bond (sister of J. Williams Thorne) 6, 63
"fusion" movement (NC) 158
Fussell, Dr. Bartholomew 43
Fussell, Dr. Edwin 24–25, 42

Gadarene swine (from Bible) 81
gambling 73–74, 85, 90, 124, 147, 149

Gap Gang 48, 158
Garfield, James 130, 131, 136, 188n26
Garrett, Thomas 43, 61
Garrison, William Lloyd 22, 23, 32, 33, 36, 42, 45, 49, 53, 60, 77, 100
Gash, Thomas L. 96–97, 183n31
Gaston, William 92, 94
George, Henry 150
Georgia 59, 136
Germany 127
Gettysburg, Battle of 62–63
gold standard 111, 122, 123, 152
Golden Rule 91, 102, 110, 116, 167
Goldsboro Messenger 125
Goodell, William 34
Gorsuch, Edward 36, *37*, 160
Graham, William A. 107, 109–10
grand juries 29, 31, 32, 37, 44, 121
Grant, Ulysses 75, 101–2, 111, 129, 130
Granville County NC 91, 96, 97, 116, 129, 133, 182n15
Greeley, Horace 41, 101, 180n29
Greenback Labor Party 112, 123, 124, 125, 126, 127, 131, 137
Greenback movement 123, 124, 125, 126, 127
Greenback Nationalist 127
Grier, Robert 38–39
Griffith, Samuel 8
Gudger, Hezekiah A. 91, 93, 96, 132
Guilford College *see* New Garden Boarding School
Guilford County, NC 68, 93, 94, 109

habeas corpus 30, 53
Halifax County, NC 107, 109
Hamilton, J.G. de Roulhac 87–88
Handbook for immigrants, 1880 140
Hanway, Castner 36–39, 43, 45, 46, 49, 160
Hanway, Washington 36, 39, 42, 52, 63, 76, 88, 153
Harnett County, NC 95, 97
Harper, Douglas 28
Harper, Ellen Watkins 71
Harris, James S. 122, 125
Harris, S.C. 116
Harrison, Thomas S. 96
Hayes, Rutherford B. 110–12, 116, 123, 126, 129
Hayes, William 120
Heaven 92, 119
Hell 92, 103
Henderson, NC 129, 133, 138, 152
Henry, Jacob 14, *15*
Hershey, Anna ("Annie") Emma Thorne (Daughter of J. Williams Thorne) 41, 72, 73–74, 76, 82, 106, 112, 117, 118, 120, 122, 127, 128–29, 131, 138, 139, 140, 141, 151, 152, 153–54, 178n40

205

Index

Hershey, Carl 106
Hershey, Edgar 118, 128–29, 140, 141, 152, 153–54
Hershey, John 74
Hershey, Peter 72, 73–74, 76, 82, 83, 118, 120, 127, 128, 129, 132, 137–38, 139
Hershey, Ralph 138, 141, 153–54
Hickman, John 60, 66
Hicks, Elias 11, 12, 19
Hicksite Quakers 11, 18–19, 21, 24, 27, 41–42, 46–47, 48, 79
Hinduism 94; Brahma 99; Vishnu 99
Hinkley, F.A. 154–55
Holden, William Woods 4, 68, 75
Hood, James Walker 43, 135
House of Commons, North Carolina *see* North Carolina House of Representatives
House of Lords (England) 142
Houston, R.J. 28–29
Hubbs, Orlando 131, 135, 136
Hudson, Erasmus 24
Hughes, Hanson T. 90, 91, 95, 97, 116–17, 157
Hull, Gilmore 54, 57
Humphrey, Anullette 139
Hunter, David 59, 61
Huntingdon, PA 127
Hyman, John 70, 84, 112, 122

Illinois 52, 72, 139, 177n14
immigration 68, 140, 143, 146, 147–48, 154; Chinese 123, 140, 143, 146–47; Hungarian 140; Swedish 140
income tax 123, 125
The Index 99–100, 101, 111, 122, 133, 185n15
Indiana 5, 136
Ingalls, John 143
Ingersoll, Robert 112, 133–35, 137, 185n16
Industrial Mutualist *see* Peers of Kosmos Compact
Isaac (Biblical patriarch) 80
Islam 80, 177n31
Israelites (in Bible) 80

Jackson, Thomas ("Stonewall") 95
Jay, Allen 68
Jefferson, Thomas 1, 10, 116, 166, 168
Jeffersonian (West Chester, PA) 25
Jepthah (Biblical figure) 80
Jesus 48, 58, 79, 81, 100, 143, 147, 167
Jews 14, 81, 93, 177n31
Johnson, Andrew 134–35
Johnson, Oliver 42, 43, 52, 57
Johnston, George 6
Johnston, William F. 37–38
Jones, Benjamin 24
Jones, Benjamin W. 76

Jones, H.G. 156
Jones, Sidney 45–46
Jones Springs, NC 69
juries 8, 25, 38, 39, 44, 53, 57, 62, 119, 120–21, 134, 136, 188n23
Justinian (Roman emperor) 167

Kelley, Abby 23–25
Kennett Monthly Meeting 41–42, 49
Kent, Esther 53–54
Kent, Henry S. 148
Kersey, Jesse 17–18, 103, 173n33
King, Edward 3–4
Kitchin, William H. ("Buck") 122, 123, 125, 186n56
Kline, Henry 36
Ku Klux Klan 74–75

labor theory of value 124, 150
Lafayette, Marquis de 7
Lancaster, PA (county seat of Lancaster County) 127, 138
Lancaster County, PA 6, 19, 20, 21, 28, 29, 32, 33, 36, 38, 43, 44, 48, 50, 52, 54, 62–63, 68, 71, 75, 140, 153
Lancaster Evening Express 67
Lancaster Examiner and Herald 57, 74
Lancaster Historical Society 160
Lancaster Inquirer 153
Latta, Dr. (anti-abolitionist census-taker) 56
Lazarus, Marx Edgeworth 41, 71–72
Lee, Robert E. 62, 95
Lewis, Elijah 36–39
Liberal Anti-Prohibition Party 137
Liberals (religious) 78–82, 110, 111, 121–22, 129, 130; *see also* National Liberal League and American Liberal Union
Liberator 22, 55
Liberia 21–22, 50
Liberty Party 22–23, 33–35
Lincoln, Abraham 52, 55–56, 57, 58, 59, 60–61, 63, 77, 134, 143
Lincoln University 50, 75, 80, 84, 160, 161
Lippincott, Barclay H. 76, 88, 90
Lippincott, Caroline Thorne Hanway (sister of J. Williams Thorne) 6, 36, 63, 76, 88, 153
Lippincott, Emma 76
London Grove, PA 24
London Grove Monthly Meeting 172n17
Longwood, PA 41, 43
Longwood Yearly Meeting of Progressive Friends 43, 45–48, 49, 50, 51, 52, 55–56, 57, 58–61, 62, 63, 66, 69, 79, 84, 90, 104, 118, 127–28, 138, 139–40, 141, 144, 146–52, 153, 154–55, 161–62, 163–64
Louisburg, NC 136
Love, Alfred 60, 62

206

Index

Love vs. Marriage 41
Lowrie, James Robinson 97
Lukens, Charles 25
Lukens, William 25
"Lunar Cycle Rule" 143
Lundy, Benjamin 15
Luther, Martin 14, 93
Lyceum movement 26, 28–29, 41, 51, 58, 72

Mabry (or "Maberry"), S.W. 113
MacElree, Wilmer W. 119–20, 186*n*39
Mackey, Edward 54, 57–58
Macon, Nathaniel 92, 94; Nathaniel Macon House **93**
Maddox, Lucy 157–58
Madison County, NC 91
"Maine Law" movement 50–51
Marlborough Monthly Meeting (Hicksite) 42
Mason-Dixon Line 8, 31, 39, 50, 172*n*12
Massachusetts 149
Massachusetts Personal Liberty Law 53
Matlack, J. Chalkley 171*n*5
May, Samuel 175*n*36
Mayflower (ship) 67
McAfee, Ward M. 157
McCreary, Thomas 31–32, 39
Means, Paul B. 89
Mendenhall, Nereus 94–95, 157
Methodism 77, 79
Mewes, Lydia Ann Thorne (sister of J. Williams Thorne) 6–7, 63
Mexico City 126
Middleburg, NC 135
Miller, Joseph 39–40, 45
Millwood Lyceum 72
Milton, John 26, 147, 150
"miscegenation" 100, 102, 108–9, 122
Mississippi 9, 136, 149, 153, 158
Mitchell, Tom 31–32
model farm 68
Mohammad 94
Monty Python's Life of Brian (movie) 21
Moore, Edward B. 59, 67–68, 136–37
Moore, Joseph 35
Moore, Samuel D. 102, 184*n*51
Mordecai, Alfred 71
Mordecai, Laura 71
Mordecai, Miriam 71
Mordecai, Rose 71
Moring, John M. 90, 91–92, 95, 182*n*14
"Moses" (poem) 71
Mott, John J. 135, 137
Mott, Lucretia 45
Mount Tambora (in modern Indonesia) 5
Moyamensing Prison (Philadelphia, PA) 38
Murray, Pauli 35

NAACP 159
Napa Register (CA) 98
National Antislavery Standard 23, 24, 56, 65
National Enquirer and Constitutional Advocate of Universal Liberty see *Pennsylvania Freeman*
National Liberal League 111, 121, 133, 184*n*14; state Liberal Leagues 100
National Liberal League of America see American Liberal Union
National Reform Association 100–1
Native Americans ("Indians") 79
Nethry, William 59
New Bern, NC 59, 102–3, 129
New Garden Boarding School 94
New Orleans, LA 102, 110
New York, NY 60, 79, 99
New York Observer 57, 178*n*33
New York Society for the Suppression of Vice 79
New York Times 98
New York *Tribune* 41
Newton, Isaac 150
Nineteenth Amendment 159
Noble, W.Y.P. 101
Norlina 159
Normans 67
Norment, Dr. Richard Montgomery ("R.M.") 89–90, 91, 95, 96, 97, 107, 130
North American Review 133, 135, 188*n*25
North Carolina 1, 3–4, 14, 59–60, 66, 68–69, 73, 74–75, 76, 78, 82, 84, 86, 87, 90, 91, **93**, 94, 96, 101, 103, 104, 105, 107, 108, 113, 116, 118, 122, 126, 127, 128, 129–31, 132, 133, 135–36, 137, 138, 139, 140, 150, 151, 152, 156, 157, 158, 159, 160, 162
North Carolina Constitution 97, 106–110, 115, 182*n*6; anti-miscegenation amendment 108–9, 112; local-government amendment 107, 112, 114–15; segregated-schools amendment 107–8, 112, 157
North Carolina House of Representatives 3–4, 14, 86, 87, 88–97, 98, 103, 104–5; Committee on Privileges and Elections 89–90; Education Committee 91
North Carolina in the 19th Century: The Great Ecclesiastical Trial of J. Williams Thorne 101–3, 109
North Carolina Land Company 68
North Carolina Senate 84–86, 87, 89, 90, 111–17, 130–31, 165–69; Committee on Buildings and Grounds 113; Committee on Corporations 117; Committee on Insurance 113
North Carolina Supreme Court 90, 91, 92, 117

207

Index

Oak Grove (J. Williams Thorne's Warren County, NC farm) 73, 118, 128, 129
Oberlin College 84
O'Hara, James 109, 122, 125
Orange County, NC 107
Orthodox Quakers 11–12, 18, 24, 69, 94
Ottawa, Illinois 52, 72, 117n14

Pacifism 47, 94, 178n40
Paine, Thomas 98
Panama Canal Zone 91
Parker, Eliza (wife of William Parker) 36
Parker, Elizabeth 39–40, 44, 50
Parker, Rachel 39–40, 44, 50
Parker, William 36, 75, 161
Paschall, John M. 85–86
Passmore, Joseph W. 153
Patton, Montraville 95–96
Peers of Kosmos Compact (Industrial Mutualist) 127
Pennock, Elizabeth 69, 83
Pennock, Joseph Liddon 24–25
Pennsylvania 1, 5, 8–10, 10–11, 15, 17, 20, 23, 30–32, 35, 36, 37, 38, 39, 40, 44, 50–51, 52, 55, 56, 57, 62–63, 65, 66, 69, 70, 73, 74, 75, 78, 83, 90, 92, 97, 99, 101, 104, 105, 112, 118, 120–121, 123, 127, 128, 129, 131, 132, 135, 137–38, 139, 140, 149, 150, 151
Pennsylvania Abolition Society (PAS) 9, 15, 21
Pennsylvania Antislavery Society (PAAS) 16, 45, 53
Pennsylvania Constitution 128; proposed prohibition amendment 143–44, 146
Pennsylvania Freeman 15
Pennsylvania Hall 16, 17, *17*
Pennsylvania legislature 30, 47, 50, 53, 66, 85, 104, 136, 143
Pennsylvania Personal Liberty Laws: amendment to 1847 law 40; law of 1826 10, 26; law of 1847 30, 32, 37, 57; pre-1826 8–10; proposed amendment to 1847 law 57
Pennsylvania School Journal 71
Pennsylvania State Teachers' Association 71
Pennsylvania Supreme Court 17, 29
People's Hall (Ercildoun, Chester County, PA) 26, *27*, 157
People's Hall (Warren County, NC) 113–14
Pharisees 103
Philadelphia, PA 5, 7, 9, 11, 14, 15, 16, 24, 31, 38, 43, 49, 53, 63, 69, 71, 75, 76, 77, 101, 103–4, 111, 152, 160, 171n5, 180n27; Concert Hall 71
Philadelphia Press 71
Philadelphia Times 103–4
Philadelphia Yearly Meeting (Hicksite) 11, 24, 42; Western Quarterly Meeting, 24, 27
Philadelphia Yearly Meeting (Orthodox) 11
Phillips, Wendell 55, 100
Pilgrims 67
The Poets and Poetry of Chester County 6
Polk, James K. 23
polygamy 49, 80, 81, 143, 148
Pownall, Levi 36
Pownall, Sarah 36
Pownell, J.D. 75
Presbyterianism 40, 49–50, 80, 178n33
Priestly, J.B. 10
Prigg v. Pennsylvania 20, 30
Progressive Friends 41–42, 43, 69; *see also* Longwood Yearly Meeting of Progressive Friends
prohibition (of alcohol) 47, 50–51, 63, 88, 105, 113–14, 130, 132, 135, 137, 141, 143–44, 146, 148, 149, 150, 151, 158–59, 188n20; high-license laws 143–44, 149, 159; local option 29, 88, 105, 159; monopolistic state liquor stores 158
prostitution 148
Prothero, Stephen 159
Puritans 79
Purvis, Robert 45
Pusey, Ann ("Annie") 73–74, 90, 118, 119
Pusey, Caleb Alfred ("Alfred") 73
Pusey, Eliza 58
Pusey, Evan 66
Pusey, Jesse D. 119, 178n40
Pusey, Mary Jones *see* Thorne, Mary Jones Pusey

"Quaker Belt" (North Carolina) 68–69
Quaker schism of 1827 11; *see also* Orthodox Quakers and Hicksite Quakers
Quakers (pre-schism) 79

Radical Club 104
Raleigh, NC 3–4, 97, 102–3, 108, 102–3, 112, 127, 132, 140
Raleigh and Gaston Railroad 66
Raleigh Daily Sentinel 93–94
Raleigh Daily Times 97–98
Raleigh News 90–91, 93, 100
Ransom, William S. 86
Read, John 7–8
Reconstruction 3, 67, 87, 92, 94, 116, 135
Reece, Daniel 12
Reid, David S. 107
Religion, Race and Reconstruction 157
Religious Freedom Amendment 100
Republican Party 33, 60, 87, 102, 110–11, 111–12, 114, 126, 130, 132, 134–35, 137, 156; of North Carolina 74–75, 84, 87, 107–9, 110, 122, 123, 125, 130–31, 132, 135, 137, 140, 158; of Pennsylvania 52, 66, 136–37, 143; of Warren County 84

Index

Rice, Edgar 161
Richardson, John 57
Ridgeway, NC 66, 126
Ritner, Joseph 17
Roanoke River, NC 3
Roberts, [first name not given] (friend of J. Williams Thorne) 78
Rohrer, John 139
Rose, Ernestine 45
Russell, Daniel L. 125
Russia 147

Sadsbury (Chester County, PA) 6, 27–28, 32, 53, 54, 66
Sadsbury (Lancaster County, PA) 6
Sadsbury Monthly Meeting (Lancaster County, PA) 6, 33, 43
Second Congressional District, NC ("Black Second") 84, 122, 125, 157
Second Great Awakening 11
Settle, Thomas 112
Shadd, Abraham 21
Shakerism 99
Shakespeare, William 142
Shelley, Percy Bysshe 140
Sheridan, Philip H. 102
Shipley, Peter 8
Shocco (township) 85
Shocco Chapel 113–14
Shocco Creek, NC 66
Shocco Springs, NC 69
Sickles, Daniel 67
slavery and antislavery 1, 3, 8–10, 14–19, 20–25, 26, 30–34, 35–36, 38–41, 42, 43, 44–46, 48, 49, 50, 51, 52, 53–57, 58, 59–63, 65, 69–70, 71, 77, 78, 79, 80, 81, 91, 94, 108, 110, 115, 122, 128, 133–35, 146, 147, 149, 151, 157–58, 160, 161–62, 163
Smedley, Dr. Robert Clemens ("R.C.") 32–34
Smith, Gerrit 33–34
Smithwick, D.T. 66, 72, 83, 156
Smythe, J.H. 109
Society for the Relief of Free Negroes Unlawfully Held in Bondage *see* Pennsylvania Abolition Society
Solomon (Biblical king) 81
Solon (Greek lawmaker) 191*n*2
South Carolina 3, 11, 59, 67, 108, 135, 168
South Carolina College, Columbia, SC 11
Spears, John A. 95, 96–97, 183*n*31
spiritualism 92, 101
The Spiritualist at Work 101
Stanly, Edward 59–60, 61
Staples, John N 93
Statue of Liberty 147
Stowe, Harriet Beecher 42
Swayne, Benjamin 19
Syracuse, NY 120

Tar River, NC 3
Tarboro, North Carolina 71
Taylor, Bayard 62, 126–27, 128, 137, 147
Taylor, Fred 62
Taylor, Joseph 62, 137
Taylor, Rebecca 62, 137
Taylor, Susanna Pusey 118–19
temperance 29, 34, 46–47, 51, 65, 84, 105, 129; education 139; *see also* "Maine Law" movement; Prohibition
Tener, John K. 161
Thompson Farm 74, 76
Thorne, Ann Eliza *see* Underwood, Ann Eliza Thorne
Thorne, Anna Emma *see* Hershey, Anna ("Annie") Emma Thorne
Thorne, Caleb Pusey ("Pusey") (son of J. Williams Thorne) 28, 58, 65–66, 73–74, 83, *83*, 88, 104, 136, 138
Thorne, Caroline *see* Lippincott, Caroline Thorne Hanway
Thorne, Elizabeth ("Eliza") Davis 83, 88
Thorne, Eugene ("Genie") (son of J. Williams Thorne) 42, 58, 73, 74, 83, 106, 112, 118, 129, 130, 131, *131*, 132, 135–36, 137–38, 140, 152, 185*n*16, 188*n*23
Thorne, George 111
Thorne, James (brother of J. Williams Thorne) 6, 13
Thorne, Joseph (of New Jersey) 171*n*5
Thorne, Joseph (Philadelphia doctor) 171*n*5
Thorne, Joseph Jonathan (father of J. Williams Thorne) 6–7, 18, 52, 63, 72, 172*n*17
Thorne, Lucretia (sister of J. Williams Thorne) 6
Thorne, Lydia Ann *see* Mewes, Lydia Ann Thorne
Thorne, Margaretta (Margaret) Williams (mother of J. Williams Thorne) 6, 13, 171*ch*2*n*2, 171*ch*2*n*5, 172*n*17
Thorne, Mary (grandmother of J. Williams Thorne) 5
Thorne, Mary Dubree *see* Fulton, Mary Dubree Thorne Bond
Thorne, Mary Jones Pusey (wife of J. Williams Thorne) 27, 40–41, 42, 43–45, 58, 66, 73, 76, 82–83, 112, 116, 117, 118–19, 120, 122, 126, 127, 129, 131, 135, 138, 140, 141
Thorpe, Margaret Newbold 69, 70, 83
Tilton, Theodore 60, 79, 99
tobacco 40, 45, 47, 66, 68, 128, 131, 161
Tourgée, Albion Winegar 109
Townsend, Washington 85, 136
Townshend, Fanny Lee 45–46
Train, George Francis 79, 181*n*33
Transylvania County, NC 97
Troy, Wesley Clark 113

Index

Truth, Sojourner 45, 46
The Truth Seeker 99, 101, 102, 106, 122, 130, 133

Uncle Tom's Cabin 42
Underground Railroad 1, 9, 32–35, **37**, 43, 50, 63, 65, 156
Underwood, Ann Eliza Thorne (sister of J. Williams Thorne) 6, 52, 63, 72
Union League 108
Unionville, PA 31
Unitarianism 11, 79, 98, 99, 115
United States House of Representatives 60, 87, 96
United States Senate 75, 84, 87, 96, 130, 143
United States Supreme Court 20, 21, 38, 134, 142, 160, 182*n*6
Uriah (Biblical figure) 80
Utah 148, 151

Vance, Zebulon 75, 112, 129–30
Vance County, NC 133, 182*n*15, 188*n*23
vegetarianism 7, 55, 67, 73, 156, 157, 161
Village Record (West Chester, PA) 31, 62, 142
Virginia 9, 35, 53, 62–63, 68, 135
Voltaire 94, 98

Waddell, William B. 136
Wahl, Albert J. 45, 46
Walker, Platt D. 91, 92, 93
Walker, Zachariah 160–61
Walnut Street (Philadelphia, PA) 104
Walton, E. Clayton 152
Walton, Lizzie 90
Warren County, NC 4, 68–72, 73, 74–76, 78, 82–86, 88, 90, 91, 92, **93**, 97, 98, 102, 104, 106, 107–8, 110, 111–12, 113–14, 118, 120, 122, 125, 126, 127, 128–29, 182*n*15, 185*n*15
Warrenton, NC 69, 83
Warrenton Gazette 82, 84–85
Washington, George 143, 146; Mount Vernon 146
Washington, D.C. 23, 54, 61, 116, 126, 132, 137
Wassom, George 122
Weaver, James B. 131

Wellman, Manly Wade 69
West Chester, PA 7, 12, 25, 28, 31, 41, 45, 58, 62, 153; Horticultural Hall 41, 45, 53
West Chester Local News 120
West Fallowfield, PA 6
West Marlborough, PA 36
West Point (U.S. Military Academy) 84
Western North Carolina Railroad 130
Westtown Friends Boarding School 12–14, 172*n*18
Whig Party 23
White, George Fox 18–19, 24
White League 102
White Mountain 68
Whitson, Thomas 32–35, 63, 175*n*36
Why Liberals Win the Culture Wars 159
Wilber, Nebraska 43
Wilkes County, NC 95
Willard, Frances 144, **145**
William I ("The Conquerer"), King of England 67
Williams, James 35
Williams, William H. 86
Williamson, Passmore 52
Wilmington, DE 66
Wilmington, NC 102–3
Wilmot, David 30, 61
Wilson, Frank 54, 56–57, 58–59, 67
Wilson Advance 125
Winch, Julie 9
Windle, Thomas 78
Wise, Isaac M. 100
women's rights 41–42, 47, 104, 138, 139, 146, 148, 149, 151, 157, 159
Woodhull, Victoria 79–80, 81
World Alliance for Human Happiness 51
World War I 159
Wyoming 151

Yadkin River, NC 3
Yardley, Will 118
Yardley family 118
Young, Brigham 81
Young Men's Christian Association 60, 78, 79, 81

Zercher's Hotel **37**

www.ingramcontent.com/pod-product-compliance
Lightning Source LLC
Chambersburg PA
CBHW032043300426
44117CB00009B/1173